D1830444

Empowerment of Woman through Self Help Groups

Empowerment of Woman through Self Help Groups

G. Sreeramulu

KALPAZ

Published by

Kalpaz Publications
C-30, Satyawati Nagar,
Delhi – 110052

Distribution Network
gyanbooks.com
India, USA, Canada, UK, Australia, France

© Publisher
All rights reserved. No part of this work may be reproduced, stored, adapted, or transmitted in any form or by any means, electronic, mechanical, photocopying, micro-filming, recording or otherwise, or translated in any language, without the prior written permission of the copyright owner and the publisher.

ISBN: 9788178355016 (HB)

15 impression 2019

Printed at: Goyal Offset Printers, Delhi.

The book is sold subject to the condition that it shall not, by way of trade or otherwise, be lent, resold, hired out, or otherwise circulated without the prior publisher's written consent.

Contents

Foreword

Since, Indian constitution has emphasized on welfare state, its primary responsibility is to improve the quality of life of the citizens. The Government of India has evolved several economic programmes, one such programme is self-help programme. Hence, the Government of India evolved different types of economic strategies and programmes for the betterment of living conditions of the rural masses. The Indian society is marred by the illiteracy, poverty, ill-health and backwardness of varied nature prevailing in both rural and urban areas. The government of India starting with the community development programme (CDP) later shifted to several other programmes under five year plans. Despite all this welfare and development programmes significant outcome in 1970's is that highly neglected section of the society is women. As per recommendations of the National Perspective Plan (1988-2000). Then focus shifted to women upliftment through economic developmental process, increase women participation in economic production activity. Then onwards the policy-makers focus their attention on shaping the socio-economic development of the rural women.

All the rural development programmes have emphasized on the integrated of women development. Thus a number of programmes have been evolved to meet the requirements of rural woman. The most important factors which influence the status of women are education, health, and employment. The education is one of the crucial and key factor to attain gender equality and women development. It can open up ample of opportunities for women to entry in to the area of productive work, decision-making process and to participate in various developmental activities in order to change their living conditions.

The successive five year of plans of Indian Government have evolved several programmes. From 6th five year plan onwards a few pilot projects were introduced in 50 blocks in the country under the caption of Development of Women and Children in Rural Areas DWCRA in 1982. Later on it was introduced through out the country. By conferring joint titles on land and house sites the status of women has been tried to improve. The National Research Development Corporation was established as part of the planning commission to provide expertise and resources to women entrepreneurs and a number of schemes were taken up in the social welfare sector to elevate the status of the rural women.

The DWCRA programme is successful programme among all the programme initiated by the Government of India. Recently the DWCRA programme is changed its nomenclature as 'SELF-HELP GROUPS'. The Government of India has given top priority and allocated special funds in 9th and 10th five year plans. Now the scheme of DWCRA programme is being transformed as Self-Help Group by providing *Micro Finance* to the members of the SHG's. The state of Andhra Pradesh has becomes a role model for the other states. The impact of SHG's are appreciated by the World Bank. Based on this experience, The World Bank officials are planning to put a condition to introduce the borrowing countries *Micro Finance* schemes. The World Bank task force committee officials praised SHG programmes as "create a silent revolution in the lives and status of the women". The women's Self-Help Groups in rural areas can create a movement for women's solidarity, to protect their interests and needs.

The author has aptly chosen this topic "Women Empowerment Through Self-Help Groups" for his research. The study mainly focused its attention on empowerment of women, topography socio-economic background of the rural women in district selected for study. It covers the problems and perspectives of Self-Help Groups and suggested several measures. The study has evaluated the implementation of several schemes in the district such as rearing goats, dairying, petty business activities, making of soft toys and so on. The findings are very much encouraging, as per the opinion expressed by majority of respondent, belonging to backward castes and SC's and ST's. As per the Study they improved their incomes through various income generating activities,

This work is a real addition to the existing social science studies on women empowerment through various economic development programmes.

Dr. P. Hussain Khan

Date: 14-02-2006
Warangal

Acknowledgements

The present book is an outcome of the research workdone at the Department of Political Science, Kakatiya University, Warangal, Andhra Pradesh, under the able supervision and guidance of Dr. P. Hussain Khan, Associated Professor in the Department of Postgraduate Studies in Political Science, to whom I am indebted for his valuable suggestions, academic inspirations and constant encouragement in completing this work.

I particularly, acknowledge my everlasting debts of gratitude to Prof. V. Satyanarayana, Prof. Ravindra Shastri, Prof. Tirupati Rao, Dr. Krishna Reddy, Department of Political Science, Osmania University, Hyderabad. Prof. P.W. Purushotham, Department of Political Science, S.K. University, Anantapur, Prof. Sangetah Venkataram, Institute for Social and Economic Change, Bangalore and Prof. P.K. Patnaik, Department of Political Science, Utkal University, Orissa for their encouragement, cooperation and help completing this work.

I acknowledge my sincere gratitude to Prof. V. Ravindra, Department of Chemistry, Kakatiya University, Warangal and Prof Chandrashekar, Department of Chemistry, Gulbarga University, Gulbarga for their help in completing this work.

The Director and Staff of DRDA Anantapur, Mandal Development Officers and staff of Kalyandurga, Gorantla and Anantapur Rural Mandals all of them deserve my appreciation for their whole-hearted and kindness in providing me necessary data and information for the work. I will be failing in my deities if I do not record my gratitude to all respondents, leaders of Self-Help Groups and village Secretaries, whose spontaneous cooperation went a long way in shaping this study.

I also thank to Sri Krishna Chandran ISEC, Bangalore, for his valuable guidance and help for data tabulation and analysis.

My deepest gratitude is due to my wife Smt. Sangeetha, who put up with all inconvenience caused by a study of this nature with immense patience. My daughter Sahana deserves a special mention, as she did not receive due attention at a tender age owing to my pre-occupation with this study.

I also thank Sri T. Srivasulu, IPS, Ex-DGP and IG and Security Advisor, Government of Karnataka, Dr. (Smt.) Sitra Sarijini Sreenivasulu and T. Janardhana Naidu, IAS, Hyderabad for their constant encouragement and help in completing this work.

My thanks are due to K. Suraj, Dr K. Sreeramulu, Dr. Sindhe Jagsannath, R. Jagadeesh Panchal and Srinivas.

I am especially grateful to my Father, Mother, Sister in-laws, Father-in-law, Mother in-law and other family members for their constant encouragement and moral help.

I am also grateful to Kalpaz Publications for cooperation and help.

Dr. G. Sreeramulu

1

Introduction

The present work intends to analyse the enacted legislations and exclusive programmes for women in India in general, Andhra Pradesh in particular. An attempt is made to explain the necessity and requirement of the schemes of economic programme for women. Who were thrown out of the mainstream of social and economic life. The policymakers recognised the necessity of such economic programmes for the upliftment of the highly neglected sections of the society, i.e., women.

In every modern state of the 19th and 20th centuries the concept of welfarism has taken a prime place in the government's objectives. Since the states declared themselves as welfare states, they have responsibilities of amelioration of various programmes for the vulnerable sections of the society. The dawn of independence has given a chance to propose several programmes. The government of India evolved several economic programmes. One such programmes is that Self Help Programmes and water shed programmes. All these programmes are designed in tune with the directives of the World Bank and IMF. After the collapse of alternative economic systems, the world economy became a single independent unit resulting in the emergence of a unipolar economic system led by the USA, thus creating a different picture in the economics. The Indian economy is in no way different from the global economy. Whatever directives flow from these international institutions have to percolate to the nook and corner of the economics of all the states.

In this background the government of India designed a programme witch answers to the needy of the society. Once the government of India opened up the controls of the economy, empetus has given to the privatisation and the state has with drawn from the responsibilities of social justice. And the slowly majority of the welfare state with drawn from the concepts of welfareism. Ultimately the majority of the third world countries are bound to follow the directives of international economic institutions. As long as the third world economies are bound to seek the financial and technical assistance from the monopolistic states, which force them to depend on the developed economies, more so from USA, it is inevitable for these economies. They cannot go for alternative economic strategies.

Since they are seeking the financial aided technology on monopolistic states they have to be bound by the conditions and stipulations by international financial agencies. Hence, the government of India evolved the economic strategies and programme in accordance with the directives given by the international agencies. Whatever the economic policy, programme or scheme are simply replicas of the US policies of incremental policies. All these policies are considered as target oriented programmes. Once the target is achieved, such policy will be disbanded. And another new targetoriented policy will be introduced to meet the requirement of the situation.

There fore, the present work deals exclusively with policy strategies and evaluation methods.

The Role of Indian Government

The Government of India, after its independence went in for social and economic transformation of the country. Before independence nearly 80 per cent of people lived in rural areas and most of them were below the poverty line. There exist illiteracy, ill-health, and backwardness of varied nature prevailing in both rural and urban areas. After 55 years, the country is facing the major difficulties which prevailed at the time of Independence.

As a result, the Government of India had to take up several policies and programmes in the direction of meeting the needs of its people. In this direction, in 1952 the Government of India introduced the Community Development Programme (CDP) as an initiation. It had also implemented several programmes under Five Year Plans. It has been working with the determination of implementing these plans to make a direct attack on poverty by developing massive resources for the development of the poor.

From 'Welfare' to 'Empowerment' Strategy

A significant outcome of the broad policy debates in the 70s was a shift from viewing women as targets of 'welfare' policies in the social sector to regard them as 'critical agent' for development. This was recognised by the VI Five Year Plan, which, for the first time, incorporated a chapter on women and development.

In the entire economy the areas that can be directly intervened by the government will be very limited and the scope to cover a substantial portion of women population under government sponsored programmes also will be extremely limited. Therefore, government's intervention can act only as indicative to the system as to which direction the natural economic development should take and such intervention can only be a declaration of the intent of the modern state.[1]

Besides these attempts, the Government of India prepared the National Perspective Plan (1988-2000) which envisaged a multipronged strategy for integrating women into the mainstream. "Shramshakti" (1988), a comprehensive report of the National Commission for self-employed Women and Women in the Informal Sector,[2] examined related issues concerning women workers in the informal sector and made valuable recommendations for improving their status.

The realisation that women had a weak and vulnerable position in the family, the most informal and primary unit, made the policy-makers focus their attention on woman in foetus, as girl child, in her adolescence and in her in-laws' family. The strategy aimed at fighting against unsafe motherhood, nutritional anemia, iodine deficiency, the vulnerable years of the infancy and building up a woman's capacity to cope up with the barriers and challenges of growth, change and stabilization.

Non-governmental organisations (NGOs) promoting women's issues gained strength. They protested against violence against women, demanded right to abortion, sought amendments in the Dowry Prohibition Act. 1961 for making the offence cognizable and non-bailable so as to increase its effectiveness and pleaded for a better deal for women in work place etc. By the beginning of the 1990s, meek and feeble grumbling of women activists had become strong, loud and bold protests.

The early 90s saw the reshaping of strategies of socio-economic development and the emphasis shifted from "development" to "empowerment". There was a realization that women have limited access to capital market, education, skill training, extension advice and participation in the decision-making process. The Constitution 73rd and 74th Amendment Acts of 1992 constitute a major milestone on the road to empowerment of women as these Amendments ensure one-third of the total seats and positions of Chairpersons in rural and urban elected bodies.

The subject of women's development is multidimensional, multisectoral and multidisciplinary. In the recent past, awareness about the contribution of women at the level of family and community has been on the increase. As the issue of redistribution with growth was considered threatening, this was subverted around mid-1970s by a call from meeting "the basic needs of the poor directly", along with efforts towards promoting economic growth. Basic needs encompassed health, nutrition, water, sanitation and shelter. Several credit, income generation, skill-building programmes were started. In this context, it was pointed out that women experienced poverty to a greater extent than men and poverty eradication intervention targeted at heads of households failed to address these. Hence, the need for reservation for women and designing of separate poverty-alleviation programmes for women was stressed. The government has been emphasising the need for development of rural women and promotion of their participation in the developmental programmes. Rural development programmes have laid due emphasis on the integrated development of women. And thus, a number of programmes have targeted to cover substantial proportion of rural women.[3]

Review of Related Literature

The studies on Public Policies in general and women in particular, along with women's development programmes in India and in the World have attracted the attention of scholars from disciplines such as Political Science, Sociology, Economics and Social Work. An array of scholarly works examining the genesis, growth, implementation, outlays and deficiencies has been brought out.

The concern over the problems of women received global treatment with the declaration of the U.N. Charter in 1945.

when the preamble itself declares that the people of the United Nations are determined to reaffirm their faith in the fundamental human rights, in dignity and worth of human persons, in the equal rights of men and women and of nations large and small. Therefore, the studies on women development, Empowerment, other related problems and the specific programmes and policies of respective governments have gained considerable importance in analysing varied facets and factors which are instrumental for the overall development of women. In spite of the above mentioned studies, a good number of studies have attempted to unevil particular sociological, economic and political factors contributing immensely to the economic, political and social empowerment of women.

It is held by observers that the last decade has seen the emergence of grass-root women's movements in many parts of the developing world. In India, e.g., Self Help Women's Groups have been formed by milk producers, street vendors and agricultural labouers. Urban women have also organised around issues of rape and dowry. In rural areas women have moblised to secure forest rights and protest against scarcity of water and fuel. In India on these issues the studies carried out by institutions and individuals are also quite relevant.

A review of certain important works is quite pertinent in the context of the present study. The researcher has been able to tap some of the significant works and also lay fingers over some of these studies which have considerable bearing on the present study.

Thus, the present work is entirely different from the above studies in respect of its importance, objectives, methodology and scope. Special Programmes under UNDP (United Nations Development Programme) and SAPAP (South Asia Poverty Alleviation Programmes) have been focussing in a few poor mandals of Anantpur District along with Mahaboob Nagar and Kurnool District of Andhra Pradesh. As a result in Ananatapur District (study area) small scale income generating activities are being promoted. It is also intended to assess the impact of the UN programmes. Finally the study aims to evaluate the impact of all these programmes on the socio-political, cultural and economic development of families on the one hand and on the other to know the status of poverty eradication programmes in Anantapur District, has its relevance. It has Difference from the other Studies carried at the State, National and International levels.

In the present study, the studies have been classified into four groups firstly, studies on public policies secondly, on specific programmes for women development, thirdly on self help groups and fourthly studies in Andhra Pradesh including the study area.

Studies on Public Policies

Fuller, Taleria Renee Studied "*Chronic Illness and Depression Among Women: The Role of Social Support*" in 2000. Using data from the 1995 Detroit Metropolitan Area Public Policy Survey (DMAPPS), this study examines the relationship between chronic illness and depression among a sample of women, and investigates the role of social support. Results show that a relationship between chronic illness and depression could not be established, and due to specified criteria, the mediating role of social support could not be properly addressed. Other interesting findings reveal the importance of socio-demographic factors in predicting both of chronic illness and depression, while the very crucial role of social support for women with and without chronic illness and/or depression was explored. The author discusses the implications of these findings, including the observation that structural constraints and limited options of those disadvantaged continues to be paramount in women's overall risk for chronic illness and depression.[4]

Schulenberg, Jennifer Lina undertook a study on "*Neuenbundeslaender : The effects of state and policy reunification on the women and families in the former German Democratic Republic*" (2001). This thesis is an investigation of the relationship between public policy and family well-being within Unified Germany through an examination of the effects of public policy on the women and families in the New Federal States as a result of reunification. Data obtained from secondary data analysis, personal observation, interviews with German sociologists and content analysis of media excerpts conceptualized within the theoretical framework of Margrit Eichler's models of the family and Myra Marx Feree's private and public patriarchy indicate that when the laissez-faire family policy structure of West Germany was imposed upon the former East Germany in an authoritarian and colialistic manner it had a predominantly negative effect on the women and families in the New Federal States. Reunification has affected women more than men as they experience higher levels of unemployment, less employment opportunities in becoming rehired, and diminished personal options. The economic situation is considerably worse for families and there is more income stratification between family types. The findings also indicate that the public policies which benefited women and family well-being in the GDR are the areas that saw the most dramatic demographic shifts where the trends in the New Federal States now resemble those in the Old Federal States as a result of adaptation to policy changes suggesting a reciprocal relationship between policy and the family that needs to be considered in public design and implementation.[5]

Farmer, Mary Jane instituted a research on "*Freedwomen and the Freedmen's Bureau: Race, Gender and Public Policy in the age of emancipation*" in 2000. It examined the gendered nature of Bureau policies as well as the ways in which freedwomen used the Bureau to protect and redefine their place in postwar southern society. Without minimizing other factors, this study demonstrates that a freedperson's gender shaped the nature and outcome of African Americans' struggle for freedom. As they stepped into freedom, African American women faced choices about marriage, children, family, residence, mobility, and labor. These choices often fueled heated contests with black men as well as with white southerners and federal officials over the meaning of freedom.[6]

Poole, Mary Elizabeth made a study on "*Securing race and ensuring dependence: The Social Security Act of 1935*" in 2000. The objective was to understand how public policy can contribute to the construction and reconstruction of racial hierarchy. A prime example of this phenomenon is the exclusion of most African American workers from the two programmes created in the Act for workers, Unemployment Insurance and Old Age Insurance (now social security). Further, this dissertation describes the participation of different groups in the development of the Social Security Act, and then analyzes the ways that the racial ideologies of these groups factored into their participation, and into the Act that resulted.[7]

Harkness, S. Suzan Jane studied "*Women and Work: Dynamics of the Glass ceiling and Public Policy perspectives*". (2000). This Reveals that some women did made headway. The analysis documented that the gap closed slightly, that women were more likely to work within the professional occupations by 1978, and that women were armed with strong human capital investments and aware of how important they were to career mobility. The analysis found that legislation enacted during the early 1960s and amended during the 1970s has had a very limited impact upon issues of equity within corporate environments, and that much of the inequity stems from discriminatory organizational factors and policies. Women's overall opportunities will continue to be limited as long as the opportunities within corporations remain hampered, unequal, and unaccommodating to the variety of women's growing presence.[8]

March, Jennifer Ann, studied "*Gendered Public Policy : How welfare reform attempts to reconstitute the nuclear family*" (2000). The premise that reforms of AFDC policy have not sought to empower women in ways which would allow them to meet their domestic and economic needs independently. The study illustrates how programme administrators were permitted and encouraged to design, monitor, and implement JOBS programmes in ways that produced budgetary savings, reduced and simplified bureaucracy, and enforced client compliance with preferred social and economic norms. These factors failed to design, monitor, and implement welfare to work programmes in ways which would address client needs because the Family Support Act lacked a genuine commitment to female economic independence. The influence of the JOBS programme's experience on the Personal Responsibility and work Opportunity Act of 1996 is also examined, underscoring the gendered interests that guide policy formation and the likelihood that new reforms will negatively impact client well-being.[9]

"*On the streets and in the state house: American Indian and Hispanic women and environmental policy-making in New Mexico*" (2000) by Prindeville, Diane-Michele, is also another important research. The study explores the politics of American Indian and Hispanic women leaders in New Mexico's environmental policy-making arena. Using non-random purposive sampling, 50 women were selected for participation who were political activists in grassroots organisations or public officials, elected or appointed to local, state, or tribal government. Personal interviews were employed to gather data on their political socialization, their leadership trajectories, their motives for engagement in public life, their political policy agendas and strategies for influencing public policy-making. The findings revealed that the leaders' motives for community service stemmed primarily from their childhood socialization in politically active families, and that they were further politicised during their youth by their participation in social movements. Many of the leaders described their political involvement as a deeply felt commitment to help others; political participation was viewed as a personal responsibility or life purpose.[10]

Aguila, Jaime R. studied *"Protecting 'Mexico de Afuera': Mecan emigration policy, 1876-1928"*, (2001). This dissertation analyzes the formalization of Mexican public policy concerning Mexican emigration to the United States from 1876 to 1928. This dissertation argues that emigration policies unfolded, at first, as reactions toward specific events, such as violence along the border and the growing economic interdependency between the two nations. Following the 1910 and 1920 Mexican Revolution, policy-making assumed a more pro-active agenda that aggressively sought to benefit the post-revolutionary state by promoting Mexican patriotism, encouraging the emigrant's return while simultaneously discouraging immigration.[11]

Grossback, Lawrence James conducted a study of *"Public Opinion and the process of Democratic responsiveness"* in 2000. It is an empirical analysis of the relationship between mass policy preferences and public policy outputs in the post-war United States. This study combines case study information with longitudinal data analysis to study both the nature of public opinion and the determinates of public policy change in five issue areas; education, the environment, employment, defense, and health care. The findings of the study are that the characteristics of a policy issue, including the length of time it has been on the public agenda and the costs and benefits it bestows, greatly affect which factors will influence the amount of resources the federal government commits to the policy area. The relative influence of the economy, election results, the parties composition of government, and public opinion is found to vary extensively across the issues studied. In only one issue domain, health care, is public opinion found to affect policy outputs over the time entire span studied. This result points to less governmental responsiveness to citizen attitudes than was found in previous studies. In addition to addressing issues related to representation, this dissertation also contributes to the literature on aggregate public opinion, public policy studies, and agenda setting within policy domains.[12]

Welsh, Michael Maurice made a study of *"Discursive policy processes and the environment lessons from case studies of public range management"* in 2001. This dissertation examines public range management for conclusions about natural resources administration and discursive public policy making. The dissertation argues against a historic and theoretical academic literature asserting the inevitable rise to dominance of organised interests in delegated forums of policy making, looking specifically at the origins and history of public range management. The dissertation analyzes five of the twenty four regional advisory council cases that grew out of the participatory component of the Bureau of Land Management's programme of rangeland reform in 1995 and mdash; four that produced noteworthy environmental protections, and one that did not. Using field research, regional history, and in-depth interviews, the dissertation develops a list of background conditions that contribute to these environmental success, and tests the validity of that list against data gathered in the unsuccessful case.[13]

"Women and Work: Dynamics of the glass ceiling and public policy perspectives", in 2001 by Harkness, S. Suzan Jane. Describes the findings and also suggest that organisational discrimination was evident and that Title VII (Civil Rights Act of 1960) has done little to ensure equal opportunity within organisations. Gender was found to have a significant impact upon career opportunity and mobility.[14]

Weldon, Sirje Laurel undertook the study on *"Explaining cross-national variation in government responsiveness to violence against women: Women's movements and political institutions in democratic policymaking"*, in 2000. In this study an attempt is made to seek to explain why some democratic governments are more responsive to the problem of violence against women than others. Specifically, why do some stable democratic governments undertake broad, multifaceted initiatives to address violence against women while other governments do not even recognize the problem, or respond only partially. The study finds that strong, independently organised women's movements interact with effective women's policy agencies to produce the broadest government responses to violence against women. These contextual variables are more important than the individual level variables (gender, policy preferences, leadership style, etc.) on which the literature on gender and public policy tends to focus. This suggests that study of gender and policy making must move beyond the study of women as policymakers.[15]

Studies on Women Programmes

Basu Rumki studied *"New Economic Policies and Social Welfare Programmes in India"* in 1996. It is suggested that India's move toward privatization and a market economy will weaken the present insufficient social infrastructure and simultaneously fail to generate sufficient trickle-down benefits to fund new infrastructure or create enough employment to eradicate poverty. Continued government social welfare intervention is essential. A variety of existing and needed social welfare programmes are discussed: (1) Poverty alleviation/employment programmes; (2) National social assistance programmes; (3) Nutritional support for primary education; (4) services for rural women and rural life insurance; (5) Agricultural strategies; (6) Assistance for small and marginal farmers; (7) social security ; and (8) Programmes for the unorganised sector.[16]

"Rural Poverty, Growth and Macroeconomic Policies: The Asian Experience" (1990) Islam Rizwanul is also another

important research. Noting that the efforts of developing Asian countries were more successful in alleviating rural poverty in the 1970s and 1980s than in the 1960s, it is contended that, while high growth is an essential precondition for poverty alleviation, it is not a sufficient condition in and of itself. Appropriate macroeconomic policies in the areas of trade exchange rates, taxation, credit, subsidies, etc., are shown to have an important role to play in poverty reduction.[17]

Weisman, Stephen R. revealed that *"Structural Adjustment in Africa : Insights from the Experiences of Ghana and Senegal"* in 1990. The effectiveness of structural adjustment (SA) policies in promoting equitable and sustainable economic growth in Ghana and Senegal is evaluated using statistical data from the International Monetary Fund, US Agency for International Development, and World Bank. SA encompasses interrelated policies for stabilizing a country's economy and engineering sustainable long-term growth. It is shown that although past SA helped create an improved framework for economic growth, it is a fragile trend that could be easily disrupted.[18]

Tripathy, S.K.; Bhuyan B, Pradhan P.N., carried out a Study on *"The Economic Impact of the Integrated Rural Development Programme"* in 1990. The impact of the Integrated Rural Development Programme in alleviating poverty in the Dhenkanai district of Orissa, India, during the Six Plan period (1980-85) was examined through an interview survey of 977 beneficiary households. Analysis reveals that 38 per cent of households below poverty level prior to onset of the programme crossed above the poverty line after programme assistance. Service and business sectors performed better than any others. Problems with the implementation of the programme included improper identification of beneficiary households, technical and economic unfeasibility of schemes, lack of working capital, supply of inferior and diseased animals in the animal husbandry scheme, lack of proper supervision, inappropriate use of assistance, and inadequate loan accounting.1[9]

Servon, Lisa J. Bates Timothy undertook the study on, *"Microenterprise as an Exit Route from Poverty : Recommendations for Programmes and Policy Makers"* in 1998. Whether and how microenterprise programmes can be used as an economic development strategy to enable low-income people in the US to achieve self-sufficiency through self-employement. A review of census and other published data provides little support for the notion that hard work and a small loan are sufficient ingredients for business success. As a poverty alleviation strategy, microenterprise is not a panacea. Nevertheless, programmes targeting the poor who do have skills, resources, and support networks can be useful vehicles for helping some to escape poverty.[20]

Chinake, Hazel studied on, *"Strategies for Poverty Alleviation in Zimbabwe"*, in 1987. Outlines a broad, appropriate, and practical strategic approach designed to alleviate poverty in Zimbabwe through a reorientation of conventional development strategies. Emphasis is placed on basic needs fulfillment as an indispensable prerequisite for socioeconomic development. Structural inequalities that must be tackled at national and global levels to ensure growth with equity, while also safeguarding the environment, are delineated. The role of social work education and practice in meeting the exigencies of the moment is also outlined.[21]

Ali Shaikh Maqsood, Sirivardana Susil, *"Towards a New Paradigm for Poverty Eradication in South Asia"*, (1996). Discusses the evolution of government policy regarding the eradication of poverty in South Asia, based on a critique and expansion of the suggestions proposed by the Independent South Asian Commission on Poverty Alleviation (ISACPA).[22]

Blank Rebecca M studied *"Poverty and Public Policy in the 1990s"* in 1995. In this study the problem of poverty in the 1990s is surveyed, and policy proposals to solve this problem are considered. Poverty today is described as a problem that disproportionately affects single-parent families headed by women. Three axes of current policy discussion of poverty the feminization of poverty, the problem of urban poverty, and the problem of increasing wage inequality are discussed. Recent changes in policy discourse, including an emphasis on responsibility and obligation, an interest in public/private partnerships, and a focus on coordinated programmes, are then assessed. It is argued that this orientation to the problem of poverty is a good one, but that changes in the labour market may hinder any attempt at reduction in poverty rates, and that an insistant racial coding of poverty threatens many viable policy proposals.[23]

Sawada Yasuyuki, Studied on *"Aid and Poverty Alleviation : An International Comparison"*, (1996). In order to evaluate the poverty alleviation effect of international aid provided by the governments of Japan, the UK, the US, and the Development Assistance Committee. It is asserted that the first necessary condition for poverty alleviation is appropriate policies on the part of the recipient nation, while the second necessary condition is the responsibility of donors to expand aid to countries where poverty is most widespread. By utilizing head count ratio data, it is argued that aid expansion by Japan is relatively inefficient and ineffective in terms of poverty alleviation, while US aid is most effective.[24]

Squire, Lyn undertook a study on, *"Evaluating the Effectiveness of Poverty Alleviation Programmes"*, in 1995. It describes the necessary component for rigorous evaluation of poverty alleviation programmes in developing countries. Poverty specific issues, e.g., empowerment of the poor, and beneficiary participation in programmes design and implementation, are explored. In addition, qualitative, quantitative, economic, and experimental approaches to evaluation are discussed. Finally, the importance of four key issues is underscored, namely, clarity of intermediate objectives, specification of counterfactuals, incorporation of all factors influencing outcomes, and allocation of resources to the activities with the highest potential returns.[25]

Amis Philip made a study on, *"Employment Creation or Environmental Improvements: A Literature Review of Urban Poverty and Policy in India"*, in 1995. The Study offers a general literature review on the question of Indian urban poverty with the object of considering the importance of an employment creation or environmental improvement approach to poverty alleviation. The literature clearly shows the importance of the labour market in terms of segments and casualisation, gender, and short-run shocks in explaining the incidence of poverty. However, the independent nature of environmental problems is also highlighted. The policy implication is that both employment creation and environmental improvements are necessary.[26]

Kabeer Naila undertook a research on, *"Targeting Women or Transforming Institutions? Policy Lessons from NGO Anti-Poverty Efforts"* in 1995. While inequalities between men and women have long been recognized in formal development policies, poverty alleviation schemes generally display a discrepancy between their declared commitment to equity for women and their actual achievements in incorporating the insights of gender analysis. Explored here are the experiences of NGOs (Non Governmental Organizations) that have successfully incorporated gender awareness into the formulation of antipoverty interventions. It is shown that increasing poor women's organizational experience is critical to ensuring that their needs and views inform the planning process. It is concluded that, unless women are empowered to take part in formulating policy and allocating recources, they will continue to be a marginalized category in development.[27]

Wegelin, Emiel A, Borgman, Karin M carried out a research on, *"Options for Municipal Interventions in Urban Poverty Alleviation"*, in 1995. It reviews the wide range of options available to municipalities in the southern hemisphere to alleviate or reduce poverty, including options for employment creation and improving low income groups' access to justice and protection from crime as well as improvements to urban service–e.g., water supply, sanitation, solid waste management, public transport, health care, and education.[28]

Palakudy, Thomas, Singh Sukhpal, carried out research on, *"The New Agricultural Policy and the Rural Poor"*, in 1993. Against the background of a rising trend in the number of small and marginal holdings in India, and the process of depeasantation and pauperization this trend points to, the new Agricultural Policy of the Government of India (1993) is examined, focusing on its relevance for enchanting the livelihood and security of the landless labour and small and marginal families in the rural sector. The policy is criticised for its total faith in the spread effect of increased agricultural production as an effective weapon for poverty alleviation, with no means to ensure that distribution is done in an equitable manner. In sum, the new policy holds little promise for the rural poor.[29]

Gordon Sara, studied, *"Social Policy and the National Solidarity Programme : La politica social y el programa Nacional de Solidaridad"*, (1993). The study focusses on the National Solidarity Programme (Pronasol), introduced by Mexican President Salinas de Gortari in 1988 to remedy the rural and urban poverty aggravated by the economic crisis of 1982.[30]

Teklu Tesfaye undertook a study on, *"The Prevention and Mitigation of Famine : Policy Lessons from Botswana and Sudan"*, in 1994. Several lessons can be drawn from the drought experiences of Botwana and Sudan in the 1980s, the former of which compensated economic losses and averted famine, while the latter underwent large declines in food entitlement and severe nutritional deterioration. Botsawana's strategy for dealing with drought and famine combined policies of steady economic growth with supplementary poverty alleviation and drought relief programmes. A responsive and accountable political system and a decentralized participatory administrative structure were maintained. While Sudan should develop policies that are compatible with its own environment, it is crucial that it recognizes the critical role of public action in promoting growth, alleviating poverty and providing timely relief responses in times of anticipated growth failure.[31]

Echeverri Gent, John carried out a study on, *"Public Participation and Poverty Alleviation: The Experience of Reform Communists in India's West Bengal"*, in 1992, and found that though effective poverty alleviation programmes require public participation, the poor do not have equitable representation. The problems stemming from this paradox of participation are demonstrated through an examination of the National Rural Employment Programme in the Indian State of West Bengal. It is shown how implementing poverty alleviation programmes through elected governing councils has simultaneously made policy more responsive to the poor while permitting the organisational interests of the ruling communist party to distort implementation. Emphasized is the importance of political competition among parties and non government organizations for maximizing responsiveness to the poor.[32]

Morrow William L, undertook the study on *"Economic Rights and the Welfare State : The Quest for Policy Integrity"*, in 1989. It is a review essay on books by: Leslie Dunbar, The Common Interest : How Our Social Welfare Policies Don't Work and What We Can Do about Them (New York :

Pantheon Books, 1988), and Charles Lockhart, Gaining Ground : Tailoring Social Programmes to American Values (Berkeley : U of California Press, 1989 [see listings in IRPS No. 62]). Solutions to the problems and failures of entitlement and welfare programmes to alleviate poverty in the US are examined, emphasising the elevation of economic rights on a par with political and civil rights;, i.e., citizens are entitled to the economic right to help themselves, and failing in their efforts, may seek assistance from the government. The political clout of an entitlement/job training constituency is not enough, however, to get entitlement programmes back on a track of success. It is concluded that entitlement programmes need to embody the ideology of a capitalist democracy and work toward the development of a sense of personal responsibility in their recipients[33].

Sherraden, Michael, studied *"Full Employment and Social Welfare Policy"*, in 1991. The modern welfare state assumes employment as a foundation on which other social programmes are built. In the absence of adequate employment, household incomes are insufficient and social programmes are under political attack and underfunded. Full employment, although not a perfect solution, is by far the most acceptable and effective strategy for combating income poverty. Those who suggest abandoning the goal of full employment in favour of expanded welfare transfers fundamentally misinterpret the economic and political character. [34]

Gaiha Raghav made a study on, *"Poverty Alleviation Programmes in Rural India: An Assessment"*, in 1991. An Evaluation of the claim by India's Planning Commission that the Integrated Rural Development Programme was responsible for a substantial reduction in rural poverty during the early 1980s. Drawing on results of a general equilibrium model applied to secondary statistical data, selected antipoverty interventions are compared from a macro-perspective, noting incentive and information-related problems and addressing some key issues in designing anti poverty interventions. The relationship between rural poverty, agricultural production and (consumer) prices is explored, and distinguishing between transitory and persistent poverty, alternative measures of persistent poverty are presented. A case is made for an interventionist antipoverty strategy, followed by a brief review of salient features and selected performance indicators of poverty alleviation programmes launched/implemented during the Sixth Plan period. Selected antipoverty interventions and possible design-related reforms are also outlined.[35]

Studies on Self Help Groups

B. Sudhakar Rao, G. Ramachandraiah, V. Krishnamurthy, Y. Gangi Reddy and R. Murugesan studied *"Self-Employment Projects–Groups Approaches"*.

The Major Objectives of the Study : (1) To identify the inhibiting factors for group approaches in entrepreneurship and project development. (2) To study the economics of group activities in rural units/micro enterprises and to highlight their contribution and (3) To arrive at measures for successful interventions.

Findings of the Study : (1) Existing skills, not generated through any training activity but based on only previous experience have taken precedence in the formation of groups. Though they have resulted in some form of income generation, their growth and sustainability have raised questions about their viability, sustenance, competitive strength, full time family employment, etc. The problems in marketability, institutional support, managerial skills, etc., need a fresh look into the interventions approach of development. (2) In terms of other infrastructure the requirements are still not satisfied in terms of road connectivity, 30 groups have felt the requirement, 67 per cent have felt the need for telephone facility. 40 per cent felt the need for training, and 32 per cent have felt the need for electricity...Likewise 40 per cent have no bank facility. (3) The groups in spite of sufficient satisfaction levels, have not been guided properly, 62 groups have felt the requirement of guidance from suitable agencies. (4) There are 37 types of activities that are surveyed and include primary, secondary and tertiary activities. The groups are also not wholly dependent on these activities, leading to the conclusion that for many members employment in the scheme is not full employment. In sheep and goat rearing the monthly average income varied from Rs. 2000 to 3800, with only one exception. Generally, the incomes are in that range except certain activities like latrine cut, brickmaking, masonry, oil mill etc. (5) The leadership ability has taken predominance over the external factors. About 99 per cent of the groups have thought that the sustainability of the project depends on the leadership emerging within the group, 94 per cent have mentioned the related success to the external factors.[36]

D.V.L.N.V. Prasad Rao instituted a research on, *"Poverty Alleviation Through Self Employment : A Case Study of East Nimar District of Madhya Pradesh"* in 1997-98. The main Objectives of the Study were : (1) To assess changes in economic conditions of the beneficiaries following the implementation of IRDP. (2) To evaluate the IRDP planning process at the grassroots level.

The Major Findings of the Study were that the occupational analysis of beneficiaries reveals that the majority of beneficiaries belonged to Bullock Pair scheme, i.e., the cultivating class (44 per cent of the Selected beneficiaries), 14 per cent of the beneficiaries utilised the Bullock cart scheme, and the next 18 per cent of the beneficiaries availed for the motor pumpset scheme. Only one person was sanctioned for a goats, and two persons received loans for business schemes. The level of income generation varied from scheme to scheme, Activities in the tertiary sector were found to be most profitable, while those in primary sector were the least. The two villages are located at far a distance from the main central service point villages. The study reveals that IRDP assistance has helped the majority of the beneficiaries to improve their income levels, which is reflected in the high degree of upward mobility along the income ladder. Though financially many beneficiaries have not crossed the poverty line, the way people expressed their feelings, the self employment schemes will be more suitable for them in future also. Simultaneously wage employment programmes will also boost their real income to cross the poverty line.[37]

D.V.V. Ramana Rao, undertook a case study on *"Impact of Institutional Credit on the Socio-Economic Condition of Rural Women in Self-Help Groups–A Case study in Bidar District of Karnataka"* in 2001. Objectives of the Study were: To document the experiences of micro-credit movement through self-help groups, which are promoted to serve the micro credit needs of the poor in the pursuit of and to develop micro-enterprises for a sustainable livelihood system.

The Major Findings of the Study are : (1) Average membership in SHGs was around 19.1 women. The main occupation of SHG Members includes agriculture labour, non-farm labour and petty business. Membership in SHGs was heterogeneous in character. The amount of savings per SHG were to the tune of Rs. 7699.8. The average savings mobilised by the groups sponsored by the cooperative banks is Rs. 39984 and the average savings of SHG groups sponsored by the NGOs is Rs. 37014. This trend indicated that the groups mobilised by the cooperative banks have mobilised more savings than the groups sponsored by the NGO organisations. The amount of membership savings in SHGs was found to be positively linked to their period of operation. (2) The average number of loans per SHG was 23.6 persons out of a total membership of 19 persons. This trend indicated that a few members have raised loans more than once and shows increased awareness in the credit linkage programmes with the Banks. The loans disbursed per SHG during 1998-99 amounted to Rs. 1,63,800 which has increased to Rs. 1,82,400. The average amount of loans disbursed per SHG during 1995-96 (Rs. 26,150) has increased to Rs. 1,09,613 during 2000-01. That means the average amount of loan disbursed has increased four times during the five years. The cumulative amount of loans disbursed by the SHGs in the past five years has been estimated to be Rs. 3,83,812. (3) Borrowings from SHGs by members indicate a linear trend over the yeayears. It is seen that both in terms of number of borrowers and total amount of loan disbursed by SHGs, a leap–frogging tendency are clearly in evidence. While the number of borrowers from SHGs rose from 23-242, the amount of loan disbursed by SHGs showed a manifold increase from Rs. 26,150 in 1995-96 to Rs. 8,76,900 in 2000-01. A similar trend could be noted in terms of per member borrowing. Which increased from Rs. 1,137 to Rs. 4,766 during the above period.[38]

D.V.V. Ramana Rao, made a case study of *"Self Help Groups, A Case Study of Voluntary Organisations"*. Objectives of the Study were : (1) To examine the organisational and managerial aspects of the voluntary agencies taken up for the study, (2) To assess the impact of their activities on Self-Help Groups. The Study found that: (1) Most of the groups are homogeneous from the same caste and tribes and same social status. Some of the groups are given revolving fund of Rs. 25,000/- from DWCRA. All the leaders are trained by the SAKTI and Treasurer is trained in maintaining accounts. Once the group is formed very rarely the members discontinued their membership. While the government supplies the self help groups with by-laws, passbooks, cashbooks and accounting forms, DRDA has sanctioned them DWCRA funds. Being voluntary organisations, the groups are sustained by their members. The success of the group depends on mutual trust and discipline of the members. To sustain these groups women leaders should be trained in management of the thrift and credit activities and other income generating activities. (2) The main successful factors for mobilising SHG's are distribution of books to school children, freedom from the clutches of money-lenders, easy availability of loans without collateral security and the recognition of SHG in the village and by the government officials. (3) Change in the status of women in the Ramanagaram project area is evident. Women are now active and participative. The organisation of women's groups has enabled a collective strength and solidarity in the women. (4) The programmes, for legal aid and counselling aims to provide support to women in distress. The gender sensitization programmes are directed to address discrimination against women on gender lines.[39]

K.P. Kumaran's study, *"Case Studies on Self-Help Groups"* (1997) was conducted in the Thirumangalam block of Madurai district in Tamil Nadu. Three types of SHGs promoted by a voluntary organisation–Association for Serva Seva Farms (ASSEFA), were studied in detail. The SHGs studied include Gram Sabha, IFAD assisted group and ASSEFA group-With three objectives : (1) To study the role of non-governmental organisation (NGOs) in promoting Socio-economic development of the poor through SHGs. (2) To study the structure and function of the SHGs with special reference to the pattern of resource mobilisation, decision making and participation of members in group activities. (3) To examine the linkages of the SHGs with other organisations including financial institutions. The study showed that the savings generated within the group and the loan provided to them by linking with financial institutions helped the members to meet their credit requirement to a large extent. Apart from taking up economic activities, these group also undertake social development programme for its members. The analysis of data on individual—se studies also showed that the programme implemented by the ASSEFA helped its members not only to achieve socio-economic development but also improve their standard of living. However, from the study the following two important points have emerged which are to be noted. The caste study showed that the group approach through SHGs is one of the best approaches for the socio-economic development of the rural poor. As the poor do not form such groups on their own based on their common problem, it the outside agencies like Government and non-Government organisations that promote such groups. As the role of NGOs in promoting such groups is limited due to several known factors, it is describes that the Government agencies also should take keen interest in promoting such groups among the poor. It is found that the repayment of Group/Bank loan among the SHG members is very high. But the amount received through these sources are not able to meet the credit requirements. Although several measures have been taken by the Govt. to link the SHGs with financial institutions the number of such groups are relatively few. Therefore, it is necessary to link the SHGs with banks and other financial institutions by further streamlining the procedure.[40]

Rahman Atiur carried out a study on *"Rural Development from Below: Lessons Learned from Grameen Bank Experience in Bangladesh"* in 1996. It discusses the success of the Grameen Bank, an innovative rural banking program, in promoting rural development in Bangladesh, particularly through poverty alleviation. The analysis draws on primary data collected in a 1990 village survey conducted in Rangpur district, involving interviews with all members (N=49) of the Gangachara branch of Grameen Bank, supplemented by data from 51 households in the adjacent villages. The organisational and management strategies of the Grameen Bank are identified, noting how it differs from other grassfoots organizations initiated by the government. The bank's socio-economic impact is assessed, and its applicability in other societies considered.[41]

Paoletti Isabella, carried out a study on *"Caring for Older People: A Gendered Practice"* in 1998. Describes some instances of the moral and relational universe in which caring practices are embedded, drawing on data from The Role of Women in the Family Care of the Elderly (INRCA, Ancona, Italy), an action project that interviewed women caregivers in Ferrara and involved them in various initiatives, e.g., self-help groups. The data were inspected, in particular, for the material and moral reasons that produce dependency of the family caregivers on the cared for. In fact, if an objective dependency of the cared for exists, in many cases, caregivers' life revolves around the cared for, even when alternative solutions are feasible. Caregivers often complain of severe psychological and physical health problems.[42]

Titus Mathew studied the, *"Developing Financial Services for the Urban Poor: The Sharan Experience"* in 1997. Early difficulties in non-governmental organizations' mobilizing, promoting, and operating of self-help groups that provide financial services are, in fact, resources for skills, methods and insights intrinsic to both working with communities of the poor and providing financial services. Transforming the experience into a systematic training process for newer entrants into the arena is an important constituent of attempting to reduce learning time and costs. Here, some of the issues experienced by Sharan, a non-governmental organization based in Delhi, India, in developing community-based financial services for the urban poor are discussed, drawing on field notes.[43]

Bhole, L.M., Bhavani R.V., undertook a research on *"Restructuring Rural Credit System: Issues and Alternatives"* in 1995. Problems of the Indian rural credit system and its reforms are reviewed and criteria and organizing principles for a decentralized rural credit system (DRCS) are formulated. A DRCS would comprise thousands of cooperative or commercial unit banks, primary agricultural credit societies, informal credit markets and local self-help groups. Models of self-help groups, interest rate policies and relationships of existing financial institutions and non governmental organizations are discussed. While reconstructing the formal centralized credit system will be difficult, a DRCs is possible with national consensus and a slow, persistent, and determined approach.[44]

Jalali, Rita made a study on *"The Grass-Roots Women's Movement in India"*, in 1990. The last decade has seen the emergence of a grass-roots women's movement in many parts of the developing world. In India, e.g., self-help women's groups have been formed by milk producers, street vendors, and agricultural laborers. Urban women have mobilized to secure forest rights and protest scarcity of water and fuel. Here, evidence from recent Indian studies is used to examine the emergence of women's organizations in traditional, patriarchal societies; the major issues that concern women's organizations in developing countries; how these organizations differe from their counterparts in developing countries; how these organizations differ from their counterparts in the West; and the impact of feminist ideology on such organizations.[45]

"Micro Finance through Self-Help Groups and Its Impact : A Case of Rashtriya Gramin Vikas Nidhi-Credit and Saving Programme in Assam" was conducted by Saundarjay Borbora and Ratul Mahanta in 1995 as a pilot project. The study tries to evaluate the RGVN's Credit and Saving Programme (CSP) in Assam over the years. The specific objectives of the study are to examine the role of micro-credit in the generation of income of the poor, to assess the role of SHGs in promoting the saving habits among the poor and the contribution of the programme in social and economic empowerment of the poor in general and of women in particular. The analysis of survey data revealed that 80 per cent of the members in the selected SHGs were from poor

families. The members of the groups were women who were engaged in gainful economic activity. Of the 45 members selected for study, only 7 had saving bank account with the post office or bank joining SHG. The programme has succeeded in inculcating the habit of saving among the members. As many as 57.8 per cent of the members could save Rs. 200 to Rs. 500 and 42.2 per cent saved Rs. 501 to Rs. 1,000 each. It also helped them to free themselves from the clutches of non-formal sources of credit. Forty-three of the sample beneficiaries could expand their income generating activities. The SHGs have helped to set up a number of micro enterprises for income generation. The CSP is found to be successful as its focus is exclusively on the rural poor; it adopted a credit delivery system designed specially for them with the support of a specially trained staff and a supportive policy with no political intervention at any stage in the implementation of the programme.[46]

"Economic and Social Empowerment of Rural Poor through Self-Help Groups" studied by V. Puhazhendhi and K.J.S. Satyasai is quote relevant because the study atempted to evaluate the performance of Self-Help Groups (SHGs) with special reference to social and economic empowerment. Primary data collected with the help of a structured questionnaire from 560 sample households in 223 SHGs functioning in 11 states representing four different regions across the country formed the basis for the study. For assessing the impact of the programme, a comparison of pre-SHG (before) and post SHG (after) situations was followed in this study. The reference year of the study was 1999-2000. With a view to quantify the economic and social empowerment of SHG members, Economic and Social Empowerment (ESE) Index was computed for each household combining the social and economic parameters using the scoring technique. The empirical findings of the study revealed that the SHG as institutional arrangement could positively contribute to the economic and social empowerment of rural poor and the

impact on the latter was more pronounced than in the former. Though there was no specific pattern in the performance of SHGs among different regions, the southern region had an edge over other regions. Confirming to this situation, the SHG programme has been found more popular in the southern region and its progress in other regions is quite slow, thus there is an uneven achievement among the regions. Older groups had relatively more positive features indicating their better performance than younger groups thus confirming the stability of the SHGs at the ground level. The involvement in the group significantly contributed to improving the self-confidence of the members. The feeling of self-worth and communication with others improved after association with the SHGs. Further the model where NGOs acted as non-financial intermediary could perform better than the other models. Hence, efforts must be made to encourage the NGOs in different regions and motivate them to actively participate in this programme. An effective networking of NGOs would be a step forward in this regard. An efficient rating system of NGOs must be developed that would help in eliminating the ineffective NGOs in this system.[47]

Kamal Vatta and Parminder Singh studied "The Performance of Self-Help Groups in Punjab : A Study of Hoshiarpur District (2000)". It is revealed that about 83 per cent of BPL groups were elegible to get bank loan but only 5 per cent of them could get it. This problem was also faced by the APL groups. The provision of even very little credit helps the rural poor to improve their income levels as illustrated by the case study of an APL SHG which availed of bank loan. Undue delays in the sanctioning of loans need to be eliminated to achieve the objective of economic upliftment of the poor. An extensive awareness campaign is needed to convince the bankers that the poor are bankable and advancing credit to them is more profitable and secure in terms of recovery. The undue delay in the advancement of loan raises apprehensions among the group members regarding the benefits of group formation, which needs to be checked.[48]

"Nature and Performance of Informal Self-Help Groups-A Case from Tamil Nadu" by M. Manimekalai and G. Rajeswari (2000) was to study the socio-economic background of SHG women in rural micro-enterprises, to examine the factors which have motivated the women to become SHG members and eventually as entrepreneurs, analyse the nature of economic activities and the performance in terms of growth indicators such as investment turnover, employment, capacity utilisation, sources of finance and supplementary finance, marketing and other related aspects and identify the problems faced by SHG women in running the enterprises and suggested policy measures. The study found that women SHGs earned the highest profit from agriculture, followed by trade related activities and catering service. A majority of the sample units did not market their products outside the district but sold their products directly to the consumers. The income of the SHG women almost doubled after taking up micro enterprises. The study reported a significant difference between the mean performance of entrepreneurs based on their age, community, education and previous experience. Among these the majority of respondents faced serious problems, in addition to non-availability of raw material, lack of infrastructure facilities including marketing, lack of support from family members in running the enterprises, etc. The provision of microfinance by the NGO to women SHGs has helped the groups to achieve a measure of economic and social empowerment. It has developed a sense of leadership, organisational skill, management of various activities of a business, right from acquiring finance, identifying raw material, market and suitable diversification and modernisation.[49]

Working of Self-Help Group with Particular Reference to Mallipalayam Self-Help Group, Gobichettipalayam Block,

Erode District, Tamil Nadu, (2000) made by S. Lakshmanan is interesting as, it reveals that the members are engaged in the making of mats which are of highe equality. Husbands of the women members support them in the proper functioning of the group-In fact they support women entrepreneurship in the rural areas. However, one of the problems faced by the group is the procurement of raw material for making the mats, besides its high cost. The study reveals that this type of SHG is really a boon in the rural areas, which gives financial autonomy to the rural women and make them economically independent.[50]

Women Self-Help Groups Affiliated to "Chaitanya" : A case study in Pune District, conducted by S.N. Tilekar, N.J. Naikade, B.J. Deshmukh and A.A. Patil (1999) had two hypotheses, First, the role of non-governmental organisations (NGOs) in mobilising savings and in disbursing credit in the rural areas is wellknown. Second many of them have done commendable work in the rural areas compared to other formal institutions. It reveals that the loans are sanctioned especially for all types of farm works, for education purpose, towards meeting the medical expenses, for carrying out the social functions, purchase of livestock and even for non-productive works.[51]

M. Anjugam and T. Alagumani studied the *"Impact of Micro Finance through Self-Help Groups–A Case Study"* (2000). The study revealed that the SHG helped them to use the loan properly and repayment was 100 per cent. It has increased the awareness of members for girl's education, improved outside contact and decision-making skill. This case study has clearly indicated that if the group formation is correct, then definitely there will be a positive impact on all aspects.[52]

M.S. Kallur, *"Empowerment of Women through NGOs : A Case study of MYRADA Self–Help Groups of Chincholi Project, Gulbarga District, Karnataka State"*, (2000) indicated that, women in India are not only poor but also are victims of a multiple socio-economic and cultural factors. Formal arrangments made through banks and cooperative institutions have failed to provide resources to them and this has prompted the non-governmental organisations (NGOs) to organise women Self-Help Groups (SHGs) to provide them credit and to encourage thrift habit among them. Finally it found that the group approach has brought to the surface many operative latent traditional values like group support thrift, group action and sustainability of women SHGs.[53]

R. Das, R.N. Barman and P.K. Baruah in their study of *"Performance of Self-Help Groups in Sonitpur District of Assam"* (1999), found that, the idea of Self-Help Group (SHG) flourished in the nineties at a time when formation of the non-governmental organisations has become a trend with the objective of improving the socio-economic conditions of both the urban and the rural poor.[54]

T.S.Raghavendra, in his study on *"Three Groups in Shimoga District Performance Evaluation of Self-Help Groups"* (2000), found a significant change in the participation of group members in diversifying income generating economic activities in rural areas. Though the credit needs of members are not effectively met, the study suggests that the programme is financially sustainable. Further, the resource constraint is a major detrimental factor to expand economic activities by these two groups. The level of education of the groups is another factor obstructing structural changes. However, the group approach is becoming more and more significant in alleviating poverty and promoting income generating activities in the rural areas. It also reduced transaction cost of lending to the rural poor and emphasised the predominance and effectiveness of group approach in rural credit delivery system. The case study clearly shows that there is a greater potential for SHGs in implementing various programmes for the rural poor in future.[55]

"Self-Help Groups in Karnataka–Trends and Implications" by S.B. Hosamani, S.R.A. Balappa and S.N.

Megeri (2000), in their study found that the success story of "Srinidhi Women Self-Help Group" in Dharwad (Karnataka) showed an encouraging trend. On an average, over the years, the group has been able to earn a rate of return of 21 per cent per annum on their savings. The women members expressed that there has been an overall increase in the purchasing power and petty business income, besides their own empowerment.[56]

T. Ponnarasi and M.P. Saravanan in their Comparative Study on *"Performance of Self Help Groups, in a case study of Agaranallur village in Cuddalore District, Tamil Nadu"* (2000) asserts that, all the five SHGs in the village have actively involved themselves in various developmental activities that have greatly influenced the socio-economic well-being of the villagers.[57]

Working and Impact of Self-Help Groups in Goa by Rekha R. Gaonkar (2000), highlights that individual loans are mostly used for productive purposes. The rate of recovery is cent per cent. Monthly interest rate charged on individual loans is high, varying from 2 to 3 per cent. The group takes decision only after free and frank discussion and all the groups maintain the records such as membership register, minutes book, cash book, savings ledger and the loan ledger. Thus the SHGs have made a lasting impact on the lives of the poor, particularly women, Whose quality of life has improved to a great extent. The members gave the following responses relating to social and economic aspects leading to improvement in their quality of life in terms of increase in the family income, increase in savings, increase in consumption expenditure, gaining self-confidence, productive use of free time, getting opportunity to improve the hidden talent and gaining greater importance in the family. It also opined that the movement of SHGs can significantly contribute towards the reduction of poverty and unemployment in the rural significantly contribute towards the reduction of poverty and unemployment in the rural sector of the economy. The SHGs can lead to social transformation in terms of economic development and social change.[58]

"Performance and Impact of Self-Help Groups in Tamil Nadu" by S. Nedumaran, K. Palanisami and L.P. Swaminathan (2000) carried out with the objectives of examing empirically the performance of self-help groups (SHGs) linked with bank and to assess the performance and socio-economic impact of SHG on the members. The study on SHGs was undertaken in two districts of Tamil Nadu, namely, Erode and Tiruchirapalli covering 30 SHGs from two NGOs (viz., MYRADA and LEAD) and 150 members from the selected SHGs. Further, the study indicated that social condition of the members considerably improved after joining the group activities. Promotion of SHGs in the rural areas, training to members and involvement of local NGOs in building the SHGs are recommended for the overall improvement of the households.[59]

Deepak Shah Studied *"Micro Financing through Co-operatives in Maharashtra : An Impact Evaluation"* (2000). The major objective of the study was to evaluate the performance of three primary Agricultural Co-operative Credit societies (PACS) affiliated to Kolhapur District Central Co-operative Bank (KDCCB) operating in the state of Maharashtra with a view to analyse the strengths, weaknesses, opportunities and threats (SWOT) for these co-operatives at the grassroot level. Apart from evaluating the performance of PACS, it also ascertains the degree of awareness of the farmers in terms of facilities being extended by these co-operatives and the constraints perceived by them to avail of such facilities. The study is based on field level survey conducted during 1997-98. It covered 60 members, i.e., 20 members from each of the three selected societies. Further it reveals that the operational element and the framework for the development of co-operatives must be formulated in accordance with the local environment. There is, therefore, a need to formulate such credit policies which safeguard the interest of those farmers who belong to the societies situated in remore/dryland areas. The aforementioned provisions and measures will certainly revitalise and reactivate some of the societies that have shown inefficient functioning over time.[60]

P.K. Awasthi, Deepak Rathi and Vimla Sahu in their study on *"Working and Impact of Self-Help Groups on Economic Status of Women in Watershed Area of Madhya Pradesh."* The impact of self-help groups (SHGs) on socio-economic status of rural women in watershed areas. Four efficient women SHGs, namely, Khiruwa, Banhari, Madera and Karondi and 70 group members were selected purposively from Karondi Mill watershed area of Katni district in Madhya Pradesh. The study revealed that after the formation of SHGs women took up saving-credit activities and participated in the development process, which are important towards the upgradation of their socio-economic status. The very backbone of SHG is saving, mutual support and co-operation of the members to attain their objectives. Together with monthly saving of Rs. 10 to 20 on an average by each member and benefits from other group activities, they have deposited Rs. 24,046 in the State Bank of India. The SHG women members had started income generating activities, viz., mahua collection, mushroom production, aamchur papad making, pisciculture nursery, etc. Traced that, the SHGs have made a positive impact in creating leadership improving liberally consciousness about health and hygiene and skill formation among the group members. The members of SHG suffered from lack of motivation, backward and forward linkages, inadequacy of infrastructure, insufficient loan, inadequate provision for marketing and availability inputs, lack of systematic monitoring and follow-up of the activities, etc. Thus there is need to evaluate the SHGs annually to assess the progress of different income and employment generating schemes under self-help group.[61]

U.B. Singh, Himmat Singh and Gurnam Singh studied the *"Role of Self-Help Groups in the Shiwalik Foothills of Haryana"* (2000). The study indicated that the SHG even with the heterogeneous socio-economic groups can operate successfully provided the intention of all the members is good. The president, secretary and cashier with reasonably good literacy level functioned with better results. The loan for purchasing buffaloes (dairying) should also have provision for building animal sheds, as the members below the poverty line group hardly have one pucca room for their living. The working of these SHGs has shown that this new concept of micro financing can do wonders to the ruralites living in remote villages in improving their economic condition and protecting them from the clutches of the village moneylenders.[62]

V.K. Singh, R.K. Khatkar and S.K. Kharinta's *"A Study on the Working and Impact of Rural Self-Help Groups in Hisar District of Haryana"* (2000). The working and impact of rural self-help groups of the seven SHGs operating in the three villagers of Hisar district in Haryana State, it was observed that micro financing through SHGs is a better system for inculcating the habit of self-help among the rural poor. The beneficiaries are involved in every aspect of financing from the very beginning.[63]

"Socio-Economic Evaluation of Self-Help Groups in Solan District of Himachal Pradesh : Impact, Issues and Policy Implications" (2000) carried out by Prem, Singh Dahiya, N.K. Pandey and Abshuman Karol, To trace a socio-economic evaluation of the working of self-help groups (SHG) in Solan District of Himachal Pradesh in terms of their impact, issues and policy implications. Thus the study found that the social impact was deep in empowering women folk, educational development of children and emancipation from social evils like drunkenness by male household members.[64]

Case Studies in Andhra Pradesh

K. Jayalakshmi did a study on *"Deepam Scheme in Andhra Pradesh"*. The objectives of the study on : (1) To examine the pre and post-status of SHGs groups and the members. (2) To look into the operational issues pertaining to the scheme. The study found that : in each of the mandals (SHG & DWACRA) together there were more than 400 groups. Each of them was saving Rs. 20-30 per month. With 10-15 in a group-It was not very homogeneous in nature with women from different social and economic status coming together and forming a group-Although there were more than 400 groups in a mandal, almost 50 per cent were dormant. Deposits with the banks enable us to assess the scenario pertaining to the dormant groups. This is assessed by the savings deposited in the banks, regular meetings, internal lending etc. From among them, the groups, which were regularly saving for more than a year and also those who have received government matching grants, were selected under the scheme. The enthusiasm for the LPG from the group was good. The study also made efforts to see whether the SHG as a movement has gained any momentum after the launching of Deepam Scheme. Retention of the Asset. In both the districts it was found that 40-42 per cent of the beneficiaries had retained the asset. The reasons for disposing the stove was hardly of any use, free wood, crop residues available around for cooking, escalation in the price of the LPG from Rs. 167.50 to 240.15, gas dealers were not supplying the cylinder at the door steps as promised by them. Some stated that there was no platform for the gas stove and thatched house dwellers decided to dispose it off. Apart from that all the beneficiaries had worked out the cost incurred for various fuels like kerosene and gas. The former seems to be cheaper than the latter. Some of the houses also utilised electric stoves. They were far and few in between.[65]

Om Prakash and T.G. Ramaiah studied the *"Evaluation of DDP in Anantapur District"* (2000). Objective of the Study, is to study the impact generated by the Watershed Programme in improving the land, water and vegetation resources in Anantapur district. Findings of the Study : (1) Water level in the wells have increased ranging from 0.3 meters to 12.7 meters. (2) 1517 wells and water bodies were rejuvenated to the real mid satisfaction of the local people. (3) Additional net sown area of 5055 hectares were brought under cultivation. (4) Reduction in migration from Anantapur district due to acute drought condition has been from 20 to 100 per cent. (5) Increase in milk yield 15,755 liters. (6) People's participation in community works and pertaining to watershed development has increased. (7) Horticulture plantation were done on 3216 hectares of private land. (8) Agricultural productivity has increased to a great extent. Policy Implication of the Study : (1) The desert development programme on watershed basis has been implemented in the Anantapur district successfully. All the Desert Development Officers in the Office of the P.D., DDP were working on deputation including the P.D., DDP. (2) Though they were working quite sincerely this is a known fact that they do also have a responsibility for their parent departments. They are placed on deputation to PD, DDP once only for 3-4 years. For the wholehearted commitment and the only responsibility to Desert Development Programme, there has to be a separate regular department commissionarate of DDP. (3) And there should be key scientific persons in the commissionarate at the district level on a regular basis to advise the WDT and for the implementation on scientific basis. (4) It was also observed that the Hydro fracturing rig was provided for the four DPAP districts of Chittoor, Warangal, Cuddapah, Rangareddy whereas the only DDP district of Anantapur where this Hydro fracturing rig was needed the most has been left behind. In Anantapur district for fracturing the rocks in the upstream of check dams is very much required. As more than 3600 watersheds have been identified the district by the APSRAC, the cost of Rs. one crore for the Hydrofracturing rig is not much, per watershed the cost comes to Rs. 3333 only. Besides each watershed may have many check dams where on the upstream fracturing of the rocks will be essential.[66]

"A report on the Quick Evaluation study of DWACRA sponsored by the Ministry of Rural Development" is quite important (1998). The objectives of the Study of DWACRA were : (1) Programme implementation to study the degree of conformity to the guidelines of DWACRA with reference to

selection of beneficiaries, selection of projects, utilisation of funds allocated, transparency and involvement of people in the programme implementation. (2) Continuity in the Activities to see what proportion of groups formed under DWACRA have continued to remain active, what are the factors behind continuation or drop out, and whether the assets created have survived and are in use. (3) To understand the impact of the programme on poverty alleviation, i.e., whether DWCRA has contributed to an increase in production, employment and living conditions of women living below the poverty line. Findings of the Study : (1) Overall, DWCRA was not able to meet the objectives that were set forth. The study showed that a large majority of beneficiaries could not utilise the programme to translate into substantial economic benefits. The average per day income of a beneficiary was reported to be only Rs. 42. (2) At the national level DWCRA programme was received well. There was widespread knowledge about the various aspects of DWCRA. However, a very small proportion of beneficiaries could tell the different components of programme. Such as lack of commitment of officials, inability to mobilise NGOs for the benefit of programme and high illiteracy of rural women were some of the reasons for this. (4) Women became more aware, there was a reduction in family size and time spent on household activities. More women were keen to spare some hours for productive work. (5) Eligible women, from both majority and minority communities, participated in DWCRA in proportion to their overall population. However, since the programme was targeted at BPL families, a greater proportion of beneficiaries belonged to lower classes and Scheduled Castes and Scheduled Tribes (SC&ST). The programme, as intended also benefited disabled women. Analysis found that 52.8 per cent of all beneficiaries were SC/ST, and 2.4 per cent were disabled. (6) DWCRA reached not only married women but it also benefited unmarried and widowed women, though their number was small.[67]

"Emergence of Women Self-Help Groups and Its Impact on Rural Development : A Case Study in Krishna District of

Andhra Pradesh" (2000) was studied by Y. Indira Kumari and B.Sambasiva Rao. The objectives were to examine the origin, concept and strategy of women self-help groups (SHGs) and the functioning of groups formed under the programme of Development of Women and Children in Rural Areas (DWCRA) in Nuzvidu division of Krishna district in Andhra Pradcesh. The primary thrust is the formation of groups of 10 to 15 women from poor households for delivery of services like credit, skill development and infrastructure support for self-employment through the strategy of group formation. The case study taken up in Nuzvidu division highlighted how the 194 DWCRA groups composed of 2512 women supported themselves for their upliftment as a part of the remedy for alleviation of poverty. Surf making, candle making, purse making, leaf plates and basket making, internal lending, etc., are some of the activities taken up by the DWCRA groups which helped them to derive DWCRA assistance and the rest of the groups functioned with their own savings. The average corpus of the funded groups was Rs. 57,232 and of the unfunded groups was Rs. 10,336, which included capital accumulated with the help of bank loan, self finance, and cumulative savings. Hence, the Government should provide more assistance to the SHGs of Nuzvidu to generate additional incomes. Along with increase in incomes, savings and their expenditure would rise which in turn would cause a rise in the standard of living of women. Despite the bottlenecks that arose in the functioning of the DWCRA scheme, it helped the majority of women of Nuzvidu division to cross the poverty line. [68]

V.M. Rao's Study *"Dairy Women and Self-Help Groups: A study in Andhra Pradesh and Karnataka"* (2000) was an attempt to present the genesis and development of self-help groups (SHGs) in India and to document the working of women managed SHGs in the study area. The data were collected from 48 women dairy co-operative societies (WDCSs) spread over six districts of Andhra Pradesh and Karnataka during April 2000 to February 2001. The study indicated that the existing formal financial institutions failed to provide finances to landless, marginalised, and disadvantaged groups. The origin of the SHGs could be traced only to mutual cooperation in India Village community. Co-operatives are formal bodies, whereas the SHGs are informal. The SHGs encourge savings and promote income generating activities through. The experiences available in the country and elsewhere suggested that the SHGs are sustainable, have replicability, stimulate savings, and in the process helped borrowers to come out of the vicious circle of poverty. A number of research studies carried out to find out the impact of SHGs revealed that they helped in improving the socio-economic conditions of members.[69]

Rayavarapu Ramakrishna studied the *"Credit Needs of the Rural Poor and the Role of Self-Help Groups"* (2000). The study aims to assess empirically the role of self help groups (SHGs) in improving the access to formal credit institutions in meeting the credit needs of the rural poor in Thumpala village of Visakhapatnam district, Andhra Pradesh. It is based on both secondary and primary data. The primary data were collected for the year 1999-2000. A total of 50 SHG beneficiaries and 25 individual Integrated Rural Development Programme (IRDP) beneficiaries were selected for the study, the latter group of beneficiaries forming the control group. The main findings of the study are : Firstly, the progress of SHG Bank linkage in India is remarkable. The number of SHGs linked to banks increased from 225 in 1992-93 to 9,620 in 1997-98. Another feature is that there is wide diversity in the regional spread of the programme. Besides, there existed wide diversity in the relative significance of various institutions in the linkage. At the national level, Regional Rural Banks (RRBs) are the major partners (66 per cent in 1997), followed by commercial banks (24 per cent in 1997) with the role of co-operatives being rather minimum in the linkage programme. Secondly, as compared to IRDP beneficiaries, those covered under SHGs fared better in respect of social empowerment and economic progress. Thirdly, access to institutional credit has been of a higher order for SHG beneficiaries compared to IRDP beneficiaries. If the SHGs are allowed to develop links with bank branches, the credit needs of the poor are met and their small savings tapped, recoveries and profitability would improve. The linkage of the SHGs with the bank will enable them to become operationally viable units.[70]

Objectives of the Study

The present work has two types of objectives, namely main and sub objectives.

(A) ***Main objective :*** Is to analyse the role of Self Help Groups (SHGs) for promoting socio-ceonomic development of women.

(B) ***The sub objectives are—***

1. To examine the relationship between SHGs and women economic empowerment (production, consumption and economic status).

2. To examine the relationship between SHGs and women social empowerment (health, nutrition and educational status of women and children).

3. To examine the relationship between SHGs and women political empowerment (improvement in the capacity or ability of women to demand or raise their voice regarding their entitlements and rights in various public forum, as well as their participation as members/presidents in panchayati raj institutions (ZP/MPPS/ VP/ Gramasabha and other local organisations like Village forest, educational and health committees).

4. To offer policy perspectives on women empowerment.

5. To find out the importance of Self Help Groups as a public policy.

6. To find out various public policies aimed at the upliftment of weaker sections particularly women.

7. To find out the role of Government in formulation of public of Policies and its impact on the socio-economic development of the Nation.

8. To study the aims and objectives of Self Help Groups and to asses the economic development of women.

9. To study the structure and working of Self Help Groups.

Hypotheses of the Study

1. All the rural development programmes including the Self Help Groups have been of greater benifitto the rural rich/ middle class peasant women than to the poor.

2. Due to the illiteracy and ignorance of the rural women, several public policies aimed at their development are not administered properly by the district administration.

3. Self Help Groups in Andhra Pradesh are not channelising the various poverty alleviation and development programmes.

Methodology

The study intends to analyse the public policy with special reference to self help groups. Further it intends to identify the policy implementation for the socio-economic, cultural and educational development of rural poor women through self help groups. Normative (Analytical), descriptive, Historical methods have been employed in this study. Successful and not successful cases of self help groups would also be observed through case study.

Sample Design

In the present work the required data has been collected randomly with the help of stratified random sample technique. Since, the research area consists of three revenue divisions, one mandal from each revenue division has been selected, for eliciting the opinion, performance and their attitude towards the governmental policies. Firstly, Gorantla mandal from Penukonda Revenue Division. Secondly, Atamakur from Anantapur Revenue Division which is nearer to the district head quarter. Thirdly, Kalyandurgam from Dharmavaram Revenue Division which consists of a large of Scheduled Caste population. Further these mandals have been selected on the basis of rainfall, economic development, illiteracy, unemployment and cultural differences. The collected sample is 450 in total, 150 from each madal it consists of both urban and rural. The groups in villages have also been chosen on the basis of facilities like distance from mandal headquarters, transport facilities, school, anganwadi center etc.

Sources of Data

The study is made on the basis of both primary and secondary sources. The macro aspect of the study is based on the published and unpublished works on the subject, reports of government and expert bodies. Exclusively in this study Reports, records, annual action plans, bulletins and documents prepared by DRDA Anantapur are the main sources of data. Information is also collected from government websites like Andhra Pradesh.com, ap-nic.in, ap-govt.in,nic.in. Secondary data has been collected from books, Journals and Newspapers In addition to these sources, and primary information collected through interviews with questionnaires served to a cross-section of the people is used for analysis.

Data Collection and Tools Used in the Study

For collecting the data, different methods of social enquiry have been adopted. A special tool was used by the investigator using the scientific process. The questionnaire process the questionnaire consists of items in all spread over behavior areas and also to collect their personal data, i.e., name, sex, age, social, economical, political, educational and cultural backgrounds.

Time Span of the Study

The questionnaires were administered during the months of March to May 2001 and October and November 2002. The groups were chosen to administer the questionnaire only after the completion of three years of period.

Data Analysis

The data had been analysed with the help of a computer. It had been transformed into computer code and ananlysed with the help of single variable or multi-variable tables. Statistical tools such as average, percentage, cross sectional, Mean, Deviation from mean, Average mean deviation and Over all Average had also been used to analyse the data.

Preliminary Survey and Pre-Testing

Prior to approach the actual field, a preliminary survey was undertaken and pre-testing was done to decide the questions to be finally included in the questionnaire. This preliminary survey was conducted in six villages of Anantapur District, i.e., two from each Revenue Division. Only after preliminary survey and pre-testing, a design was made on the variables which were included in the structured questionnaire.

Need, Importance and Scope of the Study

The study has a vast scope in terms of understanding the nature of public policy in the present context. It is intended to make a study of both public policy and self help groups for the over all development of rural and urban women. Apart from this, the aim of the study is to make an analysis of socio-economic, cultural and educational status of rural and urban women before and after joining as members of self help groups. It also intends to assess the merits and draw backs of public policy for the upliftment of women belonging to the weaker sections' women. Specific aims and objectives of self help groups would be analysed.

The researcher selected the topic and the research area because of two reasons. Primarily with the belief that the Anantapur District has been classified as one of the backward districts of Andhra Pradesh. It receives the lowest rainfall, stands first in poverty (nearly 50 per cent), dropout rate. As a result the governments at the centre and the state have been implementing a large number of programmes. Self help groups scheme is on among these and women from weaker sections even in remote villages have been involving.Thus women's participation in self help groups caused for the improvement of living conditions of families. Secondly the district administration is promoting thrift and credit groups under DWACRA programme and the present SGSY (SwaranJayanti Gram Swarozgar Yojana).

Limitations of the Study

1. The present work has certain limitations, which must be reckoned with for the purpose of specificity and the limited nature of the research undertaken. Though the concept of Self Help Groups came in to effect from 1999. But prior to this it was an integral part of AWACRA Groups. Later on these emerged as Self Help Groups. Hence, in the study DWACRA groups were taken into consideration for analysis for over a period of time.

2. The study employed only percentage, average and mean analysis. This is also to be seen in view of the purposes of the study. There is no scope for the use of other types of statistics. Since the study intends to deal with implications of public policy.

3. An attempt could have also been made to assess the impact of assistance given to individuals under

this scheme and Self Help Groups of men. This has not been attempted since the study is concentrated on women groups.

4. The study was undertaken only in a few mandals. The findings naturally have relative validity. The researcher has chosen to deal with a few variables. However it encompasses innumerable variables, which the researcher considered to be significant for the study. In judging what the significant variables are,the researcher may have been some what arbitrary.

5. The researcher was besets with time and special constraint due to his full time employment. the data might not be all exhaustive, which ideally required for this kind of study.

References

1. Robert E. Goodin and Hans Dicter Klingemann (Ed.): "A New Handbook of Political Science Political Science", Oxford University Press, 2000.
2. *Ibid.*, p. 575.
3. G. Suvarna Rani : "Development and Rural Woman of India", Kurukshetra, Aug. 1995. p. 21.
4. Urvashi Gulati: "Women's Development in India with Special Reference to Rural Women", *Ibid.*, p. 17.
5. P.Anandharajkumar, "Multiprogramme Approach to Women's Economic Independence", *Ibid.*, p. 74.
6. DAI-A 61/03, p. 1181, Sep. 2000.
7. MAI 39/01, p. 110, Feb. 2001.
8. DAI-A 61/12, p. 4915, Jun. 2001.
9. DAI-A 61/10, p. 4150, Apr. 2001.
10. DAI-A 61/10, p. 4158, Apr. 2001.
11. DAI-A 61/03, p. 1157, Sep. 2000.

12. DAI-A,60/08, p. 3123, Feb. 2000.

13. DAI-A, 61/10, p. 4142, April. 2001.

14. DAI-A 61/03, p. 1143, Sept. 2000.

15. DAI-A 61/07, p. 2908, Jan. 2001.

16. DAI-A 61/10, p. 4158, April. 2001

17. DIA-A 60-09, p. 3517, March. 2000.

18. Social Action; 1996, 46, 3, July-Sept., pp. 262-277.

19. International Labour Review; 1990, 129, 6, 693-714.

20. World Development; 1990, 18, 12, Dec., 1621-1634.

21. Indian Journal of Social Work, 1990, 51, 1, Jan., 99-106.

22. Journal of Urban Affairs; 1998, 20,4,419-441.

23. Journal of Social Development in Africa, 1997, 12, 1, 39-51.

24. International Social Science Journal 1996, 48, 2 (148), June, pp. 207-218.

25. Demko George J & Jackson Michael C (Eds.): "Populations At Risk In America : Vulnerable Groups At the End of the Twentieth Century", Boulder, Co:Westview Press, Inc, 1995, pp. 66-76.

26. IDS–Bulletin ; 1996, 27, 1, Jan., pp. 100-108.

27. New Directions for Programme Evaluation ; 1995, 67, fall, 27-37.

28. Habitat International : 1995, 19, 4, Dec. 485-497.

29. Development in Practice; 1995, 5, 2, May, 108-116.

30. Environment and Urbanization, 1995, 7, 2, Oct., 131-151.

31. Social Action, 1993, 43, 3, July-Sept. 328-338.

32. Revista-Mexicana-de-Sociologia; 1993, 55,2, April-June, 351-366.

33. Disasters; 1994, 18, 1, March. 35-47.

34. World Development, 1992, 20, 10, Oct. 1401-1422.

35. Policy Studies Journal; 1989, 18, 1, fall, 213-219.

36. International Journal of Sociology and Social Policy; 1991, 11, 1-3, 192-211.

37. Development and Change, 1991, 22,1, Jan., 117-154.

38. www.nird.org, Research Highlights 2000-2001.

39. www.nird.org., Research Highlights 1997-1998.

40. www.nird.org., Research Highlights, 2000-2001.

41. www.nird.org., Research Highlights, 1998-1999.

42. www.nird.org., Case Studies on Self, 1997.

43. Journal of Socio-Economics; 1996, 25, 2, Summer, 189-223.

44. International Sociological Association (ISA), 1998.

45. Envirnonment and Urbanisation: 1997, 9, 1, Apr., pp. 227-232.

46. Man and Development; 1995, 17, 3, Sept. pp. 46-60.

47. American Sociological Association (ASA), 1990.

48. Indian Journal of Agricultural Economics, July-Sept. 2001, pp. 440-450.

49. *Ibid.*, pp. 450-1.

50. *Ibid.*, pp. 452.

51. *Ibid.*, pp. 454-5.

52. *Ibid.*, pp. 457.

53. *Ibid.*, pp. 458.

54. *Ibid.*, pp. 459.

55. *Ibid.*, pp. 465-6

56. *Ibid.*, pp. 466.

57. *Ibid.*, pp. 465-7.

58. *Ibid.*, pp. 469.

59. *Ibid.*, pp. 469-70

60. *Ibid.*, pp. 471.

61. *Ibid.*, pp. 472-3.

62. *Ibid.*, pp. 472-3.
63. *Ibid.*, pp. 476-7.
64. *Ibid.*, pp. 481-82.
65. *Ibid.*, pp. 482.
66. *Ibid.*, pp. 486-87.
67. www.nird.org. Research Highlights 2000-01.
68. *Ibid.*, Research Highlights 1998-1999.
69. www.Andhra Pradesh.com.
70. Indian Journal of Agricultural Economics, July-Sept. 2001, p. 485.
71. *Ibid.*, pp. 467-8.
72. *Ibid.*, pp. 469-70.

2

Public Policy: A Theoretical Perspective

The public policy is framed in accordance with the needs and basic requirements of the people and area for the growth of social justice and maintenance of social order. As such, public policy may be regarded as a cumbersome process or a net result of the institutionalization of general will of the masses. The administrative and political structure of Indian democracy, evolved the plans and programmes after serious deliberations both inside and outside the organisation in conformity. At the time of policy making due attention is always paid to the ideological aspirations, prescribed norms of socio-political system within the prevailing legal and constitutional framework, social environment and cultural ethos of the people.[1]

Meaning of Public Policy

The study of Public Policy has attained vital importance in modern times. Through the evaluation of several public policies, it seeks to improve the quality of life at all the citizens and also aims to bring about social transformation and social change. Such policies could be broadly categorised into two types. They are: (i) the policies which are known as comprehensive and lead to structural transformation; and (ii) incremental policies, which are reformative in nature.[2]

As a concept in political science, "Policy" has a least two quite distinct meanings. On the one hand, "Policies" are often considered to be ways of doing things by decision or by rules these are called Administrative Policies. On the other hand "policies are often regard as substantive programmes, referring specifically to the content of what is being done."[3]

Thus, public policy has not been the central focus of the political science discipline. Political scientists had largely concerned themselves with the institutions and structures of the government and the political behaviour and process rather than the content of public policy itself.[4] Emphasising the need for the research on public policy studies, Harold D. Lasswell observed: "Of all specialists in several fields of knowledge, political scientists are the ones who are most obeviously concerned with policy structures and functions. Possessed of large literature on government, law and politics, the professional student of government is expected to study important decisions made at the national, international or sub-national levels and to contribute to our knowledge on factors-combination that helps to explain how and why they occurred.[5] Public Policy involves the deliberative choice of collective goals and the implementation of public decisions. When enacted, such decisions are considered authoritatively binding upon all members of the society. The political system is the vehicle for enacting these decisions.[6] Thus, such public policies require to be studied in depth by political scientists in areas concerning formulation, implementation and evlauation of Government programmes for the upliftment of the people.

The study of public policy has attained considerable prominence in political science due to scientific, professional and political purposes.[7] Different political scientists have defined public policy in different perspectives.

Thomas R. Dye viewed public policy as "whatever the government chooses to do or not to do".[8]

Carl J. Friedrich opined: "Public Policy is a proposed course of action of a person, group or government within a given environment providing opportunities and obstacles which the policy proposes to utilise and overcome in an effort to reach a goal."[9]

Robert Evestone holds that "the relationship of a government unit to its environment is known as public policy".[10]

According to Richard Rose, public policy be considered as "a long series of more or less related activities and their consequences for those concerned rather than as a discreet decision".[11]

David Easton has opined that public policy is "the authoritative allocation of values for the whole society".[12]

Laswell and Kaplan have observed it as "a projected programme of goal, values and practices."[13]

Thus, the above views converge on the basic theme of specific governmental actions as well as the overall programmes of actions towards a given goal. The public policies that are formulated, are in tune with the basic objectives of the country as enshrined in the constitution and also for bringing about a suitable transformation in society.

A comprehensive study of public policy begins with a systematic enquiry into the various forces that shape the policy which are known as the inputs into the policy. The analysis of the policy content includes the decisions and actions of the government in pursuance of the policy. The examination of the accomplishments of public policy, which is known as the the policy outcome, is equally significant. It helps us understand as to how far the intended results have been achieved and the problems appearing from time to time have been overcome. In the final analysis, the feedback of a public policy influences the future decisions of the government. Therefore, proper analysis of public policies enables the decision-makers to choose the right policy, allocate appropriate priorities and adopt efficient means of implementation.

The study of public policy has attained greater attention of the political scientists in contemporary times as it analyses the causes and effects of governmental activity. Thomas R. Dye aptly states: "This involves a description of the content of the public policy; an assesment of the impact of environmental forces on the content of public policy; and inquiry into the consequences of various public policies for the political system, and an evaluation of the impact of the public policies on society, in terms of both expected and unexpected consequences".[14] Public policy is the policy of the Government through which it materialises the desires of the society. It is an instrument to effect the desired changes.

Thus, Public Policy is, the proposed action of the Government with which it will perform the regulative, instributive and extractive activities in the society and, in turn, the Government will be influenced by the society through the feedback mechanism:

(a) The goals with which policy analysis is concerned.

(b) The means for achieving those goals.

(c) The methods for determining the effects of alternative means on goal achievement, and

(d) The profession of policy analysis which is applying these methods in relating means to goals.[15]

Policy analysis is an appropriate tool in approaching policy questions. Policy analysis enables us to describe and explain the causes and consequences of public policy.[16]

Public Policy and Public Administration

Academic study of public administration between the world wars preached a dichotomy between politics and administration. Academics deliberately chose to confine the area of the discipline by drawing narrow boundaries because they wished to establish their autonomy from political science, law and other related disciplines by concentrating on the internal relationships of public administration system which were not being covered by any other discipline. They wanted to improve public administration without entering the political arena. Their model was depoliticised, professional, morally irreproachable and efficient public bureaucracy, and their method was scientific inquiry. Their preoccupations were civil service, legislation, governmental reorganisations, budgeting systems innovative management techniques. In this way they protected their embroynic discipline while meeting a felt public need. Academics brought into the discipline their own values-belief in rationality, one best way, and goals of efficiency and economy.[17]

With the New Deal, serious objections were raised, challenging this introverted view of public administration. White ended his Introduction To The Study of Public Administration (1926) with a reference to morale, the key to which was to be found in trusted political and administrative leadership.[18] Gullick said that at the beginning of the Roosevelt era, his programmes involve a new and revolutionary extension of the theory and practice of public administration, concerned not with checks and balances or with the division of policy and administration, but with the division between policy veto on one side and policy planning and execution on the other.[19] In reaching this conclusion, he demolished the politics-administration dichotomy. J.M. Gaus, in Frontiers of Public Administration rightly emphasised the significance of public policy in the administration intended to carry out the public welfare and also suggested that public administration was not the managerial aspects of enforcing the law but the state in action as broad as government itself. The objective of public administration was not blind obedience to the master's dictates but the good as the helpless power of the government elite or mechanical business efficiency tantamount to economy, penny-pinching and profit makings. It was the life, humane, warm, progressive and protective of individual rights. A good administration was a political participant in public policy making.[20] Appleby left in the field of public administration a bias on behalf of administrative pluralism, a system in which governmental administration is immersed in group competition over the shape and content of public policy.

"Public Policy is the reconciliation and crystalization of the views and wants of many people and groups in the body social... The reconciliation of diverse interests in the public interest is a joint undertaking by both legislative and executive branches and the crystalization occurs when a law is passed. Then, when the law is executed, it is the public administrator who is primarily involved... But in a complex age such as ours, legislation cannot be sufficiently detailed to cover every contingency; hence government officials must exercise discretion not only in the execution of a law but also in its interpretation.[21]

Administration makes policy, initiates legislation, amplifies legislative enactment's, represents pressure groups, acts as a pressure group itself, and is caught up in many ways in the tug of war between the two major parties.[22] Administration relates to the ends of a state in the determination of policy. The administrator not only carries out public policy but recommends it, and he often takes an active part in securing its enactment into law.[23] The textbooks on public administration confronted with the obvious concern of public administration with public policy have revised their definitions to reflect the public policy orientation, i.e., "Public administration consists of all those operations having for their purpose the fulfillment or enforcement of public policy".[24]

"Public administration may be defined as the co-ordination of individual and group efforts to carry out public policy".[25] "As a study, public administration examines every aspect of government's efforts to implement the laws and to give effect to public policy."[26]

"Public administration,", claims Appleby, "is policy making". But it is not autonomous, exclusive or isolated policy making. It is policy making in a field where mighty forces contend, forces engendered in, and by, society. It is policy making subject to still other and various policy-makers. The legislature can authorise any new programme. But based on past experience, the experts in the administrative branch will be relied upon to work out the details of legislation, and then will take the responsibility for making it a success in practice. These programmes will not succeed, no matter how well-supported financially, unless the administrators made sound decisions in initiating and carrying out the different projects.

Public Policy and Public Opinion

The influence of public opinion over government policy has been the subject of great philosophical controversies in the classic literature on democracy. Edmund Burke believed that democratic representatives should serve the interest of the people but not necessarily confirm to their will in deciding questions of public policy. In contrast other theorists have evaluated the success of democratic insitutions by whether or not they facilitate popular control over public policy.[27]

V.O. Key in his most acclaimed work, "Public Opinion and American Democracy", said that government attempts to mould public opinion towards support of programmes a: l policies it expouses. The perfect congruence between public policy and public opinion could be government of public opinion rather than by public opinion.[28]

In order to support the notion that public opinion has an important influence over public policy, there is very little direct evidence in the existing research literature. Many studies reveal the options of any knowledge or opinion about public policy on the part of the masses of citizens. This suggests that mass opinion has little influence over the content of public policy. Policy studies suggest that masses of people have little knowledge of and interest in or opinion about a great many political questions which clearly imply that public opinion has little impact on the content of public policy. Likewise, studies indicate that public opinion is unstable and inconsistent ; also imply that public opinion has little bearing on pulbic policy.

However, it is said that policy makers are not completely free from the influence of public opinion voting behaviour of Congress men on roll call voters correlates very closely with the characteristics of their constitutencies. In modern liberal democracies, while framing the policies, the public opinion will be considered by decision makers.

Factors Influencing the Public Policy

In order to have a better understanding of public policy, one has to analyse and enquire into the factors that shape the public policy in a given political system. The institutions, the process which are working as the agents in a political system, which are coming from the environment that shape the public policy, should be studied thoroughly. The factors which influence public policy may be powerful in one political system but the same may be weak in another. In other words, the factors that influence public policy may differ from one political system to other.

The problem of assessing the independent effect of mass opinion on the decision makers is that their actions help to mould mass opinion. Public policy may be in accordance with mass opinion, but it is considered that whether mass opinion shaped public policy or public policy shaped mass pinion.

The other factors which influence the generation and initiation of policy measures may be broadly mentioned as elite attitudes, political parties and interest groups, etc.[29] These forms of inputs are instrumental for generation of public policy within a political system.

Policy Initiation

All the studies on public policy begin with an enquiry into the institution of policy. While discussing the different variables involved in shaping the policy, it is pertinent to bring Dye's analytical models which explain different forces involved in moulding public policy. They are:[30]

(i) Systems theory portrays public policy as an output of the political system; different forces in society in the shape of demand influence the governing elite to formulate policies.

(ii) The elite theory suggests that the mass do not possess the calibre to demand and support policies. Hence, it is left to the governing elite to chalk out public policy, enlighten people about the policy and also to implement it.

(iii) Group theory insists that public policy is shaped out of the actions of the interest groups. It is the result of the equilbrium reached in the group struggle at any given time.

(iv) Incrementalism views public policy as a continuation of past govermental activities with only incremental modification.

(v) In the rational model, a particular policy is selected from a number of alternative policies as the most efficient one to achieve the goal.

(vi) Finally, the structure of governmental institutions may have greater share in policy outcomes.[31]

Public policy may be initiated according to any one of these models or it may be the outcome of the combination of a number of models.

Policy Implementation

Political system reacts by the inputs, particularly by the demands. Demands and supports should be equal, so that political system will maintain a kind of equilibrium. In accordance with the demands there will be the policy outcome from the political system. The political system will try to implement to clear distinction between policy implementation, policy performance and what is generally referred to as policy impact. Policy impact studies and examinees the linkage between the specific programme approaches and observes its consequences. The study of policy implementation, on the other hand, highlights one of the forces that determines policy impact by focussing on those activities, while effectively rendering the public services. Policy impact studies generally are concerned with "what happened"? Whereas implementation studies lay emphasis on why it happened this way.

There is no common agreeable definition of the policy implementation in the literature of political science. "Policy implementation encompasses those actions by public and private individuals affecting the achievement of objectives set forth in prior policy decisions.[32]

Policy implementation model directs attention to a set of variables and their inter relations that determine policy performance within a particular jurisdiction. Therefore, the selection criteria for assessing the performance is a crucial stage in the analysis. An analysis of policy implementation requires more than the measurement of programme performance. The principal goal is to derive explanation from the events and factors that intervene between the articulation of a particular policy and the results that occur within the states and localities.

The formal and informal attributes of the organisation responsible for implementation affects it as the ability to carry out the policies stated, no matter what the attitudes of its agencies, staff, structure, and relations with other officials and units of the Government, will tend to limit or enhance the prospects for the effective implementation. One important factor is the experience and competence of the staff to perform the tasks required of them. Obviously, the staff that lacks sufficient training and knowledge in the area of policy will have difficulty in coping with the type of the tasks they must perform.

The status of the agency within the hierarchy of the parent organisation of which it is a part or the local government structure also affects its administrative capacity. An organisation without sufficient financial and political support and without the necessary independence to make decisions and hire qualified personnel will face severe setbacks in administrative programmes.[33]

National Policy for Women Welfare

The constitution of India itself demands for social, economic and political justice to all the sections of society and directs the government to take special care of the underprivileged people.[34] India accepted a socialistic form of state a form of Government. Ultimately, the state had committed to the happiness of its citizens. Measures for providing welfare services to the weaker sections of the state became an integral part of its functions and responsibilities.

As a result, the Government of India decided to take steps directed for social change based on three major areas, viz. Constitutional and Legal reforms, planned development based on mixed economy and state support to social welfare activities. All these three steps have their impact on the status of women.[35]

Social Legislation

The Constitution of India came into force on January 26, 1950 provided social rights to women with men. However, in actual practice, a few forms of inequalities persisted even, today. Legal measures have been enunciated in India from time to time to protect and promote the welfare of women, leading to an improvement in their status. The women specific laws enforce different aspects which endanger the situation of women and make their condition alarming. These can be broadly categorised into three aspects namely, social, economic and political aspects. The major issues relating to social legislation comprise of family, marriage, adoption, abortion, maintenance and, above all, with same legislations that protect women from violation and atrocities.[36]

The above mentioned problems of women have been sought to be removed by the enactment of the Hindu marriage and divorce act (1956), Hindu Guardianship Act (1956), Hindu inheritance Act (1956) providing equal share to women in property, establishment of the principle of monogamy are some of the important innovations introduced in the Indian Social Structure affecting women's status and role. The termination of pregnancy Act 1971, the Maternity Benefit Act 1961, the Dowry Prohibition Act 1971, the Immoral Traffic Prevention Act 1986, and the equal remuneration Act 1976 are some of the measures of relief for all women irrespective of caste, creed or religion. In 1984, the government conceded to the demand of women to establish family courts for speedy conduct of matrimonial disputes through the provision of informal procedure of conciliation. Hence, Laws are being used as an instrument to remove social disabilities and for empowering women.

Constitution and Women Policies

The Preamble to the Constitution of India assures "to secure to all its citizens: Justice-social, economic and political, liberty of thought, expression, belief, faith and worship ; Equality of status and opportunity ; and to promote among them all fraternity assuring the dignity of the individual and unity of the nation". To attain these National objectives, the constitution guarantees certain fundamental rights and freedom such as freedom of speech, protection of life, personal liberty and prohibition of discrimination or denial of equal opportunity.[37] Thus, a few specific articles which are related to women are:

Right to Equality

Article 14: equality before Law. the state shall not deny to any person equality before the law or the equal protection of the laws within the territory of India.

Article 15: Prohibition of discrimination on grounds of religion, race, caste, sex,or place of birth. This Article permits the State to make special provisions for women and children.

Article 16: equality of opportunity in matters of public employment. The main objective of article 16 is to create a constitutional right to equality of opportunity and employment in public offices. No citizen shall or any of them, be ineligible for, or discriminated against in respect of, any employment or office under this Article is confined to citizens as distinguished from other persons. Further, it is confined to employment or appointment to an office under the state.

Article 21: Protection of life and personal liberty. No person shall be deprived of his life or personal liberty except according to procedure established by law. The expression procedure established by law in Article 21 has been judicially construed as meaning a procedure which is reasonable, fair and just.

Right Against Exploitation

Article 23: Prohibition of traffic in human beings and forced labour. Traffic in human beings and beggar and other similar forms of forced labour are prohibited and any contravention of this provision shall be an offence punishable in accordance law.

Right to Constitutional Remedies

Article 32: the Supreme Court shall have power to issue directions or writs, including writs in the nature of habeas corpus. Mandamus, Quo warrant and certiorari. Whichever may be appropriate for the enforcement of any of the rights conferred on this part. The right guaranteed by this Article shall not be suspended except as otherwise provided for by this Constitution. Segregating prostitutes' children by locating separate schools and providing separate hostels, would not be in the interest of such children and of society from their mothers and be allowed to mingle with others and become part of the society.

Directive Principles of State Policy

Though the provisions contained in this part shall be enforceable by any court, but the principles therein laid down are nevertheless fundamental in the governance of the country and it shall be the duty of the state to apply these principles in making kaws.[38]

Article39: The state shall, in practice, direct its policy towards securing (a) that the citizens, men and women equally, have the right to an adequate means of livelihood; (b) that there is equal pay for equal work for both men and women; (c) that the health and strength of workers, men and women, and the tender age of children are not abused and that citizens are not forced by economic necessity to enter avocations unsuited to their age or strength; (d) that children are given opportunities and facilities to develop in a healthy manner and in conditions of freedom and dignity and that child and youth are protected against exploitation and against moral and material abandonment.

Article 42: Provision for just and human conditions of work and maternity relief–the State shall make provision for securing just and humane conditions of work and for maternity relief.

Article 44: uniform civil code for the citizens–The State shall endeavour to secure for the citizens a uniform civil code throughout the territory of India.

Article 45: Provision for free and compulsory education for children–the State shall endeavor to provide, within a period of ten years from the commencement for all children until they complete the age of fourteen years.

Thus the constitution of India has given special attention to the needs of women to enable them to exercise their rights on equal with men and participate in national development.[39]

Women and Economic Development

After independence, the various problems of poverty leading to various imbalances and discriminations for a vast number of people posed a formidable problem to Indian rulers. Plannced Development was considered to be the most efficient way of meeting the problems. The policy measures had serious implications for Indian women. India adopted a path of development based on mixed economy with an emphasis on industrialisation.[40]

Institutional Set up

The central social welfare board is a national body in women's development at three levels-policy, programmes and implementation. The Board frames policy at the central level through links with voluntary women's organisation, makes its own development programmes for women on the basis of funds given by the government, and implements programmes through its welfare extension projects which reach remote areas of the nation.[41]

The Union Government established the Board in 1953 to promote welfare and development services for women, children and other under previleged group. Agencies administering programmes for women's developments are disperssed in different departments and agencies of government at the centre, the state and the local level. At the crentral level, the planning commission, ministry of education and social welfare, with its two specialized agencies, the central and the national council for women's education, ministry of Health and Family Planning, Ministry of Home Affairs and Ministry of Labour and Employment, shares the responsibility of implementing women's development programmes.

Five Year Plans Approach for Women's Development

The planners and policy makers realized the importance of women in the process of economic development and designed several programmes for the benefit of women. These programmes laid emphasis on the provision of minimum health facilities including family welfare, nutrition, child welfare, literacy programmes etc. Further, several other programmes have been introduced to improve the economic and social status of women including rural women.

First Five Year Plan: During the first Five Year Plan, social services like health, education, sanitation, housing and rehabilitation were given priority. The Central Social Welfare Board was set up in 1953 and grants-in-aid were extended to promote welfare of women. The central board, through the State Social Welfare Board provided assistance to voluntary agencies to improve the welfare of women. This paved the way for the growth of women's organizations and starting of Mahila Mandals at various levels.

Second Five Year Plan: During the Second Five Year Plan period attention was paid to protect the women from injurious work and maternity benefits were extended to women. The Central Social Welfare Board took up welfare extension projects. One in each district in the country each serving a group of 25 villages.[42] The Central Board had set-up two Advisory Committees to study the social and moral hygiene problems and the other care services.

Third Five Year Plan: During the Third Five Year Plan Period a strategy for the development of women was formulated and the education of girls was focused. Central and State Welfare Boards assisted about 6,000 voluntary organizations in the country to extend health and education services to women. Community development programmes were implemented along with extending assistance to about 1700 Mahila Mandals Training courses were organised for adult women to enable them to take up employment and holiday homes were constructed for children.

Fourth Five Year Plan: During the Fourth Five Year Plan period special attention was paid to welfare programmes of women. The Central Social Welfare Board continued to promote educational, cultural and recreational activities for women and children. Basic training programmes, for women and young girls in handicrafts, nutrition, health and maternity services were grounded. Block level women welfare centres were established and local mahila mandals were allowed to organize welfare programmes for women with the help of village panchayats. It was also recognized that the family and child welfare programme is the single largest effort directed towards the welfare of women and children.

Fifth Five Year Plan: The Fifth Five Year Plan assigned high priority to the removal of poverty and self employment. The First Non-Congress Government at the Centre (Janata Government) changed these priorities and gave importance to the claims of women in need of care and protection for low income families. Literacy programmes to train women in the age group of 15-35 years, health care and home economy were stressed.[43] The Committee appointed by the Government of India in 1971 to examine the status of women pointed out the following:

1. Majority of the women are not enjoying the rights that are guaranteed by the constitution.
2. The status of women is lowered due to the increasing incidence of dowry.
3. The incidence of suicide among young married women is high.
4. The women are still ignorant of their legal rights regarding marriage, divorce, inheritance and maternity benefits.
5. There is a wide gap between the enrolment of girls and boys in formal educational institutions.
6. The dropout ratio of girls in the schools is very high.

With the above findings, to improve the wellbeing of women, this committee suggested several developmental programmes in the areas of education, health, family planning, nutrition, employment and so on. In 1976 the Bureau of Women's Development and Welfare was established to initiate steps for women's development.

Sixth Five Year Plan: During the Sixth Five Year Plan period attempts were made to improve the working conditions of women and to raise their economic and social status. Vocational Training Centres and Industrial Training Institutes for women were started. Under the Integrated Rural Development Programme the beneficiaries covered under TRYSEM were women. The new programme-Development of Women and Children in Rural Areas (DWCRA) –was started in 1982-83 to train women in a large variety of economic activities. Non-formal education centres for girls were set-up and scholarships were extended to girls belonging to Scheduled Castes and tribes. Functional literacy programmes for adult women were grounded.[44]

Seventh Five Year Plan: During the Seventh Five Year Plan period, women development programmes were executed with the purpose of providing employment and income generating services, education and training services, legal and support services. Establishing of an apex body for women's training is urged and is reponsible for reorientation of the administrative machinery at all levels to the issues of women development. A reservation of 30 (thirty) per cent seats in all elected bodies is stressed as a transitionary measures to ensure that women have the opportunity to enjoy equal political status with men. The focus of the programmes has been shifted from welfare to development and there is more involvement of women in the planning and implementation process at all levels. Beneficiary oriented schemes for women were executed. Minimum needs programme is strengthened and legal enactments were made providing access to property, maternity and other benefits for women.

Eighth Five Year Plan: The important objective of the Eighth Five Year Plan was to extend the reach of services to women, both qualitatively and quantitatively. The strategy of women development during the Eighth Plan period aims at the following:[45]

1. To remove the socio-cultural and administrative constraints for the realization of full utilization of women potential and to ensure that the benefits of development from different sectors do not bypass women.

2. To integrate the issues relating to women in the total endeavours of development.

3. To strengthen the women groups at the grass-roots levels and offer a package of services to them such as family welfare, education, health, nutrition, drinking water etc.

4. To introduce special programmes for adolescent young girls.

5. To ensure equal share in the parental property.

6. To strengthen the development of women and children in rural areas programmes.

7. To cover larger number of women under special extension services.

8. To implement vocational training of women activity as the thrust area.

9. To retain girls in schools upto elementary stage of education.

10. To sanction women's colleges and universities and women's study centres.

11. To execute programmes for the rehabilitation of destitute women and women in distress.

12. To support voluntary organizations to promote and accelerate the process of women's development.

Thus greater emphasis has been placed on the programmes of development of women and children during the Eighth Five Year Plan period.

The Ninth Five Year Plan: The Ninth Five Year Plan came into effect from April 1, 1997. In the preparation for the Ninth Five Year Plan an approach paper has been developed by the Planning Commission and accepted by the National Development Council (NDC). This document becomes the basis on which the Ninth Five Year Plan developed.

In the approach paper, the focus is on, among the other things, empowerment of women and people's participation in planning and implementation of strategies. To ensure consistent gender perspective in the plan and to have a strong sub-plan, the regional consultations and sectoral studies undertaken and have brought some new concerns to the policy issues.

An important objective in the Approach paper is the empowerment of women. In planning process, empowerment, at the outset, means choices for women and opportunities to avail of these choices. The supportive environment should be provided to women at all stages by the home, school, government and workplace.[46]

Centrally Sponsored Schemes

The following Rural Development Programmes are initiated by the Government of India being implemented by the District Rural Development agencies in Andhra Pradesh:

1. Integrated Rural Development Programmes (IRDP).
2. Training for Rural Youth for Self-Employment (TRYSEM).
3. Development of Women and Children in Rural Areas (DWCRA).

Integrated Rural Development Programmes (IRDP): IRDP is a beneficiary oriented programme with the objective of assisting the families below the income level of Rs. 11,000 per year and 30 per cent benefits are allocated for women. Under the programme, income generating assets are being provided to the beneficiearies with a package of assistance consisting of subsidy from the District Rural Development agencies besides term loan from the bank.

The State and the Government of India have to share 50:50 out of which Rs. 46 crores is earmarked to 61,300 women headed families in the State which is 40 per cent of the physical and financial targets of the proposed targets during 1997-98.[47] During 1996-97, through IRDP, 1,22,863 women benefitted by Rs. 8830.88 lakhs against the target of one lakh beneficiaries.

Training for Rural Youth Self-Employment (TRYSEM): The programme is to train rural youth in the age group of 18 to 35 years for the provision of self/wage employment. As against the proposed Rs. 12.66 crores, the Government of India and State Government have to share equally out of which Rs. 5.06 crores has to be earmarked to women, i.e., to cover 10,760 candidates which is 40 per cent of the proposed targets of physical as well as financial achievements.

Development of Women and Children in Rural Areas (DWCRA): The DWCRA Scheme, a sub-scheme of IRDP, was introduced in 1983-84. The programme was meant for the development of women and children in rural areas by providing a revolving fund of Rs. 25,000/-to a group of 10-15 women belonging to poverty group for undertaking economic activities and ancillary services like nutrition, health, child care, family welfare, immunisation, literacy adult education facilities which are covered for the beneficiary family. During 1997-98, it was proposed to form 25,000 groups in the state. The total outlay of the project is Rs. 62.50 crores.[48] Up to 1994-95, the scheme was extended to all religions in Andhra Pradesh.

The DWCRA Scheme is implemented by the District Rural Development Agencies (DRDA) through Mandal Praja Parisads. For implementation of the scheme, a Women Project Officer was appointed.

The scheme was implemented throughout the State as against the expenditure of Rs. 2735.45 lakhs during the year 1995-96 and an amount of Rs. 2423.90 lakhs was spent up to December 96. The coverage of the group was 17,165. During 1995-96, 5,663 TV sets were distributed to DWCRA groups. The TV facilitates women to mobilise and articulate their problems.[49]

Mahila Samriddhi Yojana

The Mahila Samriddhi Yojana (MSY), launched on 2nd Octobver, 1993, is one of the most innovative schemes for the economic betterment of rural women. The scheme has been launched to deal with predicaments of women workers at home and their workplaces. It is an important step to remove the social handicaps such as fads, taboos which inhibit rural women to come out of the household. It encourages and promotes thrift and enable women to come out of the narrow confines of their home to go to post office to deposit their hard earned savings and to give them the discretion and the authority to utilise their income in a manner they think appropriate. It also provides an interface of women with government functionaries and enables them to face their problems of life with strength, courage and confidence. The response has been tremendous.[50]

The incentives given to the account holders are:

The government contributes 25 per cent on the completion of 12 months for each deposit upto a total deposit of Rs. 300 in a year. For example, a depositor will get Re. 1 as an incentive on completion of 12 months on a deposit of Rs. 4. Again, a depositor will get Rs. 75 as incentive money on a deposit of Rs. 300 made on 9.11.93, the depositor would be Rs. 375 including the incentive money of Rs. 75 on 9.11.94.

In case Rs. 4 is deposited on 9.11.93 and another Rs. 16 on 16.11.93 the depositor would get back Rs. 5 on 9.11.94 and Rs. 20 on 16.11.94. Thus an incentive at the rate of 25 per cent admissible on deposits upto Rs. 300.

Indira Mahila Yojana (IMY)

The Indira Mahila Yojana was launched in Aug. 1995 in 200 blocks of the country. The main objective of Indira Mahila Yojana is to give a forward thrust to the education, awareness, income-generation capacities and the empowerment of women. The platform for the forward thrust is to be the self-help group at the grass-root level.

The scheme emphasises the constitution of Indira Mahila Block Societies (IMBS) at the block level and Indira Mahila Kendras (IMK) at the Anganwadi level. At the grassroot level under every Anganwadi, there should be women's self-help groups.[51]

The IMY is aimed to empower women through a sustained process of awareness generation and their direct access to resources, thereby they can share and demand social and economic development. The main objectives of IMY are:

(i) To generate awareness in women through provision of information on different developmental programmes and issues of specific concern to women;

(ii) To ensure convergence of sectoral services at the Panchayat, block and district level through active involvement of women;

(iii) To optimize the utilisation of scarce resources in speeding up the process of mainstreaming women in development;

(iv) To initiate the process of awareness generation/ education to enable them to understand and analyse their problems and find solutions through their collective interactions; and

(v) To help women become self-reliant and independent by their economic empowerment through income generation activites.[52]

Rashtriya Mahila Kosh (National Credit Fund for Women)

The Rashtriya Mahila Kosh (RMK) scheme aims at economic empowerment of poor women by meeting their credit requirments. The economically disadvantaged and illiterate women find it difficult to borrow even small sums of money for their economic activities. Most of their borrowings are met through private money-lenders at exorbitant rates of interest. Keeping in view the shortage of micro-credit facility for poor women and to utilize the income generation skills of millions of such women in the country, the Government of India established the Rashtriya Mahila Kosh (National Credit Fund for Women) with a corpus of Rs. 31 crore in 1993.[53]

Primary Objective of the Scheme to promote credit as in instrument of socio-economic change, the Govermnet established the Rashtriya Mahila Kosh (National Credit Fund for Women) as a registered society, it tries to fulfil the need for a quasi-informal credit delivery mechanism which is client-firendly, has simple and minimal procedures and has flexible repayment schedules. Since its inception, the Rashtriya Mahia Kosh (RMK) has given credit to the tune of over Rs. five crore.

RMK can act as an advocate or agent for influencing development and micro-finance policy and creating a more enabling policy and legal environment for the spread of micro-finance activities in India. Being a creation and a representative of the government, RMK has a particular advantage in this area.[54]

Swaranjayanti Gram Swarozgar Yojana

To begin with, IRDP was the only self-employment programme. Beginning with Training of Rural Youth for Self Employment (TRYSEM), a number of allied programmes have been added over the years such as Development of Women and Children in Rural Areas (DWCRA), Supply of Improved Toolkits to Rural Artisans (SITRA), and Ganga Kalyan Yojana (GKY). The multiplicity of programmes, being viewed as separate programmes in themselves, resulted in a lack of proper social intermediation, absence of desired linkages among these programmes inter se and the implementation being more concerned with achieving individual programme targets rather than focussing on the substantive issue of sustainable income generation. To rectity the situation, Government have decided to restructure the self-employment programmes. A new programme known as "Swarnjayanti Gram Swarozgar Yojana" (SGSY) has been launched from April 1999. This is a holistic programme covering all aspects of self employment such as organisation of the poor into self help groups, training, credit, technology, infrastructure and marketing. SGSY will be funded by the Centre and the States in the ratio of 75:25.

With the coming into force of SGSY, the earlier programmes IRDP, TRYSEM, DWCRA, SITRA, GKY and MWS are no longer in operation. The unspent balances, as on 1.4.99, under these erstwhile programmes, will be pooled under the head SGSY and utilised as per the new guidelines.

The objective of SGSY will be to bring the assisted poor families (swarozgaris) above the poverty line in three years, by providing them income-generating assets through a mix of bank credit and government subsidy. It would mean ensuring that the family has a monthly net income of at least Rs. 2000. Subject to availability of funds, the effort will be to cover 30 per cent of the poor families in each block during the next five years. Quality will be the hallmark of SGSY, which has to be imaginatively used to bring people above the poverty line.[55]

The Swaranjayanti Gram Swarozgar Yojana (SGSY) has been launched with effect from 1.4.1999 as a new Self-employment Programme. With the coming into effect of the SGSY, the earlier Programmes of Integrated Rural

Development Programme (IRDP), Training of Rural Youth for Self-Employment (TRYSEM). Development of Women and Children in Rural Areas (DWCRA), the Ganga Kalyan Yojana (GKY) as well as the Million Wells Scheme (MWS) are no longer in operation. The brief details of the Programme are indicated in the following paragraphs:

Objective

The objective of the SGSY is to bring the assisted poor families (Swarozgaris) above the Poverty Line by providing them income-generating assets through a mix of Bank Credit and Governmental Subsidy.

Strategy

The SGSY is different from earlier Programmes, in terms of the strategy envisaged for its implementation, and has been conceived as a holistic Programme of self-employment covering all aspects of self-employment, viz, organisation of the rural poor into Self-Help-Groups and their capacity building, training, planning of activity clusters, infrastructure build-up and technology and marketing support.

Target Groups

Below the Poverty Line families in rural areas constitute the target group of the SGSY. Within the target group, special safeguards have been provided to vulnerable sections, by way of reserving 50 per cent benefits for SC/STs, 40 per cent for women and 3 per cent for disabled persons.

Funding Pattern

The Swarnjayanti Gram Swarozgar Yojana (SGSY) is financed on 75:25 cost sharing basis between the Centre and the States.[56]

Women Welfare Policies in Andhra Pradesh

In India, Andhra Pradesh has been in the forefront in implementing various developmental programmes for women.

The Department of Women Development and Child Welfare has undertaken various economic and developmental programmes and relief measures for the welfare of women. In Andhra State, initially the programmes for women's welfare were limited to the activities with four women welfare centres. With the formation of Andhra Pradesh State on 1.11.1956, the programmes of the department were extended throughout the State and multifarious activities were undertaken for the upliftment of women belonging to economically backward classes through different schemes like providing shelter to aged women, destitutes, working women and job-oriented technical training courses, etc.[57] Programmes of this Department can be broadly classified into three programmes, (a) Welfare Programmes, (b) Developmental Programmes and (c) Welfare-cum-Developmental Programmes.

Institutional Services

State Homes: State Homes are meant for women discharged from correctional institutions and who are unable to protect themselves from adverse social forces and also for those women who voluntarily seek shlelter. They are given free lodging and boarding at the rate of Rs. 210 per month per head.

There are five State Homes in the state located at Hyderabad, Mahaboobnagar, Srikakulam, Kurnool and East Godavari. Women, according to their necessity, stay for 3 to 5 years. During the period, they are given graining in the Training cum Production Units in printing of book, binding work, screen-printing, and cloth weaving, mat-weaving, cane and bamboo work. Marriages are also performed at government cost, as a part of rehabilitation, if any suitable persons come forward to marry. The expenditure of State Home during 1996-97 was Rs. 52.40 lakhs.[58]

Service Homes: These homes are meant for destitute women, helpless widows and deserted wives who are in the age group of 18-35 years. Rehabilitation will be made through job courses and training-cum-production. During their stay with children who are below the age of 5 years are provided with free food, shelter, clothing and medical aid. Scheduled Caste women are permitted to stay for five years. The dietary charges are Rs. 210/-per month per head (adult) and Rs. 210/ per child.

There are 6 Service Homes in the State located at West Godavari, Ananthapur, Nellore, Krishna, Kurnool and Hyderabad.[59] Initially these homes provided training in tailoring and coaching to appear for 7th class and 10th class examinations subsequently. Several units have been introduced like toy-making, weaving, banian and socks making, leather units and card board units. The expenditure for the year 1995-96 was Rs. 60.86 lakhs. The budget allocation for the year 1996-97 was Rs. 59.75 laksh.[60] Each home is managed by a superintendent who is assisted by a Matron, two teachers, one craft instructuress, part-time teacher skilled workers and other ministerial staff.

Working Women's Hostels: These hostels provide food, shelter and other facilities including security to the working women who are away from their families on payment of charges prescribed by the Government. Those who earn monthly income of less than Rs. 3,000 are eligible for admission. There are 18 working women hostels in the state. Sanctioned strength of each hostel is 50 women. They are located in Srikakulam, Vizayanagaram, Visakapatnam-2, Vijayawada, Guntur, Nizamabad, Karimnagar, Ananthpur, Tirupathi, Medak, Mahaboobnagar, Khammam, Warangal, Hyderabad-2, East Godawari, West Godavari, Krishna, Guntur, Kurnool. The budget allocated for the year 1996-97 is Rs. 90.77 lakhs.[61]

Women Welfare Branches: These are the primary institutions of the Department (WD & CW). Children in the age group of 3-6 years are given pre-school education. For the age-group of 15-35, training is given in crafts, nutrition and child care education. There are 46 such centres in the

State of which 33 are for SCs and 13 are for STs. The sanctioned strength in each centre is 30 children and (3) women with one teacher, one part-time instructuress and 2 ayahs.

The State Government has launched a special project for girl child under which 100 girls will be adopted in each district and imparted education and vocational training courses. Because, Andhra Pradesh continues to be the top of the list of child labour for the last 3 decades. At present there are 565 special school (Bala Jyothi Schools) in which children who are withdrawn from child labour.[62]

Rehabilitation of Girl Child Labourers

The State Government initiated a new scheme of identifying girl child labourers in the State with a view to rehabilitate them. Rs. 1 crore was released for the rehabilitation of girl child labourers.

Girl Child Protection Scheme

This scheme was launched by the State Government during the year 1995-96. Rs. 24 crores were released for the scheme and extended to all districts. During the financial year 1996-97, Rs. 25 crores were released for the scheme and 80 per cent of the amount disbursed. In 1996-97, the target girls were 60,000. So far 45,000 girls were identified.[63]

State Action Plan for Women 1994-2000 AD

The Government of Andhra Pradesh launched the Andhra Pradesh State Action Plan for women 1994-2000 AD. The main objective of the Action Plan is to integrate women at all levels into the mainstream of developmental and economic activity. In Andhra Pradesh, women are encouraged to come to the forefront in all spheres. A separate department exclusively for Women Development and Child Welfare was constituted at the inception of the State in 1953. A women's Co-operative Finance Corporation was set up in 1975 for providing needy women skill training and extending loan facilities for augmenting their earnings and thereby improve their status socially and economically.

Some of the policy decisions taken by the State Government in the recent past in support of women's development include:[64]

1. 30 per cent reservation of seats in panchayat raj institutions.
2. 30 per cent reservation in government and other public sector jobs.
3. Minimum 30 per cent coverage under loaning by Finance Corporation namely the Scheduled Tribes, Physically handicaped Minorities Corporation and the State Financial Corporation.
4. Free education upto graduate level.
5. Entrustment of Fair Price Shops.
6. Grant of individual or joint land and house site pattas.
7. Equal property rights for daughters and sons under the Hindu Succession Act since May, 1986.

The State Government has decided to formulate a perspective Plan of Action for Women with a time frame that will take the State into the next centuary. This document lists out the specific actions that the Government of Andhra Pradesh propose to launch and pursue during the next six years to ensure that the policy initiatives already undertaken are consolidated and tangible gains accrue to women.

UNDP Programmes in Andhra Pradesh

UNDP is the UN's largest source of grant assistance for development. Believing that freedom from poverty is a fundamental right, UNDP assists Governments and Civil society organisations in developing economic and social policies to address the cause of poverty.

Andhra Pradesh is situated in the South of India with a population of about sixty seven million (8 per cent of India), living in 23 districts or 1104 mandals or 30,000 inhabited villages. The State has 22 out of 33 Million women illiterate while, 100,000 infants out of 1.75 million from every year take leave before attaining one year (IMR 64).[65]

Because of the above reasons UNDP has been implementing several developmental programmes for women in the state. The thrust of UNDP interventions in the state is aimed at realization of what has come to be known as Sustainable Human Development, a term that warrants action on all critical issues in such areas as employment in the small scale and informal structure, biodiversity, fuel Celebes development, information technology for poverty reduction. UNDP supports programmes aimed at capacity development for strengthening decentralisation, sustainbale livelihoods, empowerment of women, and safeguarding and regeneration of natural resources.[66]

South Asian Poverty Alleviation Programme (SAPAP)

SAPAP has focussed on 20 poor mandals in the Mehaboob Nagar, Kurnool and Ananthapoor Districts of the southern state of Andhra Pradesh. It adopted a targeted rather than a holistic approach to poverty alleviation within a specific community. The primary target for the schme was poor women, especially those of the Scheduled Castes (SC's), Scheduled Tribes (ST's) and other backward classes (OBC's) and form an integral part of the programme, in Andhra Pradesh SAPAP participating for the promotion of small scale income generating activites. It is being managed by a small core professional team supported by 23 community co-ordinators and 88 community volunteers.

Adarana Project

ADARANA-or benevolence-is a project pioneered by Government of Andhra Pradesh to empower B.C. Artisans in the State by providing improved hand tools, power tools and small technological equipment. ADARANA aims at providing modern and improved hand-held tools to the Artisans with a view to improving their productivity, minimising human drudgery, improving product/service quality and help modernize process operations. The ultimate goal is to contribute to increased income levels and improved standards of living of Artisans.

It was proposed to cover 10.00 lakh Artisans during 1998-1999 and 1999-2000. A budgetary allocation of Rs. 100.00 crores and Rs. 121.00 crores for the respective financial years was made towards subsidy component of the programme. The loan component was met from term loan assistance of National Backward Classes Finance Development Corporation for providing tools costing up to Rs. 5000 and from Commercial Banks for tools costing above Rs. 5000.

During the year 2000-2001 the assistance under B.C. Corporation is to be extended mainly to Self Help Groups and the assistance to such groups will be minimum 5011/o during current year and it will gradually increase to 1001)/o in the future. For this purpose a District Level Committee will be constituted to select Self Help Groups in the District for extending assistance and this Committee will consist of Collector as Chairman, P.D., DRDA, P.D., WW & CD and Executive Director, S.C. Society as Members. Necessary adequate care will be taken to ensure that groups having creditability will be extended financial assistance. In 4 Districts reformulation of economic assistance scheme will be taken up in which it is proposed to extend term loan from B.C. Corporation in all the schemes so as to ensure timely grounding and to prevent undue delay which usually take place whenever bank loan component is included in economic assistance programme. For extending financial assistance to Self Help Groups involvement of N.G.Os. will also be examined and considered. The MPDOs are being requested to have active involvement in identification, grounding, monitoring of schemes and recovery of loans.

Janmabhoomi Programmes for Women Empowerment

The Government of Andhra Pradesh has taken up the theme of women's empowerment as one of main agenda items to tackle rural poverty and socio-economic issues. Self Help movement through savings has been taken up as a mass movement by the women–a path chosen by the women to shape their future destiny. Development Agenda of the state in the last few years has been to place the people, especially women in the forefront has enabled formation of a large number of Self Help Groups throughout the length and breadth of the State. There are more than 20 lakh women from poor families who have become members of these groups. Majority of them are saving one rupee a day. State Government is consciously making an effort to assist these Self Help Groups by providing Revolving Fund under DWCRA. There are 79,000 DWCRA groups in the State covering 11.25 lakh women and Rs. 125 crore was provided as revolving fund as against a saving of Rs. 120 crores by the groups. About half of the DWCRA groups in the country are available in our State itself.

Recently, our Government has made special efforts to assist these women in marketing their products without any middlemen. In the last three months Rs. 1.50 crores worth DWCRA products were sold by the women. These melas provided an opportunity for the women to expose their products to the urban consumers and also understand customer's choices in a competitive market environment. Similarly, DWCRA /SHGs Bazaars are being set up in several districts to replicate these initiatives at the district level. DWCRA/SHGs Bazaars taken up in Guntur, Khammam and the other districts were very successful and response is encouraging. It is also planned to establish a marketing outlet at Hyderabad exclusively for the sale of DWCRA/SHGs products to provide an opportunity for the women coming from the districts.

Training for capacity building of the women will be taken lup by organising training for the women in Mahila

Pranganam, and other local institutions. Similarly, District Rural Development Agencies have identified 6000 cluster volunteers to support the groups at the village level. These volunteeers, are selected by the DWCRA/SHGs and their expenditure too is borne by them. The cluster volunteers, DWCRA group leaders. Additional Grama Sevikas, Lady VDO's and others will be trained in the District Training Centres.

Greater support will be provided to the DWCRA/SHG groups by dovetailing with poverty alleviation programmes like IRDP. It is planned to provde at least 50 per cent of IRDP subsidy and credit to the women groups through CMEY, S.C. Corporation, Minorities Corporation by covering them under Group Loans. Social and Economic infrastructure support will be provided to the women through establishment of DWCRA/SHG Bazaars and Technicial Resource Centres.

Department of Rural Development for Women's Development

In Andhra Pradesh the Department of Rural Development was established to implement several specific programmes for Women. The objective of the department is integrated real development through implementation of antipoverty programmes including Self-Employment wage employment and area development program. The broad goals of the Department are (1) To eradicate poverty in rural areas, (2) To empower grass root level people's organizations, (3) To mobilize self-help groups of poor women, (4) To co-ordinate voluntary efforts in poverty eradication, (5) To ameliorate deterioration of natural resources and enable common property resource management by stakeholders, (6) To develop skills in rural communities to handle self-employment programmes and micro-enterprises, (7) Enable technology to be accessible to rural areas, (8) To narrow down gap between urban-rural Sectors.

The District Rural Development Agencies (DRDAs) help the Rural Development Department in implementation, monitoring and evaluation of various Rural Development Programmes at district level. These DRDAs are registered societies under the Registration of Societies Act. At present, there are (22) DRDAs in our State. There is no DRDA for Hyderabad, as Hyderabad District is an urban district.In order to implement watershed programmes and other programmes. Implementation of these programmes are entrusted to one and same District Level Agency which is implementing IRDP at the District Level. The Agency is headed by District Collector as its Chairman.[67]

Mutually Aided Cooperative Societies

Government of Andhra Pradesh has passed a reforming cooperative Act called mutually Aided cooperative societies Act (MACS, ACT 1995) which will help such women who are engaged in income generating activities by forming groups to form into a federation called Mutually Aided Cooperative Thrift Socieities (MACTS).

The objectives of MACTS are (1) Providing credit to poor women without security. (2) Reduces money lender exploitation at low rate of interest. (3) Assets creation. (4) To improve economic status of women. (5) Creation of micro enterprises. (6) Avoiding long loan sanction procedure and delay. (7) To undertake sustainable employment generation activities. (8) Generate lively hood to poor women.

Deepam Scheme

Government of Andhra Pradesh is implementing Deepam Scheme under food, civil supplies and consumer afffairs and Dept. Deepam scheme is an ambitious programme of extending domestic LPG connections to Women of Below Poverty Line families living in rural and urban areas.The Objectives of the Scheme are (1) Providing relief to women from drudgery of cooking with firewood. (2) Improving their health (3) Preventing health hazard and. (4) Reducing dependence on forest for firewood and improving the environment by preventing felling of trees. (5) Govt. of

Andhra Pradish initially proposed to release 15 lakh connections, spending Rs. 150 Crores towards refundable Security Deposit @ Rs. 1,000 per connection.

In rural areas Beneficiaries are members from DWACRA Groups and BPL families.

In India in general and in Andhra Pradesh in particular welfare programmes for a women are being implemented. All the programmes discussed above have contributed top some extent for the wellbeing of women such as, social, political, economic and cultural aspects. But, still there is a need for a unique programme for women's development.

References

1. B.M. Verma, Decentralisation in Administration, Public Policy for Eradication of Poverty, Uppal Publishing House, New Delhi, 1990 p. 33.
2. Ram Reddy, G. and Hara Gopal,G. Public Policy and the Rural Poor in India, New Delhi: Concept Publishing Co., 1985, p. 1.
3. International Encyclopaedia of Social Sciences-The Mac Millan Compay and the Free Press, 1968, p. 204.
4. Dye Thomas R. "Policy Analysis", Alabama: University of Alabama Press, 1976, p. 2.
5. Laswell Harold D. "The Policy Orientation of Political Science", Laxmi Narayan Agarwal, Agra, 1971, p. 4.
6. Joyce M. Mitchell, Wiliam C. Mitchell Rand M.C. Nully and Company, "Political Analysis and Public Policy: An Introduction to Political Science", Chicago, 1969, p. 391.
7. Dye Thomas, "Understanding Public Policy", New Jersey, Prentice Hall Inc., Englewood Cliff JN: 1971; p. 2.
8. *Ibid.*, p. 3.
9. Friedrich Carl J. "Man and His Government", New York: McGraw Hill, 1963, p. 4.

10. Everstone Robert, The Thread of Public Policy: A Study in Policy Leadership, Indiana Polis: Bobbs Merril, 1971, p. 18.
11. Rose Richard (ed.) Policy-making in Great Britain, London: Mc Millan Co., 1969, p. 2.
12. Easton Davind, The Political System, New York, Knopf, 1953, p. 5.
13. Laswell, Harold D. and Abraham Kaplan, Power and Society, New Heaven: Yale University Press, 1970, p. 37.
14. Dye Thomas R., *op. cit.*, p. 5.
15. Stuart S.Nagel, "Policy Analysis", in G. Ronald Gilbert (ed.) "Making and Managing Policy", New York, Marcel Dekkar, 1984, pp. 87-106.
16. Sapru, R.K., *op. cit.*, p. 34.
17. Dr. (Mrs.) Om Prie Srivastava, Public Adminstration Andmanagement, Vol. I, Himalay Publishing House, Bombay, 1991, p. 126.
18. *Ibid.*, p. 126-7.
19. *Ibid.*, p. 127.
20. *Ibid.*
21. *Ibid.*, p. 128.
22. *Ibid.* p. 129.
23. *Ibid.*
24. *Ibid.*
25. *Ibid.*
26. *Ibid.*
27. Dye Thomas R., *op. cit.*, p. 296.
28. Key V.O. Jr. "Public Opinion and American Democracy", New York, Knopf, 1967, pp. 422-3.
29. Dye Thomas R. *op. cit.*, pp. 300-5.
30. *Ibid.*, p. 5.
31. James E. Anderon, public policy markting. Praegar publications, New York, 1975, p. 24.

32. Charles O. Jones and Robert D. Thomas. "Public Policy-making in a Federal System", Sage Publications, London, 1976, p. 45.

33. Bailey S.K. and Mosher, E.K. ESCA: The Office of the Education Administraters Law, Syracuse University, Syracuse, 1968, p. 56.

34. Hender Mahajan, "Status of Women and Socio Economic Programmes Under India's Seventh Five Year Plan" in R.K. Saptu (ed.) Women and Development, Ashish Publishing House, New Delhi, 1989, p. 118.

35. Nerra Desai, "Changing Status of Women, Policies and Programmes" in Amit Kumar Gupta (ed.) Women and Society, Developmental Perspective, New Delhi,1986, p. 1.

36. Rath N., Womens Specific Legislations in India and Germany: A Comparative Study, Nabak Usha Chaudhary Centre for Developmental Studies, Occassional paper No. 10, Bhubavaneshwar, Orissa, 1994, p. 97.

37. Pylee, M.V., Constitution of India (Bombay, Asia, 1962), p. 149.

38. *Ibid.*

39. Kitchlu T.N. "Women's Rights, Legislative Measures", In Yojana, Nov. 15, 1991, Vol. 35, No. 20, New Delhi, p. 16.

40. Neera Desai and Maithreyi Krishna Raj, Women and Society in India, Delhi, Ajanta Publications, 1987, p. 44.

41. *Ibid.*, p. 329.

42. Government of India. Second Five Year Plan-1956-61, New Delhi, 1961, p. 602.

43. Government of India, Five Year Plan–1974-79, New Delhi.

44. Manorama Year Book, 1998, p. 527.

45. *Ibid.*, p. 528.

46. Anitha Anand, "Engendering The Plan", in The Hindu, April 6, 1997, p. iv.
47. Women Sub-Plan, 1997-98, *op. cit.*, p. 41.
48. *Ibid.*, p. 42.
49. Eenadu, January 21, 1997, p. 9.
50. Meenaxi Anand Choudhary, All About Mahila Samriddhi Yojana, Kurukshetra Sept. 1994, p. 26.
51. Indira Misra, "Self-employment Through IMY", in Yojana, April 1997, Vol. 41, No. 4, p. 36.
52. Dr. S.C. Joshi, "Indira Mahila Yojana: Empowerment of Women", Kurukshetra, March 1996, p. 24.
53. Economic Empowerment of Women through Rashtriya Mahila Kosh Scheme, Kurukshetra, May-June, 1995, p. 71.
54. www.gdrc.org. Need for Micro Finance.
55. Swarnjayanti Gram Swarozgar Yojna–Guidelines, Govt. of India, Ministry of Rural Development New Delhi, pp. i-ii.
56. www.rural.nic.in.
57. Activities for Women and Children in the State of Andhra Pradesh, Dept. of Women Development and Child Welfare, Hyd. 1997, p. 3.
58. Budget Management 1997-98 (Telugu). Women Development and Child Welfare, Government of Andhra Pradesh Press, Hyderabad, 1997, p. 3.
59. Activities for Women and Children in the State of Andhra Pradesh, *op. cit.*, p. 4.
60. Budget Management 1997-98, *op. cit*, p. 5.
61. *Ibid.*, p. 6.
62. Deccan Chronicle, Sept. 13, 1997, p. 4.
63. Eenadu, Oct. 4, 1997, p. 7.
64. A.P. State Action Plan for Women 1994-2000, Dept. of Women Development and Child Welfare, Govt. of Andhra Pradesh, Hyderabad, 1995, p. 14.

65. Suresh Bhargava, Empowering Women at the Village Level, UNICEF Representative, A.P., Karnataka, www.gdrc.org.

66. www.undp.org.-UNDP Children and Work.

67. www.ap.nic.in.introduction.

3

Evolution, Aims and Objectives of Self Help Groups

This Chapter is devoted to the evolution of SHGs and its credit facilities, and their Meaning, Aims, Objectives and Implementation process.

The concept of globalisation has created a gulf between the rich and the poor, and the third world economies becoming more vulnerable on all fronts. This is a matter of great concerne for the political scientists and the economists to preserve the privileges of the vulnerable sections of the society including women. The policy makers consciously evolved the policies to preserve the equality of gender social justice.

Issues of gender, equity and justice assumed added significance in the context of the awareness movement organised for women. With the women's concern gaining prominence in both governmental and non-governmental organisations during the 80s, women's issues became important on the agenda of all political parties. The recently constituted Commissions for Women both at Central and State levels are acting as platforms to ventilate the issues of women. They are working as springboards by creating gender consciences among the women. Both of these women's commissions are working along with political parties for the empowerment of the women. The governments recognised the necessity of the empowerment of women by involving them in the economic activity. Once, they participated in the development process, they are proving their ability on par with men.[1]

As is known, the goals of poverty eradication and empowerment of women can be effectively achieved if poor women are involved in groups for community participation as well as for assertion of their rights and their social status. The organisation of Self Help groups could be either based on trade or locality. Proper training is essential for building the organisations of the poor women.If they were properly given the esential training by providing credit and financial aasiatance, they will strive to defend their family requirements and they will effectively defend theit rights. By mobilising, concientising and organising them through a participatory process. This would enable them to participate in various programmes as effective partners and articulate their hopes and aspirations. In India, various modes of participatory development process have been tried by various voluntary organisations. The development process has given women not only a new sense of dignity and confidence to tackle their problems with a sense of solidarity to work together but also a measure of economic independence. It helped them to improve their living conditions and acquire small assets. It has also been demonstrated that the poor women's creativity, group dynamics and self-management are major elements in tackling the gender and equity issues.[2]

In the recent past, the Government of India has been focussing on women for development.The National Commission appointed by the Government of India recommended new strategies for the credit mechanism to assist poor women who are unfamiliar with the complexities of institutional finances. The Commission identified the need and strongly recommended the setting up of an exclusive credit policy for poor and self-employed women.The commission alaso confirmed the scientific credit policy, which is already practiced by these organisations. such as SEWA

(Ahmedabad), WWF (Madras), Samakhya (Hyderabad) and Annapurna Mahila Mandal (Bombay) for poor women in rural and urban areas.[3]

Rural Poverty and Credit in Perspective

The extent of poverty generally depends upon the extent of ownership of productive assets and the access to gainful employment opportunities. It is well established that due to lack of such productive assets and regular employment, the burden of unemployment/underemployment and poverty falls mainly on the rural poor. There is a clear inverse relationship between the assets held by the households and the incidence of poverty and the consequent needs to incur debt for meeting household expenditure. The question that arises is how do the poor who, by definition, lack adequate purchasing power, make both ends meet and survive. Generally, the gap between current income and consumption is usually bridged through occasional hand loans from relatives and friends. In some cases, the rural poor are even compelled to borrow on extremely exploitative terms making them labourers bonded to the creditors.[4]

Poverty eradication as the primary objective, the co-operative movement in the country, started at the turn of this century, probably represents one of the earliest examples of self help to bring together people of small means of fostering thrift and mutual help for the economic betterment of the members. Over the years, the co-operatives have, however, failed to attain their objectives. On account of their large size and the heterogeneous economic status of their members, the decision-making is invariably delegated to small groups of usually well-off and influential members. Such influential members are able to corner most of the benefits at the cost of those who are poor and do not command the ownership of productive assets or influence. Besides, since their resource base is poor, the co-operative societies heavily depend on the resources handed down vertically from the higher refinancing institutions for their operations. Against this background, evolving an alternative mechanism for meeting the economic aspirations and the credit needs of the rural poor in the form of SHGs seems a logical development.[5]

Evolution of Self Help Groups

In India soon after Independence,there has been an aggressive effort on the part of the Government, which concerned to improve the access of the rural poor to formal credit system. Some of these measures have been institutional, while some others were through implementation of focused programmes for removal of rural poverty. Reaching out of the far-flung rural areas to provide credit and other banking services to the hitherto neglected sections of the society is an unparalleled achievement of the Indian banking system. The main emphasis in the spread of the banking network and introduction of new instruments and credit packages and programmes was to make the financial system responsive to the needs of the weaker sections in the society comprising small and marginal farmers, rural artisans, landless agricultural and non-agricultural labourers and other small borrowers falling below the poverty line.[6]

With the implementation of the above policies, further the Government of India in its developmental planning emphasised the promotion of agriculture and other allied economic activities through credit intervention for ensuring integrated rural development and securing the prosperity of the rural areas. In pursuance of this, formal credit institutions have been guided by the principle of growth with equity and a large share of the credit disbursed for various activities was channelised towards the weaker sections of the society.

Consequently, thanks to the implementation of several poverty alleviation programmes, the number of people below the poverty line has declined from 272.7 million in 1984-85 to 210.8 million in 1989-90, IN 1991-2000 which constitutes over 21 per cent of the population. The number of operational holdings is expected to have crossed the 100 million mark with more than 80 per cent being small and marginal holdings. This institutional credit system needs to meet the challenge of delivering credit to an ever increasing number of rural people who need greater access to formal credit. It may have to reinforce its own structure at the grass roots levels and also have to devise new ways of reaching out to the rural poor.[7]

As a result of the experience of the implementation of the above discussed Poverty Alleviation programmes led to the introduction of the Integrated Rural Development Programme (IRDP) on 2 October 1980 with the specific objective of raising the poor rural families above the poverty line. Credit support from banks was considered as an important input in taking up economic and gainful activities by such families.

In spite of these impressive achievements in the expansion of the credit delivery system and the special programmes, nearly half the indebted rural households are still outside the ambit of the institutional credit system. They approach the moneylenders for meeting their consumption and production needs in the absence of institutional support. Some of the poor who have not been reached even by the vast network of the institutional credit delivery system, have organised themselves into self-help groups (SHGs) and many such groups have come into existence either spontaneously or with the active involvement of the Voluntary Agencies (VAs) which motivated the rural poor to pool their meager financial resources for meeting their small and frequent consumption and production credit needs.

Initiatives by NABARD

The potential of SHGs to develop as local financial intermediaries to reach the poor gained wide recognition in many developing countries especially in Asia-Pacific Region. Many NGOs have played an active role in fostering the growth of SHGs in furtherance of their socio-economic agenda. Considering the immense potential of SHGs in meeting the development aspirations of the unreached rural poor, National Bank for Agriculture and Rural Development (NABARD), the apex development institution with exclusive focus on integrated rural development, supported and funded in 1986-87, a MYRADA-sponsored action research project on Savings and Credit Management of Self-Help Groups. Therefore, in collaboration with some of the other member institutions of Asia Pacific Rural and Agricultural Credit Association (APRACA), NABARD undertook a survey of 43 NGOs spread over 11 states in India to study the functioning of SHGs and possibilities of collaboration between banks and SHGs in mobilisation of rural savings and delivery of credit to the poor.[8]

Pilot Project–The History of SHGS

Encouraged by the results of the studies of SHGs experiences, NABARD in consultation with RBI, Commercial Banks (CBs) and NGOs, launched the pilot project of linking SHGs with Commercial Banks in 1991-92 and issued detailed guidelines in February 1992. RBI had advised Commercial Banks in July 1991 to extend finance to SHGs as per NABARD guidelines. Subsequently, the linkage project was extended to RRBs and Cooperatives.

The linkage philosophy was based on the[9] informal credit system, that is, the moneylenders were holding their sway over the rural poor because of their responsiveness, flexibility and sensitivity to the credit needs of the poor. The poor require credit very frequently, in small quantities, without much hassles and for the activity of own choice. The moneylender is always there at his doorstep for supplying the credit promptly, but with an exploitative term of high interest rate, forcing the poor to coughup all his surpluses/income and making him/her, thereby, move downhill along the poverty line. The moneylender has a vested interest in the perpetuation of poverty.

The formal credit system has the resources, manpower and technical capability to handle any volume of credit dispensation. The pilot project on linking SHGs with Banks was launched aiming at combining the positive factors of both the systems and ensuring advantages to both formal credit system and SHGs. The traditional attitude of a banker that the poorest of the poor is not reliable and the banks are not meant for them were the myths to be dispelled. The distinct advantages envisaged under the project for Banks and SHGs are that the Banks were advised to win the confidence and trust of the rural poor.

As the pilot study intended to found its impact of SHGs with Banks, however, during the pilot phase of the project, a number of other studies have aslo been conducted, aiming at comparing the advantages expected and the reality.

Linkage Between Banks and SHGs

The National Bank continues to provide 100 per cent refinance to banks at an interest rate of 6.5 per cent per annum. Other support measures provided include facilitating training of bank officials and field staff of NGOS, SHGS, Federations of NGOs/SHGs and other related institutions through financial assistance, faculty support etc. As many as 550 NGOs are participating in the programme. Women SHGs constituted about 94 per cent of the total groups linked. On the whole, the programme benefited 5.60 lakh rural poor families in 280 districts. The Southern region continues to dominate the linkage programme with a share of 65 per cent, followed by Western (11 per cent), Eastern (11 per cent), Central (10 per cent) and Northern regions (3 per cent). Andhra Pradesh, Karnataka and Tamil Nadu states have taken the lead in promoting SHGS, and in establishing Bank-SHG Linkage. The bank linkage is generally established after the successful functioning of individual groups for about six months to a year. The concept of SHGs has not been as successful in the North East and some of the Eastern states. Area-specific programmes need to be formulated to meet the varying socio-cultural practices.

After successful experimentation in Cauvery Grameena Bank, Mysore (Karnataka), in association with an experienced NGO, namely MYRADA, more and more RRBs are involving themselves as SHGs. Some government agencies like Zilla Panchayat have also taken initiatives to promote SHGS; and such efforts are supported by the National Bank through assistance in organising training programmes for the staff.

Notwithstanding 100 per cent refinance from the National Bank, commercial banks perceive this activity as unprofitable. Hence, only regional rural banks and cooperative banks take up such financing. RBI has been prevailing upon commercial banks to formulate their respective policies on micro credit and promotion of SHGS. The National Bank has been organising SHG workshops involving bankers and development personnel to accelerate the process of SHG-Bank Linkage. RBI has issued a circular to commercial banks to reckon micro credit extended directly to individual borrowers or the rough intermediaries as part of their priority sector lending. The circular also stated that micro credit should form an integral part of the bank's corporate credit plan, and should be reviewed at the highest level on a quarterly basis.[10]

SHG Concept

The establishment of the SHGs could be traced to the existence of one or more common problem areas around which the consciousness of the rural poor was built and the process of group formation initiated. The group, thus, was usually responsive to a perceived need. Such groups have been formed around specific production activities and often they have promoted savings among their members and used the pooled resources to meet the emergent needs of the members of the group including consumption needs. Sometimes the internal savings generated were supplemented by the external resources loaned/donated by VAs promoting the SHGs. Since the SHGs have been able to mobilize savings from persons or groups who were not normally expected to have any "savings" and also to recycle effectively the pooled resources amongst the members, their activities have attracted attention as a supportive mechanism for meeting the credit needs of the poor.[11]

Group Approach

Group approach has been extensively adopted in promoting income generating enterprises among the poor and weaker sections, in particular, with women as one significant group under the overall financial support and guidance from NABARD and SIDBI; NGOs are being linked with commercial banks for making available credit to NGOs through commercial banks or even directly. In many states and districts, SHGs are being formed with the support of NGOs that are linked to commercial banks, NABARD and SIDBI. Under rural development programmes, including DWCRA (Development of Women and Children in Rural Areas), the impact of support given to SHGs has been quite visible. From April 1999, six rural development programmes, including DWCRA, have been integrated and the present nomenclature of the programme is Swarnjayanti Gram Swarozgar Yojana (SGSY), which focusses on cluster approach for groups of poor. Women continue to be given special attention.

Focus in the recent periods is on organising marketing efforts, and for technology upgradation and diversification of activities for groups associated with this programme. SHGs can contribute towards improving the quality of lending by offering loans in a prompt and simple manner, ensuring need-based loans, and keeping the loansize within the repaying capacity of the borrowers. Undoubtedly, SHGs have the advantage of intimate knowledge about their members as compared to the bank staff.[12]

SHGS in Andhra Pradesh

Several development agencies have promoted and inspired formation of diverse kinds of thrift and credit groups in Andhra Prdesh to channelise the various poverty alleviation and social development programmes. These groups vary widely in terms of their membership, size, decision making process, methods of group action etc. Majority of the NGOs in Andhra Pradesh, as in other states, are basically involved in the provision of social services to their target beneficiaries, and their attitudinal orientation, methodology adopted, and systems and procedures are so designed that they require social mobilisation on a large scale. With their diversification in economic sphere especially in thrift and credit activities, their resourcefulness needs to be harnessed and synthesisted with SHG-Bank Linkage programme. There is need to design a comprehensive training strategy for personnel of NGOs in various aspects of managing SHGs to secure proper focus.

Similarly, the district administration is promoting thrift and credit groups under DWCRA programme and the present SGSY (Swarnjayanti Gram Swarozgar Yojana), a UNDP project for institutional development at grassroots for poverty alleviation is being implemented in the three districts of Anantapur, Mahabubnagar and Kurnool, which envisages use of thrift and credit groups promoted under the project as a conduct for channelising their health, nutrition, education and other development programmes under the approach referred to as community based convergent services. World Bank Project on District Poverty Initiatives (DPIP) is being implemented in the six districts of Adilabad, Anantapur, Chittoor, Mahabubnagar, Srikakulam and Viziyanagaram. The project basically aims at improving capacities of community-based micro credit system and their synthesis with other local common interest groups. An attempt is being made to synthesise these patterns with the SHG concept of NABARD and assimilate them under SHG-Bank Linkage Programme. However, the induced formation of groups needs to be cautiously pursued without undermining the autonomy of groups a critical element in the effective functioning of the SHGS. Nevertheless, the groups so formed do provide the opportunity to financing banks to expand their exposure to SHGS.[13]

Women's Self Help Groups (SHGs)

The government of Andhra Pradesh has taken up the theme women's empowerment as one of the main strategies to tackle socio-economic poverty. Self Help movement through savings has been taken up as a mass movement by women– a path chosen by them to shape their destiny for the better. The Development agenda of the State in the last few years of placing the people, especially women, in the fore-front has enabled formation of a large number of Self Help Groups (SHGs) throughout the State where the majority of women are saving one rupee a day. The State government is consciously making an effort to assist SHGs by providing Revolving Fund under various programmes.[14]

SHGs—A Movement

There are about 4.01 lakhs women SHGs in Andhra Pradesh, covering nearly 53.64 lakhs of poor rural poor women. Andhra Pradesh alone has about half of the SHGs existing in the country. Upto 1994, only 10,000 groups were functioning and in the last six years, there was a massive scaling up in SHG activities. The SHGs are not only resorting to thrift but are also taking small loans out of the corpus available with the group. The group corpus consists of savings, government assistance and also bank loan. Members use the loan out of the group corpus for their personal needs initially. However in the long run, such loans are utilized for income generation activities. An amount of Rs. 1043.78 crore is mobilized as corpus with these groups so far and it is estimated that it would increase to Rs. 1,500.00 crores in the coming year. The SHGs are also popularly called DWCRA groups in Andhra Pradesh. This name became popular after the DWCRA programme (Development of Women and Children in Rural Areas) through which women's groups were assisted initially.

SHG—Convergence of Other Schemes

Socio-economic survey of such SHGs conducted by District Rural Development Agency (DRDA) in different districts has indicated that the scheme has helped women earn additional monthly incomes ranging from Rs. 1500/- to Rs. 1800/- depending on the economic activities taken up. In addition, women have taken up initiatives in improving their socio-economic status by participating in governmental programmes such as family welfare, promoting their nutritional and educational status, awareness on environment, public health through sanitation and clean drinking water. A large number of the women from SHGs participate in Janmabhoomi (A Government programme envisaging over-all development of village) regularly as active partners for the development of their villages.[15]

Capacity Building

Special programmes have been designed for training and capacity building of the SHGs. Training for skill development and awareness generation through exposure visits is taken up in all the districts for 10,000 volunteers supervising and guiding the SHGs. Regular training programmes are being organised for value addition to DWCRA products and their better packaging, and to develop marketing skills among women. Women are exposed to the best and relevant technologies displayed at TTDCs in all districts. The information about their functioning is obtained on a quarterly basis for monitoring and evaluation. Well-known agencies like ORG-Marg (a private consultancy firm) are associated for evaluation and monitoring of SHGs and to suggest measures for their sustainable growth.[16]

Marketing

Marketing support is provided to the SHGs through DWCRA Bazaars (market outlets), which have been set up in all the districts, and a permanent DWCRA Bazaar is nearing completion at Hyderabad. Products worth more than Rs. 100.00 crores were sold through DWCRA Bazaars in the last two years. Training and Technology Development Centers (TTDC) have been established in each district to introduce innovative technologies for the qualitative improvement of products made by the SHGs.

The SHGs are assisted in many districts to develop the branding of their products, for example—Stree Prakasham in Ongole district, Mahila in Adilabad district etc. Women are encouraged to participate in fairs taking place at the national level and in other states. Collaboration with the Hindustan Lever Limited has been secured by SHGs of Nalgonda district where MACS has been appointed as stockiest points and groups and sales points for marketing DWCRA products. Leading super bazaars like Food World and the Trinethra super market have come forward to tie up with SHGs to market DWCRA products.

Some DWCRA products are in high demand. The pickle producing SHGS of Guntur district got orders worth Rs. 6.00 lakhs, the lace groups of west Godavari district got export orders.

Coverage of the Rural Women

It has been planned by the government to cover all the rural poor women under SHGs in the next 4 to 5 years. It is programmed to cover at least one woman from a BPL (Below Poverty Level) family as a member of SHG in next two years. So far, all the habitations in the State have at least one SHG.[17]

Financial Support During 2000-01

The government released Rs. 44 crores during 2000-01 to assist 44,000 groups covering 6.6 lakhs women @ Rs. 10,000 as revolving fund to each group. This is in addition to Government of India grant of Rs. 4.5 crores. NABARD, Commercial Banks and Regional Rural Banks are providing direct assistance to the SHGs under the "Self-Help Linking Scheme" of NABARD.[18]

Institutional Building

SHGs are encouraged to come together as Cooperative Societies at the village level and mandal level by federating them under Mutually Aided Cooperative Societies Act 1995. Nearly 250 societies have been formed so far. These societies will be accessing credit from financial institutions, donor agencies, DRDAs and voluntary organizations and help the members of women SHGs in availing bigger loans for economic activities, and also help in collective bargaining in the marketing of products, purchasing raw materials etc.

Due to this massive Self-Help movement, there is a perceptible improvement in the socio-economic status of the rural women. Due to the constant efforts of the government, women have become very active, assertive and are concerned with the issues relating to them and their surroundings.

Meaning, Aims and Objectives of Self Help Groups

Under Swarnjayanti Gram Swarozgar Yojana (SGSY), the beneficiaries are known as swarozgaris. The swarozgaris can be either individuals or groups. SGSY lays emphasis on the group approach, under which the rural poor are organised into Self-help Groups. In either case, the list of Below Poverty Line (BPL) households identified through BPL census duly approved by the Gram Sabha will form the basis for identification of families for assistance under SGSY.

Self Help Groups broadly go through three stages of evolution :

1. Group formation.
2. Capital formation through the revolving fund and skill development.
3. Taking up economic activity for income generation.

SHG is a group of rural poor who have volunteered to organise themselves into a group for eradication of poverty of the members. They agree to save regularly and convert their savings into a Common Fund. The members of the group agree to use this common fund and such other funds that they may receive as a group through a common management.[19]

The poor may organize themselves, into small groups up to 20 persons, known as Self Help Groups (SHGs) to inculcate the habit of thrift and credit operations among themselves.

SHGs may be organised in clusters of blocks/districts either by reputed voluntary agencies/NGOs and/or at the initiative of branch managers of commerical, cooperative and regional rural banks.[20]

Under SGSY, a self-help group may consist of 10 to 20 persons. In the case of minor irrigation, and in the case of disabled persons, this number may be a minimum of five (5).

All members of the Group should belong to families below poverty line. The group shall not consist of more than one member from the same family. A person should not be a member of more than one group.

The SHG will be an informal group. However, the groups can also register themselves under the Societies Registration Act, the State Cooperative Act or as a partnership firm. The SHGs can be further strengthened and stabilised by federating them at, say village level. This would facilitate regular interaction and exchange of experiences including flow of information from DRDAs and other departments.

An external facilitator working closely with the communities at grassroot level can play a critical role in the group formation and development effort. The facilitator may or may not be an official. In some cases, NGOs can not only make available the facilitator but also help in building their capacity. DRDAs may support such sensitive support mechanisims in the shape of NGOs or community based organisations or a team of dedicated functionaries of the Government who are fully engaged in the task of initiating and sustaining the group development process.[21]

Formation of Self-Help Groups

(i) SHG is a group of rural poor who have volunteered to organise themselves into a group for eradication of poverty of the members. They agree to save regularly and convert their savings into a Common Fund. The members of the group agree to use this common fund and such other funds that they receive as a group through a common management. The group formation will keep in view the following broad guidelines. Under SGSY, a self-help group may consist of 10 to 20 persons. In the case of minor irrigation, and in the case of disabled persons, this number may be a minimum of five (5).

(i) The group corpus fund should be used to advance loans to the members. The group should develop financial management norms covering the loans sanction procedure, repayment schedule and interest rates.

(ii) The members in the group meetings should take all the loaning decisions through a participatory decision making process.

(iii) The group should be able to prioritise the loan applications, fix repayment schedules, fix appropriate rate of interest for the loans advanced and closely monitor the repayment of the loan installments form the loanees.

(iv) The groups should operate a group account so as to deposit the balance amounts left with the groups after disbursing loans to its members.

(v) The group should maintain simple basic records such as Minutes books, Attendance register, Load ledger, General ledger, Cashbook, Bank passbook and individual passbooks.

50 per cent of the groups formed in each block should be exclusively for the women. In the case of disabled persons, the groups formed should ideally be disabled persons, the groups formed should ideally be disability-specific wherever possible; however, in case a sufficient number of people for

formation of disability-specific groups are not available, a group may comprise of persons with diverse disabilities.

Aims of the Self Help Group

The aim of the SHG is to bring out all round sustainable development of the member's families, villages.

Objectives

Its objectives are multifaceted oriented with the intention of Poverty eradication, such as Socio-economic activities, political and economic development of the village. It also intends for the promotion of economic activities :

1. To create appropriate awareness among the members for their all round development in the society.

2. To promote co-operation and self-help attitude, good habit of savings among the members and voluntary collective work.

3. To promote savings attitude and habit among the members for their future and to encourage the members to commit themselves to regular savings.

4. To meet the credit needs of the members in time for consumption, income generation, asset formations and other appropriate purposes.

5. To help members in acquiring and use of appropriate technical knowledge and managerial skills in relation to their occupation in order to increase productivity.

6. To create awareness and work for human health development.

7. To improve the basic facilities of the village viz., drinking water, sanitation, etc.

8. To arrange for the availability of improved agricultural equipments, implements, etc., for the villagers and to run a service centre for the benefit of the members.

9. To give special attention to population control measures.

Rules and Regulations

Certain rules and regulations are to be followed for the effective function of SHGs. These are related to Admission, Group Meeting, Participation, Duities and responsibilities, and also includes the formation of executive committee, Savings, Credit managements and other regulations.

Functioning of the Groups

1. The Group meetings should be held once a weak and regularly on any convenient day, place and time as decided by the group.

2. The members should attend all meetings in time without fail.

3. The members who are unable to attend the meeting for genuine reasons has to inform the Group in person or through a messenger in advance or at least at the same meeting. The member who fails is liable to pay a fine for the absence as decided by the group.

4. The latecomers for the meeting and those who walk out in the middle without intimating the chairperson are liable to pay a fine as decided by the group.

5. If a member is absent for three consecutive meetings without specific reasons his/her membership shall be suspended or cancelled with or without notice.

6. Unrelated issues/points should not be brought for discussion in the Group meeting.

7. The members should not use vulgar words or physical force against any member during the meeting and the violators or those who misbehave have to pay a fine as decided by the Group or their membership shall be cancelled.

8. The members should not sleep or stay separate from the Group during the meeting.

9. All the members have to sign in the minutes book at the end of the meeting after the recorded proceedings of each meeting are read out and confirmed.

Participation of the Group Members

All the members should participate in the discussion and decision making process orally and mentally in the Group meetings.

Equal opportunity and encouragement should be given to all the members for their full participation in the meeting and in all the activities of the Group.

All the members should attend the related/trainings/ workshops/seminars, exposures, etc., within and outside the village without fail. The violators are liable to pay a fine except for the genuine reasons.

The members should co-operate and participate in all the developmental activities related to the members families, village, the group, environment, etc., appropriate actions against those who do not cooperate/paricipate shall be taken by the Group.

The members should participate in researching/learning dissemination and adoption of appropriate technologies for development.

The illiterate members should evince interest and make an effort to become literates. The Group shall run a learning centre at the convenient time for this purpose.

All the members should involve in regular savings and credit management activities with a special focus.

All the members should work with concern towards creating/building socio economical safety society and stress on population control.

The Members Duties and Responsibilities

1. All the members should promote and protect and cooperation and be united in the Group.

2. The member should create equal opportunity and give encouragement to all the members in the Group.

3. The members should mobilise, use and manage the needy resources properly/judicially.

4. It is the responsibility of all the members to take necessary collective sanction against willful defaulters and recover the loan amount.

5. The members should take responsibility carefully for their all-round development and should also take leadership responsibility in the Group with service motive.

6. All the members should involve in planning, implementing, monitoring and evaluate the development programmes of the family, village and environment time to time and to pay attention to the results of evaluation with proper action.

7. The members should promote and protect the unity and integrity of the group and the village.

Members Savings in the Group Related

1. Each and every member should save at least Rs. 5 per week and Rs. 20 per month in the Group, which should be maintained in each individual member's name.

2. Savings amount may be withdrawn by the members only at critical circumstances with prior approval of the Group. However the members should maintain a minimum balance of Rs. 1000/- (or as decided by SHG) in their savings account.

3. No interest will be paid for the members savings with the group. But 12 per cent interest shall be paid for the amount kept in the Group as fixed deposit for a minimum period of six months.

4. The members should save from the family income earned only, but not the borrowed money for interest.

5. The members will not be encouraged to adjust their savings amount against their loan due to the Group, except in extreme circumatances.

The Credit Policy of SHGS

1. The credit can be given to the needy members of the Group for the purposes such as Consumption, Income Generation, and asset creation, clearing the old burden loans, socio religious and any other appropriate purposes.

2. The credit shall be given to the members of the group only after a careful study, through discussion and unanimous decision on the quantum of credit, rate of interest and the payment schedule for each loan.

3. The loanee should give a written agreement to the Group for the loan amount as per the official procedures in the presence of the witness to the Group at the time of borrowing.

4. The loan amount should be granted on the basis of priority.
5. The loanee should repay the credit/loan amount with service charge as per the repayment schedule agreed upon.
6. The members who are irregular for the SHG meetings or irregular in savings are not eligible for credit/loan from the group.
7. All the members shall have equal opportunity for loan from the Group on eligibility/priority basis.
8. The funds of the Group should be revolved to the optimum extent for the benefit of all the members.
9. The Group can avail loan from the Bank and other credit institutions, NGOs, other Group and any other available sources for its activities and the same has been repaid in time as the terms and conditions agreed upon.
10. As well, the Group can receive donations, grants, subsidy, charity from Govt. NGOs other organisations.[22]

Strengthning of Self Help Groups

Every SHG that is in existence at least for a period of 6 months and has demonstrated the potential of available group enters the second stage, wherein it receives the Revolving Fund and also embarks on further strengthening of its entire team. DRDA will arrange to provide the revolving fund to such groups, meeting their share from out of 10 per cent of SGSY-SGSY Fund.

Principles for the management of Revolving Fund are as follows :

1. The revolving fund is provided to the groups to augment the groups corpus so as to enable a greater

number of members to access loans and also to facilitate the increase in the per capita loan available to the members.

2. As the revolving fund becomes part and parcel of the group corpus, the group should follow same norms for utilisation as in the case of their own saving fund.

3. The group should discuss the credit requirements of the members and advance loans from out of the corpus (savings + interest + revolving fund) to a few members and fix repayment schedule and interest rates. From the amounts recovered from the loans, new members could be covered.

4. The revolving fund imparts credit discipline and financial management skills to the members, so that they become credit-worthy and bankable in the eyes of the bank.

5. On receipt of the revolving fund, the group shall utilise the fund in the manner and for purposes it deems fit. The idea is that the group should develop the capacity to utilise funds it has received from outside. The revolving fund can be used by the group for purchase of raw materials, marketing or infrastructure support for income generating activities. It can alternatively be used for lending to individual members for their own purposes. The members shall inculcate the habit of prompt and full repayment of the loans taken by them from the revolving fund.

6. Those groups that have received the revolving fund under DWCRA or any other programme shall not be eligible to receive the revolving fund under SGSY. However, there is no bar on such groups receiving credit and subsidy under group loaning under SGSY, after they have demonstrated their functioning as a viable group.

7. At the end of six months from the date of receipt of the revolving fund, the SHG will be sujbected to another grading test to see if it has been functioning effectively and is capable of taking up an economic activity through higher levels of investment. It is important that the bank should be satisfied about the grading of the SHG at this stage. Therefore, the choice of the agency carrying out the grading as well as the criteria should be to the satisfaction of the bank.[23]

Loan-cum-subsidy for the Group Activity

Group activities stand a better chance of success because it is easier to provide back-up support and marketing linkages for group activities. SGSY will primarily follow the group approach. The groups should demonstrate minimum levels of group dynamism, as detailed above before considering for assistance with loan-cum-subsidy for the group under SGSY. The group loans are entitled to 50 per cent subsidy subject to a limit of Rs. 1.25 lakhs.

DRDAs should conduct training programmes to the members and the representatives of the groups so that the groups become fully selfmanaged and evolve into strong groups. The cost of the group formation and development should be met from the SGSY Revolving Fund (10 per cent of SGSY).[24]

Criteria for Allocation of Funds to the States

Swarnjayanti Gram Swarozgar Yojana is a centrally sponsored scheme and the financing of the programme will be shared between the Centre and the States in the ratio of 75:25. The central allocation earmarked for the States will be distributed in relation to the incidence of poverty in the states. However, additional parameters, like absorption capacity (based on past trend in utilisation of SGSY funds) and special requirement will also be taken into consideration during the course of the year. Devolution of funds to the districts will be indicated by the states and approved by the Government of India. Government of India will release the funds directly to the DRDAs. Devolution to the Blocks may be decided by the Governing Body of the DRDA based on the level of poverty and other local factors. Re-allocation may be made by the DRDA within a district. This can be made during January for the remainder of the financial year.[25]

(Diagram)

1.	Secretary, Ministry of Rural Development	Chairman
2.	Deputy Governor, Reserve Bank of India	Member
3.	Secretary, Dept. of Agriculture and Cooperation	Member
4.	Secretary, Dept. of Expenditure	Member
5.	Special Secretary, Banking Division, Ministry of Finance.	Member
6.	Secretary, Dept. of Women and Child Development	Member
7.	Secreatry, Dept. of Small Scale and Agro related Industries.	Member
8.	Secretary, Dept. of Science and Technology	Member
9.	Secretary, Ministry of Welfare	Member
10.	Managing Director, NABARD	Member
11.	Advisor (Rural Development), Planning Commission	Member
12.	Additional Secretary and FA, Ministry of Rural Development.	Member
13.	State Secretaries of Rural Development.	Member
14.	Chairman-cum-Managing Director of all Commercial sector banks	Member
15.	Director General, CAPART	Member
16.	Director General, NIRD	Member
17.	Chairman, Indian Bank Association	Member
18.	Joint Secreaty (IRD) Dept. of Rural Development	Member Secretary

Structure of SHGS

For the effective administration of this programme, both the Central and the state governments have set up separate departments to implement these programmes in the country.

Central Level

The Administrative set up of SHGs starts at the Central Level with the Ministry of Rural Development in The Department of Rural development, Government of India, New Delhi which has the overall responsibility of policy formulation, monitoring and evaluation of the programme and for release of central share of funds. A Central Level Coordination Committee (CLCC) has been constituted as under to assist the Department. The CLCC will meet once in six months.[26] The Secretary, Department of Rural development is the Chairman and there are other members who are the secretaries or Joint Secretaries representing various ministerial departments and states. The Non-Official members are also represented in the Committee.

The functions of the above said Central Committee are as follows:-

1. To review and ensure effective implementation of the programmes.
2. To review linkages for support services for SGSY.
3. To review progress of these programmes in physical, financial and qualitative terms including credit assistance.
4. To consider concurrent evaluation reports.
5. To provide a forum for a continuous dialogue with the State Government and Bankers.
6. To review the credit arrangements and recommend changes and improvements as and when necessary.

7. To look after the framing and revision of guidelines for the above mentioned programmes.

8. To review the block plans, district plans, annual plans.

State Level

(Diagram)

In Andhra Pradesh The Ministry of Panchayati Raj, The Department of Rural Development or any other Department to which the subject of rural Development is allocated is responsible for planning, implementation, monitoring and evaluation of the SHG programme at the State level.The Secretary Rural Development will be the Chairman and the Joint /Deputy Secretary, Department of Rural Development as Member-Secretary and there are various Heads of Departments including a representative from the Government of India.[27]

1.	Chief Secretary/Development Commissioner	Chairman
2.	Secretary, D/o institutional finance	Member
3.	Secretary, D/o Planning	Member
4.	Secretary, In-charge of Women's development	Member
5.	Concerned Heads of the Line Departments As and when required.	Member
6.	Secretary in charge of Welfare of SC/STs	Member
7.	Representative of NABARD (local Head of Regional Office)	Member
8.	Representative of RBI	Member
9.	Representatives of concerned implementing Banks at State Headquarters.	Member
10.	A representative of the Government of India, Not below the rank of Deputy Secretary.	Member
11.	Director, SIRD	Member
12.	Convenor, SLBC	Member
13.	Secretary, in charge of Rural Development	Secretary

Functions of the State Level SGSY Committee are as under :

1. To provide leadership and guidance in the planning implementation and monitoring of the programme.
2. To review the district-wise progress under SGSY and suggest remedial actions.
3. To monitor and evaluate the implementation of the programme with reference to the objectives of the programme.
4. To review the involvement of reputed NGOs in the SGSY and provide directions if necessary.
5. To provide a forum for a meaningful dialogue between the policy makers at the State level and the implementers at the field level as well as bankers.
6. To discuss any other issue relating to SGSY.
7. To secure inter Departmental Coordination and linkages for the programmes.
8. To consider needs and changes in the administrative set up for the implementation of the programme of the SHG and approve the establishment pattern.

District Level:

(Diagram)

This programme is implemented through District development Agency (DRDA) at the District level. In Andhra Pradesh, the DRDA is genrally headed by the Collector,who acts as the Chairman. The Project Director of DRDA functions as the Member secretary.

The Composition of DRDA

1.	District Collector/Chief Executive Officer	Chairman
2.	DDM of NABARD	Member
3.	LDO of RBI	Member
4.	District level Coordinators of the Implementing banks	Member
5.	Concerned Heads of district level Line departments	Member
6.	General Manager, DIC	Member
7.	District KVIB Officer	Member
8.	Project Director, DRDA	Member
9.	2-3 NGO representatives	Member
10.	Lead Bank Officer	Convenor

The Chairman of DRDA is empowered to form an executive committee and this executive committee will assist the DRDA. This executive committee consists of all the District Level Officers and other officers found necessary for the planning and implementation of the programme. The governing Body of the DRDA should meet once in a quarter and the executive committee.

The Functions of the District SGSY Committee (DRDA)

The DRDA will be the overall in charge of the planning and implementation, monitoring and evoluation of the SHG programme in the District :

1. To keep the District Level Agencies and Mandal Level Agencies informed of the basic parameters, the requirements of the SHG programme and the tasks to be performed by all these agencies.

2. Monitoring and review of the overall progress in physical and financial terms.

3. Sorting out inter-agency differences and to prepare items for consideration of State Level Committee.

4. Assessing training needs of Swarozgaris and also review the arrangements for training including identification of appropriate institutions and also.
5. Monitor the recovery position bank-wise and block-wise so as to initiate corrective measures where necessary.
6. To coordinate and oversee the services, preparation of perspective plans and annual action plans of the Mandals and finally prepare a district plan.
7. To evaluate and monitor the programme to ensure its effectiveness.
8. To secure Inter-Sectional and Inter-Departmental Co-ordination.
9. To give publicity to the achievements made under the programme and disseminate knowledge and build up awareness about the programme,and
10. To send periodical reports to the state government in the prescribed formats.

Mandal Level SGSY Committee

(Diagram)

In Andhra Pradesh SHG programme is implemented at The Mandal Level. The director of DRDA is generally its Chairman. The meetings of this committee shall be convened by the MDO. The Lead Bank Officer, DDM, NABARD and the Lead District Officer, RBI may attend the meetings as special invitees. They may attend as many meetings as possible in each mandal, so that they are familiar with the ground level problems and can help in sorting them out.

The Mandal Level SGSY committee' s composition will be as follows:

1.	Project Director–DRDA	Chairman
2.	Project Officer (Self-employment)	Member
3.	Branch Managers of all implementing Bank branches in Block	Members
4.	Mandal Level/Sub-Division Level Officers of the concerned line departments	Members
5.	NGOs representative (One)	Member
6.	Mandal Development Officer	Convenor

The meetings of this committee shall be convened by the MDO. The Lead Bank Officer, DDM, NABARD and the Lead District Officer, RBI may attend the meetings as special invitees. They may attend as many meetings as possible in each Mandal, so that they are familiar with the ground level problems and can help in sorting them out.

The main functions of Mandal Level SGSY Committee are :

(a) Selection of key activities at the beginning of the programme;

(b) Selection of villages and number of Swarozgaris to be covered each year;

(c) Distribution of the work among the bank branches;

(d) Monitoring of the performance by different agencies;

(e) Co-ordination issues in respect of infrastructure, credit, technology and marketing.

(f) Review of incomes being earned by Swarozgaris;

(g) Review of the recovery performance; fixing dates for recovery camps etc;

(h) Conduct of sample checks of verification of assets;

(i) Drawing up of the monthly report (the monthly report may be drawn by MDO based on information furnished by the banks. A review of the report in the monthly meeting will help the Mandal level committee in identifying different problems. It is, however, not necessary to hold up the preparation of the report in the absence of this monthly meeting);

(j) Review of progress of Swarozgaris in crossing the poverty line.

Controlling and Monitoring Set Up

For the purpose of the effective monitoring of the implementation of SGSY, the banks may set up SGSY cells in their controlling offices such as zonal/Regional offices. These cells should make periodical review of the flow of credit to SGSY Swarozgaris, ensure the implementation of the guidelines issued by Reserve Bank of India and the Government of India, collect data from the branches and make available consolidated data to the Head Office of the bank.[28]

Monitoring and Evaluation are the integral components of any programme and so also of SHGs. Monitoring is an on-going process and the regular systematically meetings of all the functionaries can be effectively utilised to accomplish this effectively. This programme needs to be constantly monitored for mutual understanding, understanding of the problems and theirs solutions jointly by the SHG functionaries and women. Evaluation of the inherent problems at a regular interval is necessary to assess how far the programme has achieved its objectives, for identification of the inherent problems or the problems which have emerged during implementation to correct the course and keep the direction clear.

Therefore, Income generating activities are given importance in India, particularly in rural areas with development strategies. SHG s have been designed as a new model for integrating women in the main development scheme. The success of SHGs depends on proper identification of the participants, assessment of their needs and problems, trust on the part of the officials in the potential opportunities for the development of women and their own capacities for self–employment.

References

1. Kusum Lata Tiwari, "Women and Development", Kurukshetra, August, 1995, p. 54.
2. Meenaxi Anand Chaudhry, "Empowaearment Strategies for Rural Women in India" Kurukshetra,March,1996, p. 21.
3. Indira Misra, "Reaching out to Poor Women: RMK'S Mission", Kurukshetra, August, 1995, p. 84.
4. National Bank, NABARD, Annual Report, 1990-1991, Mangalore, p. 18.
5. *Ibid.*, p. 18.
6. Financing A Self Help Groups, A Reference, NABARD, Bangalore, p. 1.
7. National Bank, NABARD, *op. cit.*, p. 19.
8. Financing A Self Help Groups, *op. cit.*, p. 9.
9. The Myrada Experience: Self Help Groups Reading Materials and Related Literature, Gulbarga, 2001, p. 127.
10. National Bank, NABARD, *op. cit.*, p. 28.
11. Archana Sood "Success Story of Matsyafed Cooperative" Kurukshetra, August, 2000, pp. 11-12.
12. *Ibid.* p. 15.
13. www. Andhra Pradesh.com, Self Help Groups.
14. *Ibid.*
15. *Ibid.*
16. *Ibid.*

17. *Ibid.*
18. *Ibid.*
19. Sawaranjayanti Gram Swarojgar Yojna, Guidelines, Government of India, Ministry of Rural Development, New Delhi, p. 16.
20. *Ibid.* p. 16.
21. *Ibid.* p. 17.
22. *Ibid.* p. 49.
23. *Ibid.* p. 19.
24. Sawaranjayanti Gram Swarojgar Yojna, Guidelines, *op. cit.*, p. 52.
25. *Ibid.* p. 51.
26. *Ibid.* p. 50.
27. *Ibid.* p. 48.
28. *Ibid.* p. 48.

4

Self Help Groups in Anantapur District

Profile of the District

Anantapur district is one of the most backward and drought-prone areas of Andhra Pradesh. Historically known as the 'Stalking ground of famines' Anantapur is in the Rayalaseema Region of Andhra Pradesh. The district deduces its name from 'Anantapur', its headquarters town. It is generally held that Anantapur is known after the big tank, 'Anantasagaram' (boundless Ocean) near the Western and Eastern sluices of which the villages of Anantasagaram and Bukkarayasamuda wre constructed by Cikkayodeya, the minister of Bukka (AD 1344-1377), the Vijayanagara ruler'[1]. Some authorities asserts that 'Anantasagaram' was named after Bukka's queen, while some others conted that it must have been known after Anantarasa Chikkavodeya himself as Bukka had no queen by that time.[2]

Historical Background

Anantapur District was formed in the year 1882 having been separated from Bellary District. Later on, it was expanded with the additional Revenue mandals of Kadiri,

Mudigubba, Nallamada, N.P. Kunta, Talupula, Nallacheruvu, O.D. Cheruvu, Tanakal, Amadagur and Gandlapenta (Erstwhile Kadiri Taluk) from Cuddapah District in the year 1910. During the year 1956, the present Revenue Mandals of Rayadurg, D. Hirehal, Kanekal, Bommanahal and Gummaghatta (Erstwhile Rayadurg Taluk) District were added to Anantapur District. The District has been divided into 3 (Three Revenue Divisions vi, Anantapur, Dharmavaram and Penukonda Divisions.

Boundary and Topography

The district lies between 130-14' and 150–4' of the northern latitude and between 760–47 and 780–26' of the Eastern longitude[3]. It is the Western most district in the state. it is roughly long is shape with the longer side running North to South. It is bounded by Kurnool district on the North, cuddapah district on the East, Chittoor district on the South-East and by Karnataka State on the south and west of the District.[4] It forms part of the Northern extremity of the mysore plateau and slopes from South to North.[5] The district with an area of 19, 126 sq. kms. ranks third among the districts and accounts for 6.9 per cent of the total geographical area of Andhra Pradesh. The district has three natural zones. before the implementation of mandal system in Andhra Pradesh this district was divided into three administrative revenue divisions viz., Anantapur, Dharmavaram and penukonda.[6] There were sixteen administrative blocks in the district as given in Table 4.1 After the introduction of the Mandal system in the state by the Telugu Desam Government on 15th of january 1987 the entire state has been devided into 1104 Mandala Praja Parishads.[7] Consequently, the district of Anantapur has also been drawn into a division resulting in the formation of 63 Mandals. (Vide Table No. 4.1). This districts 14 Assembly and 02 Parliamentary constituencies. (4.2)

Table-4.1 : Division-wise Distribution of Mandals in Anantapur District

Anantapur Division	*Dharmavaram Division*	*Penukonda Division*
1. Anantapur Rural@	23. Battalapalli	45. Amarapuram
2. Raptadu	24. Chennekottapalli	46. Gudibanda
3. Garladinna	25. Kanaganapalli	47. Rolla
4. Atmakur	26. Ramgiri	48. Agali
5. Kudur	27. Kalyandurga@	49. Hindupur*
6. Singanamala	28. Beluguppa	50. Parigi
7. Bukkaraya Samudram	29. Kambadur	51. Lepakshi
8. Narpala	30. Kundurpi	52. Chilamattur
9. Tadipatri*	31. Brahmasamudram	53. Gorantala@
10. Yadiki	32. Settur	54. Kadiri
11. Peddapappur	33. Rayadurg	55. Mudigubba
12. Putlur	34. D. Hirehalli	56. N.P. Kunta
13. Yellanur	35. Gummagutta	57. Talupula
14. Guntakal	36. Kanekal	58. Nallacheruvu
15. Gooty*	37. Bommanahall	59. Nallamada
16. Pamidi	38. Penukonda*	60. O.D. Cheruvu
17. Peddavadugur	39. Somabdepalli	61. Tanakal
18. Urvakonda	40. Roddam	62. Amadagur
19. Vajrakarur	41. Puttaparthy	63. Gandlapenta
20. Vidapanakal	42. Kottacheruvu	
21. Dharmavaram*	43. Bukkapatnam	
22. Tadimari	44. Madakasira	

Source : District at Glance–Booklet Released by the Office of the Distinct Collector, Anantapur, AP, 2002.

Note : *Indicate Erstwhile administrative Blocks–Kadiri was divided into Kadiri East and Kadiri West.

@-Mandals Chosen for Present study.

Table 4.2 : Assembly and Parliamentary Constituencies in Anantapur District

S. No.	*Name of the Assembly Constituency*	*Name of the Parliamentary Constituency*
1.	Kadiri	1. Anantapur
2.	Nallamada	2. Hindupur
3.	Gorantla	
4.	Hindupur	
5.	Madakasira	
6.	Penukonda	
7.	Kalyandurg (SC)	
8.	Rayadurga	
9.	Urvakonda	
10.	Guntakal	
11.	Singanamala (SC)	
12.	Anantapur	
13.	Dhrmavaram	
14.	Tadipatri	

SC: Reserved for Scheduled Castes.
Source: A.P. Year Book 1990, Data News Features, Hyderabad, pp. 113, 123.

Climate and Rainfall

This district possesses and extensive dry area and hence the agricultural conditions are often precarious. Like its neighbouring districts of Cuddaph and Kurnool, Anantapur is no less notorious for its appressive heat. Monsoons evade this part due to its unfavourable location. Keeping far away from its East Coast, it does not enjoy full benefits of North-East monsoon and being cut off by the high Western ghats the South-West monsoons are also prevented. As a result of bad seasons, Anantapur district has witnessed frequent droughts. The rainfall is only 550 mm which is the lowest when compared to other parts of the state. Hence, this district is also declared to be one of six districts in the country affected by severe drought frequently.[8]

Soils

Anantapur district can be divided geographically into three regions from the point of view of soils. The Northern region comprises of Gooty, Uravakodnda, Singanamala and Tadapatri taluks with larger areas of black cotton soil. The Central region covers Anantapur, Dharmavaram, Sathyasai and Penukanda taluks largely composed of non-vegetational poor red soil. The southern region constitutes Hindupur, Madakasira, Chennekothapalli and Kadiri taluks with rich red soil and better vegetation. The soil of Anantapur district is said to be deficit in Zinc. The physiography of Anantapur is rightly described as 'no high mountain ranges, no thick forests, the paucity of perennial rivers, a low rainfall, an enervating climate '-these are part of what nature has given to their land and no wonder its material progress is hampered.[9]

Infrastructure: Anantapur district headquarter is on the Hyderabad-Bangalore and Hyderabad–Tirupati railway line with broad gauge and meter gauge railway traffic. The important towns in the district are also well connected by a good net-work of roads kept under the control of Zilla Praja Parishad and Roads and Buildings department. Apart from these, a stretch of national highway No. 7 also passe through Anantapur from Hyderabad to Bangalore. There are 932 post offices, 154 Telegraph offices and 60 Telephone Exchanges functioning in the district.[10] Only about 383 villages (39.1 per cent) of the Total villages enjoy electricity and the Agricultural Sector consumes nearly 51.2 per cent, Industry accounts for 26.8 per cent, while the households consume about 11 per cent of the total electricity power consumption in the district.

Anantapur–A Drought Prone District

Drought is a situation of continuous dry weather causing distress. This district is geographically situated in an unfavourable natural zone and it is the driest part in the state as stated earlier. Lack of perennial rivers and almost total dependence of cultivation on rainfall, make the district vulnerable to frequent droughts. It is estimate that drought occurs once in three years in Rayalaseema region where Anantapur is an integral part.[11]

According to the estimates made by the Ministry of Food and Agriculture Government of India, of the area affected by scarcity conditions in the Southern region there fourths are concentrated in Andhra Pradesh. The affected areas consitute 57 per cent of total area and 47 per cent of the population of the state and Rayalaseema region forms the major part of this chronic famine area. The government of Andhra Pradesh has identified 71 Taluks in 10 districts in the state as chronically drought–affected areas. of these 33 taluks have been declared as the 'hard core' of such areas where the scarcity conditions are most acute. The irrigation commission also identified 600 taluks in 7 districts of Andhra Pradesh as drought-prone arweas. As per the above sources it is clear that all the fourteen taluks of Anantapur district come under drought affected areas. The fifth Five Year Plan of Andhra Pradesh rightly described the situation of Rayalseema; 'nature is unfourable to this area, rainfall is scanty and uncertain, surface water has been almost exhausted.

Literacy

The literacy percentage of Anantapur district is lower than that in the state as a whole. There are as many as 3,060 educational institutions all over the district. Anantapur has recorded a literacy rate of 56.69 per cent as per 2001 provisional census. The rural male literacy is 65.13 and female is 38.3 and Urban Male literacy is 80.10 and female is 59.99.[12]

Demography

As per 2001 (provisional Census) Anantapur district has a total population of 3639304 Lakhs. The proportion of rural male population 1391209 and female all together 1328016 in total 2719225 with 74.72 per cent to total district population. The proportion of urban male population is 468293 and female is 451786 all together 920079 with 25.28 per cent to the total population of the district. The details have been given in table (3,4.5&6)[13]

Table-4.3 : Itemwise Distribution of Population in Anantapur District

S. No.	*Total Area*	*Total*
1.	Total Area	19130 sq. km.
2.	Population	3639304
3.	Density of Population (Persons sq. km.)	190
4.	Men	1859502
5.	Women	1779802
6.	Total Rural Population	2719225
7.	Total Urban Population	920079
8.	% of Scheduled Castes	18.38
9.	% of Scheduled Tribes	3.22
10.	Sex–Ratio (Female ? 1000 Males)	957
11.	Literacy rate	56.69%
12.	Revenue Mandals	63
13.	Gram Panchayats	866
14.	Revenue Villages	964

Source: Provisional Census 2001 at www.manage-disaster.org p. 1.

Table-4.4 : Social Development Indicators of Anantapur District

S. No.	*Item*	*Total*
1.	Below Poverty Line	51.1%
2.	Nfant Mortality Rate (IMR)	9
3.	Maternal Mortality Rate	0.86
4.	Birth Rate	20.3
5.	Death Rate Rate	6.0

Source: Provisional Census 2001 at www.manage-disaster.org p. 1.

Table-4.5 : Place and Sexwise Distribution of Population in Anantapur District

S. No.	Place	Male	Female	Total	% to total District Population	Population AP
1.	Rural	1391209	1328016	2719225	74.72	55223944
2.	Urban	468293	451786	920079	25.28	20503597
3.	Total	185902	1779802	3639304	100.00	75727524

Source: Provisional Population, paper 2 AP, Census of India, 2001. pp. 244-251.

Table-4.6 : Distribution of Child Population from Age Groups of 0-6

S. No.	Place	Male	Female	Total
1.	Rural	178919	171985	350904
2.	Urban	54919	53307	108226
3.	Total	133838	225292	459130

Source: Provisional Population, paper 2 AP, Census of India 2001, pp. 244-251.

Table-4.7 : Literacy Rate in Anantapur District

S. No.	Place	Male	Female	Total	% to Total Literacy
1.	Rural	789605	442931	1232536	70.46
2.	Urban	331103	239057	570160	29.54
3.	Total	1120708	681988	1802696	100.00

Source: Provisional Population, paper 2 AP, Census of India 2001, pp. 244-251.

The literate population of the district consists of 442931, 1232536 rural male and female respectively. With 70.46 per cent to the literate population of the district. Whereas the urban literate population of the district are 331103, 239057 male and female respectively with the percentage of 29.54 to the total literate population of the district. Details have been given in table (7).[14]

Education

There are 3174 primary schools, 86 Upper primary schools, 428 High schools, 12 higher secondary schools with a total of 4190 schools in the district. There are 3523 schools education committees, 992 Panchyat education committees and 61 mandal education committees. The total numbers of teachers in the district are 18463 and 3606 vidya volunteers.

Table-4.8 : Land Utilisation in Anantapur District for the Year 1999-2000

S. No.	*Classification of Area*	*Area in Hectares*	*% to the total geographical area*
1.	Total Geographical Area	19,13,492	100.00
2.	Forests	1,96,778	10.28
3.	Barren and Uncultivated Land	1,72,949	9.03
4.	Land put to Non-Agricultural Use	1,61,754	8.45
5.	Cultivable	83870	4.38
6.	Permanent Pastures and Other Grazing Lands	23,341	1.24
7.	Land Under miscellaneous tree crop, groves not included in net areas sown	11256	0.59
8.	Other fallown Land	115649	6.04
9.	Current fallown land	171514	8.96
10.	Net Area sown	976381	51.03

Source: www.Andhra Pradesh.com (statistics, Agriculture Table–4.2).

Agronomic Profile

The economy of Anantapur is centered on agriculture as the main profession and agriculture continued to be the chief source of living inspite of drought condition arising from insufficient rainfall and inadequate irrigation.

Land Utilisation

The patterns of land utilsation in the district as evident from the Table. 6.4 reveals that the percentage of forest area to the total geographical area in Anantapur is only 10.28 and relatively it is the lowest among the other districts in the state. It is also clear that nearly 51.03 per cent of the total geographical area comes under cropped area.

It is also to be noticed that in recent years. Forest areas have been allotted for cultivable purpose and consequently there has been considerable decline in forest area and significant increase in the area sown in the district.

Cropping Pattern

Of all the food crops in the district, Jowr tops fist and then follows rain fed cereal Rice, Bajra and Ragi. Among commercial crops groundnut is the major crop. Table 4.9 shows the area under different crops in the district.

Table-4.9 : Details of Principal Crops Irrigated Area in Anantapur District (Acres in Hectares)

S. No.	*Crops*	*Total Acres*	*% to Total Geographical Area*
1.	Rice	58056	0.03
2.	Wheat	335	0.01
3.	Jowar	41475	2.17
4.	Bajra	185	0.09
5.	Maize	2604	0.14
6.	Ragi	6570	0.34

Source: Directorates of Statistics Andhra Pradesh at www.ap.nic.in.

By the whole of food crops in the district Rice tops first and then follows Jowar, Ragi and Maize. Rice was irrigated in 58.056 hectares and Jowar was in 41,475 hectares. Table shows the area under principle crops irrigated are during 1999-2000.

Table-4.10 : Commercial Crops in Anantapur District During 1999-2000

S. No.	*Name of the Crop*	*Area in Anantapur District*	*% in Anantapur District*	*Area in Andhra Pradesh*	*% in Andhra Pradesh*
1.	Cotton	9453	35.81	1045704	51.87
2.	Sugar Cane	884	3.35	231453	11.48
3.	Tobacco	66	0.25	172402	8.55
4.	Onions	1770	6.71	35017	1.74
5.	Chillies	5199	19.69	267789	13.28
6.	Garlic	-	-	792	0.05
7.	Turmeric	25	0.09	64182	3.18
8.	Bananas	194	0.73	37692	1.86
9.	Potatoes	10.	0.05	1774	0.09
10.	Sweet Potatoes	33	0.13	2013	0.1
11.	Others	-	-	157186	7.8
12.	Total	26395	1.00	2016004	100.00

Source: Directorates of Statistics, Andharapradesh at www.ap.nic.in.

Table 4.10 reveals that the pattern of commercial crops in Anantapur district during 1999-2000. Among these crops cotton stands first, which is irrigated in 9453 hectares with 35.81 per cent to the total area irrigated for commercial crops. In Andhra Pradesh which is 1045704 (51.87 per cent). Followed by Challies in 5199 hectares with 19.69 per cent, in Andhra Pradesh 267789 (23.28 per cent) Sugar cane in 884 hectares with 3.35 per cent, in Andhra Pradesh 231453 (11.48 per cent) The other crops irrigated in 8761 with 33.19 per cent) whereas in Andhra Pradesh irrigated is 157186 (7.8 per cent).

Irrigation: The main cause for the backwardness of Anantapur district is lack of irrigation facilities. Table 6.7 gives the position of irrigation in the district.

An analysis of Table 4.11 reveals that only 13.3 per cent sown area enjoys irrigation facility in the district during 1988-

89 as against 18.9 per cent in Rayalseema region, 33.6 per cent in Andhra Pradesh and 27.66 per cent at All India level.

Table-4.11 : Place Wise Distribution of Irrigated Land (Area in Hectares)

S. No.	*Place*	*Net Area*	*% of net Irrigated Area to net Area Sown*
1.	Anantapur District	1,132,085	13.3
2.	Rayala Seema Region	4,71,757	18.9
3.	Andhra Pradesh	35,22,487	33.6
4.	All India	38,80,500	27.7

Source: (1) Season and Crop Report of Andhra Pradesh (988-89 p. 92).
2. India Agriculture in Bureau-Directorate of Economics and Statistics, Department of Agriculture and Co-operation, Ministry of Agriculture and Rural Development, New Delhi, 1988, p. 225.

Table-4.12 : Sources of Irrigation in Anantapur District

S. No.	*Source*	*Land in Hectors*	*% to Total Irrigated Area*
1.	Canals	28,956	17.78
2.	Tanks	62,881	38.61
3.	Tube wells	168	0.10.
4.	Wells	62,258	38.21
5.	Other Sources	8,620	5.30
6.	Total	1,62,883	100.00

Source: Bureau of Economics and Statistics, Andhra Pradesh, 1999-2000, Hyderabad.

Table 4.12 shows the extent of area irrigated from different sources in the district. It is evident that tanks constitute the major source of irrigation, which account for 38.61 per cent of the total irrigated area followed by wells with 38.21 per cent of the total irrigated area. Most of the tanks and the wells are rainfed under the condition of inadequate and uncertain rainfall. The district suffers from lack of assured irrigation facilities. Hence, in the absence of adequate rainfall, these sources are not real sources of irrigation at all.

Table-4.13 : Year Wise Distribution of Women Groups in Anantapur District from 1987 to 2000-2001

S. No.	*Year*	*Scheme*	*No. of Groups*	*Total No. of Member*	*Revolving Fund released to Groups (Rs. in Lakhs)*
1	*2*	*3*	*4*	*5*	*6*
1.	1987-88	DWCRA	100	1887	15.20
2.	1988-89	DWCRA	100	1788	15.20
3.	1989-90	DWCRA	150	2365	22.80
4.	1990-91	DWCRA	100	1539	15.20
5.	1991-92	DWCRA	50	685	7.60
6.	1992-93	DWCRA	30	464	4.56
	1992-93	SplDWCRA	277	4063	40.63
7.	1993-94	DWCRA	180	2741	27.36
	1993-94	IRDP	1200	18715	S187.15
8.	1994-95	DWCRA	2585	36473	331.57
	1994-95	IRDP	1100	16500	167.20
9.	1995-96	DWCRA	600	9000	60.00
10.	1996-97	DWCRA	455	6825	113.75
	1996-97	IRDP	553	8295	82.95
11.	1997-98	DWCRA	62	930	15.50
12.	1998-99	DWCRA	416	6240	65.00
	1998-99	Addl.DWCRA	920	11726	203.85
	1998-99	SESHG	1098	18274	109.80
13.	1999-2000	SESHG	215	2857	21.50
14.	2000-2001	SESHG	2302	23850	200.00
		Total	12475	166841	1706.82

Source: Compiled form The Major Constrains of DRDA Anantapur.

In the light of above geographical, demographic and agronomic limitations and drawbacks the district of Anantapur continued to be a place of famines and droughts. Further, as its economy is based on agriculture, it is certain that there would be fluctuations in yields and outputs of different crops, which destined to pose serious problems. The cultivation under rainfed conditions in this district is not always a profitable proposition. Hence, the farmers often require credit and are forced to borrow from different sources.

Table 4.13 describes that the formation of women groups (DWCRA & SHGs) and yearwise assistance extended by govt. in the form of revolving fund. The groups started to function in the year 1987-88 under the scheme known as DWCRA. This scheme continued up to the year 1993-94. In the year 93-94 women were assisted under the scheme of (IRDP) integrated Rural Development Scheme. It is found from the above table that there exists both the schemes were continued up to 96-97. During 98-99 all the schemes converted in to SESHG.[15] In Anantapur district women groups started to form in the year 87-88 with 100 groups and 1817 members. This has gone down up to 30 groups and 464 members in the year 92-93. In spite of the fluctuations, the maximum groups of 2585 formed with 36473 embers in the year 94-95 followed by 2302 with 23850 members in 2000-2001. The year wise revolving fund released to groups also shows the fluctuation. The highest fund was released is the year 94-95 with Rs. 331.57 Lakhs, followed by 98-99 with Rs. 203.85 and in 93-94 with Rs. 187.15 Lakhs. The lowest amount was in the year 92-93 with Rs. 4.56 Lakhs followed by 87-88 and 88-89 with 1520 Lakhs.

Table-4.14 : Mandal Wise Distribution of Groups in Ananatapur District (Up to 31-1-2002)

S. No.	*Mandal*	*Assisted Groups*	*Un Assisted Groups*	*Total*
1	*2*	*3*	*4*	*5*
1.	Anantapur	350	69	419
2.	Raptadu	196	16	212
3.	Garladinne	207	-	207
4.	Atmakur	256	46	302
5.	Kudur	255	85	340
6.	Singanamala	183	-	183
7.	B.K. Saganamala	263	72	335
8.	Narpala	291	34	325
9.	Tadipatri	161	-	161
10.	Yadiki	133	10	143
11.	Peddapappur	136	52	188
12.	Putlur	119	50	169
13.	Yellanur	133	4	137
14.	Guntakal	225	24	249
15.	Gooty	210	-	210
16.	Yadiki	178	-	178
17.	P.Vadagur	215	18	233
18.	Uravakonda	157	90	347
19.	Vajrakarur	260	22	291
20.	Vidapanakal	170	48	218
21.	Dharmavaram	276	30	306
22.	Tadimarri	257	54	311
23.	Bathalapalli	282	108	390
24.	C.K. Palli	403	-	403
25.	Kanaganapalli	233	52	285
26.	Ramagiri	231	1	232
27.	Kalyandurg	480	129	609
28.	Beluguppa	362	141	503
29.	Kambadur	395	223	618
30.	Kundurpi	321	118	439
31.	Bramhasamudram	269	43	312

(Contd.)

(Table Contd.)

1	2	3	4	5
32.	Settur	236	24	260
33.	Rayadurg	181	32	213
34.	D.Hirehall	112	11	123
35.	Gummagatta	199	51	250
36.	Kanekal	261	142	403
37.	Bommanahall	218	141	359
38.	Penukonda	315	131	446
39.	Somandepalli	282	-	282
40.	Roddam	290	80	370
41.	Puttaparthu	311	26	337
42.	Kothacheruvu	245	44	289
43.	Bukkapatnam	253	30	283
44.	Madakasira	346	200	546
45.	Amarapuram	187	120	307
46.	Gudibanda	172	154	326
47.	Rolla	160	106	266
48.	Agali	185	89	274
49.	Hindupur	241	61	302
50.	Parigi	234	38	272
51.	Lepakshi	161	57	218
52.	Chilamathur	203	63	266
53.	Gorantla	400	44	444
54.	Kadiri	236	92	328
55.	Mudigubba	279	198	477
56.	Nallamada	198	69	267
57.	N.P. Kunta	226	51	277
58.	Talupula	286	22	308
59.	Nallacheruv	219	38	257
60.	O.D.Cheruvu	162	94	256
61.	Tanakal	278	30	308
62.	Amadagur	176	9	185
63.	Gandlapenta	167	36	203
	Total	14972	3768	18740

Source: Compelled form The Major Constrains of DRDA Anantapur, 2002.

An analysis of Table 4.14 shows that there are as many as 18740 groups upto 31st January 2002 in Ananthapur District of which the highest number of 618 are found in Kambadur Mandal followed by 609 groups in Kalyandurgam mandal and 503 groups in Beluguppa Mandal. The least number of 123 groups are found in D.Hirehal Mandal. Here an attempt is also made to identify the groups that are assisted and unassisted. The total number of assisted groups is 14972 whereas the unassisted groups are 3768. The highest number of assisted groups are found in Kalyandurgam Mandal with 480 groups followed by 400 groups in Gorantala Mandal. Whereas the highest number of unassisted groups are found in Kambadur Mandal with 223 groups followed by 200 groups in Madakasira Manda.

Table-4.15 : Numberwise Distribution of Groups in Anantapur District Up to 31-1-2001

Sl. No.	*Group Range*	*No. of Mandals*	*% to Total number of Mandals*
1.	1-100	0	0%
2.	101-200	9	14.20%
3.	201-300	25	39.68%
4.	301-400	18	28.57%
5.	400-500	7	11.11%
6.	501& Above	4	6.35%
	Total	6363	100.00

Source: Compiled form The Major Constraints of DRDA Anantapur, 2002.

An Analysis of Table 4.15 gives the range of SHG Groups found in various Mandals. It is evident from the table that in allmost all mandals of the district more than 100 groups have been working. There are 9 (14.29 per cent) Mandals where from 101 to 200 groups are found. The highest number of 25 (39.68 per cent) of SHG groups are ranging from 201-300 followed by 18 (28.59 per cent) groups ranging from 301 to

400. The range of 401 to 500 groups are found in 7 (11.11 per cent) Mandals and in 4 (6.35 per cent) Mandals, the number of groups is 501 and above.

Table-4.16 : Groups Formed by NABARD in Anantapur District in 1999-2000

S. No.	*Mandal*	*NABARD Linkage*		
		Groups	*Maching Grant*	*Bank Loan*
1	*2*	*3*	*4*	*5*
1.	D. Herehal	4	3500	14000
2.	Bommanahal	17	60750	249000
3.	Vidapanakal	14	38000	222000
4.	Vajrakarur	15	59000	29600
5.	Guntakal	13	24500	220000
6.	Gooty	64	359500	2629000
7.	Peddavadagur	29	122250	491000
8.	Yadiki	1	3250	13000
9.	Tadipatri	52	92625	1063500
10.	Peddapappur	11	20250	177000
11.	Singanamala	31	99750	979000
12.	Pamidi	18	38625	212000
13.	Garladinne	27	167250	739000
14.	Kudair	9	50750	245500
15.	Uravakonda	18	88750	415000
16.	Beluguppa	45	182500	823000
17.	Kanekal	40	179125	766500
18.	Rayadurg	19	91250	395000
19.	Gummaghata	12	42125	188500
20.	Brahmasamudram	26	110500	487000
21.	Settur	22	75000	383000
22.	Kudurpi	29	73000	329000
23.	Kalyandurga	66	2247500	898000
24.	Atmakur	29	135000	696000
25.	Anantapur	22	121250	645000
26.	Bukkarayasamudram	23	35000	635000
27.	Narpala	20	89625	408500

(Contd.)

(Table Contd.)

1	2	3	4	5
28.	Putlur	9	12250	154000
29.	Yellanur	30	92500	650000
30.	Tadimarri	31	200750	854000
31.	Bathalapalli	53	198625	851500
32.	Raptad	44	219675	1262700
33.	Kanaganapalli	5	19250	77000
34.	Kamabadur	17	64750	259000
35.	Ramagiri	18	67500	285000
36.	Chennekothapalli	39	138750	687000
37.	Dharmavaram	54	275000	1722400
38.	Mudugubba	94	268650	1230600
39.	Talapala	69	24500	1032000
40.	N.P. Kunta	14	30250	121000
41.	Tanakal	41	92250	477000
42.	Nallacheruvu	13	27750	203000
43.	Gandlapenta	28	111000	568000
44.	Kadiri	65	253125	1194500
45.	Amadagur	6	12500	93000
46.	Obuladevacheruvu	13	48250	200000
47.	Nallamada	57	167150	870600
48.	Gorantala	30	82500	330000
49.	Puttaparthi	21	48250	193000
50.	Bukkapathnam	10	15250	71000
51.	Kothacheruvu	66	202775	821100
52.	Penukonda	63	257750	1068000
53.	Roddam	14	69500	298000
54.	Somandepalli	57	318500	1471000
55.	Chilamatthur	14	60000	240000
56.	Lepakshi	10	90000	385000
57.	Hindupur	72	681250	3070000
58.	Pargi	29	226000	970000
59.	Madakasira	67	273750	1325000
60.	Gudibanda	81	376000	1504000
61.	Amarapuram	27	85150	344600
62.	Agali	8	37250	149000
63.	Rolla	6	29000	141000
	Total	1951	7981275	39792500

Source: Compelled Form The Major Constrains of DRDA Anantapur, 2002.

Table 4.16 analyses the groups formed under NABARD are 1951. The highest number of 94 groups are found in Mudigubba Mandal. And the lowest group of one is found in Yadiki Mandal. Matching grant was also released to groups based on the performance, savings, and continuity of the groups.[16] The highest amount of rupees Rs. 3,76,000 and Rs. 3,59,500 in Gudibanda and Gooty Mandal respectively. Along with matching Grant, the Banks also sanctioned loan to groups. The highest amount of Rs. 30,70,000 to Hindupur Mandal and 26,29,000 to Gooty Mandal.

Table-4.17 : Groups Formed by NABARAD in Anantapur District in 2000-2001

S. No.	*Mandal*	*NABARD Linkage*		
		Groups	*Maching Grant*	*Bank Loan*
1	*2*	*3*	*4*	*5*
1.	D. Herehal	5	12250	116500
2.	Bommanahal	44	125775	503100
3.	Vidapanakal	41	108500	595000
4.	Vajrakarur	78	304750	1339000
5.	Guntakal	65	164650	1017400
6.	Gooty	98	450500	2594000
7.	Peddavadagur	36	88500	454000
8.	Yadiki	36	117000	468000
9.	Tadipatri	48	99625	470500
10.	Peddapappur	17	47250	189000
11.	Singanamala	58	170000	1056000
12.	Pamidi	57	160625	727500
13.	Garladinne	58	156350	625400
14.	Kudair	12	36000	335000
15.	Uravakonda	62	175250	990000
16.	Beluguppa	34	128250	513000
17.	Kanekal	89	362000	1480000
18.	Rayadurg	44	252500	1285000
19.	Gummaghata	33	108000	472000
20.	Brahmasamudram	73	246250	1050000
21.	Settur	26	92500	442000
22.	Kudurpi	35	135250	541000
23.	Kalyandurga	58	189000	814000

(Contd.)

(Table Contd.)

1	2	3	4	5
24.	Atmakur	50	22800	912000
25.	Anantapur	15	55000	257000
26.	Bukkarayasamudram	52	179250	1339000
27.	Narpala	19	82000	353000
28.	Putlur	33	77125	607000
29.	Yellanur	20	100000	400000
30.	Tadimarri	40	327000	1418000
31.	Bathalapalli	83	334250	1402000
32.	Raptad	29	135500	700000
33.	Kanaganapalli	42	125750	503000
34.	Kamabadur	69	231750	1057000
35.	Ramagiri	50	143000	597000
36.	Chennekothapalli	97	497000	2043000
37.	Dharmavaram	58	335500	1956000
38.	Mudugubba	99	239400	1089600
39.	Talapala	60	120500	482000
40.	N.P. Kunta	21	28750	226000
41.	Tanakal	52	121500	486000
42.	Nallacheruvu	35	87375	403500
43.	Gandlapenta	30	74000	471000
44.	Kadiri	110	342000	1639000
45.	Amadagur	28	39750	250000
46.	Obuladevacheruvu	27	60500	247000
47.	Nallamada	49	107975	484400
48.	Gorantala	65	174125	722500
49.	Puttaparthi	47	155750	631000
50.	Bukkapathnam	107	385750	1550000
51.	Kothacheruvu	47	194000	1014000
52.	Penukonda	114	445500	2089500
53.	Roddam	39	119500	512500
54.	Somandepalli	34	154625	643500
55.	Chilamatthur	25	62750	419000
56.	Lepakshi	42	91750	442000
57.	Hindupur	68	548750	2255000
58.	Pargi	34	193750	870000
59.	Madakasira	128	512925	2512700
60.	Gudibanda	29	104250	477000
61.	Amarapuram	16	62000	253000
62.	Agali	19	75500	302000
63.	Rolla	16	112500	545000
	Total	3105	11197075	52638600

Source: Compelled form The Major Constrains of DRDA Anantapur, 2002.

Table 4.17 analyses the groups formed under NABARD linkage during the year 2000-01. In total in the district, there are 3105 groups. Out of which the highest number of groups 128 and 114 are found in Madakasira and Penukoda mandal respectively. The lowest number of 5 groups are formed in D. Hirehal Mandal. Out of the total matchning grant of Rs. 11197075 lakhs, the highest amount of Rs. 5,12,925 is to Madakasira Mandal followed by Rs. 4,45,500 is to Penukonda Mandal. out of Rs. 52638600 of Bank loan, the highest Rs. 25,12700 in Madakasira Mandal followed by Rs. 22,55,000 in Hindupur Mandal.

Table-4.18 : Seshg (Self Employment to Self Help Groups) State Plan 2000-2001

S. No.	*Mandal*	*SESHG (State Plan)*	
		Groups	*Matching Grant*
1	*2*	*3*	*4*
1.	D. Herehal	31	348000
2.	Bommanahal	32	314500
3.	Vidapanakal	30	269400
4.	Vajrakarur	49	490000
5.	Guntakal	46	356500
6.	Gooty	31	239100
7.	Peddavadagur	36	298400
8.	Yadiki	43	312000
9.	Tadipatri	39	296000
10.	Peddapappur	15	101000
11.	Singanamala	46	454000
12.	Pamidi	31	310000
13.	Garladinne	46	457000
14.	Kudair	28	238000
15.	Uravakonda	38	357000
16.	Beluguppa	45	450000
17.	Kanekal	42	416000

(Contd.)

(Table Contd.)

1	2	3	4
18.	Rayadurg	23	159000
19.	Gummaghata	28	229000
20.	Brahmasamudram	83	678000
21.	Settur	40	330000
22.	Kudurpi	32	320000
23.	Kalyandurga	47	441300
24.	Atmakur	25	236000
25.	Anantapur	43	346000
26.	Bukkarayasamudram	54	504000
27.	Narpala	42	390000
28.	Putlur	40	284000
29.	Yellanur	29	208000
30.	Tadimarri	31	286000
31.	Bathalapalli	36	352000
32.	Raptad	47	466000
33.	Kanaganapalli	58	519000
34.	Kamabadur	31	301000
35.	Ramagiri	44	438000
36.	Chennekothapalli	57	570000
37.	Dharmavaram	46	435000
38.	Mudugubba	69	680000
39.	Talapala	49	411200
40.	N.P. Kunta	39	288700
41.	Tanakal	42	328000
42.	Nallacheruvu	49	395000
43.	Gandlapenta	10	84000
44.	Kadiri	39	308000
45.	Amadagur	36	283000
46.	Obuladevacheruvu	44	339000

(Contd.)

(Table Contd.)

1	2	3	4
47.	Nallamada	35	270000
48.	Gorantala	58	497000
49.	Puttaparthi	50	421000
50.	Bukkapathnam	33	269000
51.	Kothacheruvu	45	443000
52.	Penukonda	49	465000
53.	Roddam	36	359000
54.	Somandepalli	47	468000
55.	Chilamatthur	44	366000
56.	Lepakshi	44	381000
57.	Hindupur	36	343000
58.	Pargi	46	430000
59.	Madakasira	46	443000
60.	Gudibanda	15	108000
61.	Amarapuram	45	301000
62.	Agali	25	202000
63.	Rolla	24	193000
	Total	2519	22175100

Source: Compiled form The Major Constrains of DRDA Anantapur, 2002.

Table 4.18 reveals the formation of groups (SESHG) in Anantapur district and the amount released under matching grant in the district during the year 2000-01. Under SESHG scheme there are as many as 2519 groups out of which the highest number of 83 and 69 is found in Brahma Samudram and Mudigubba Mandals respectively.[17] The lowest numbers of 10 groups are found in Gandlapenta Mandal. Out of the total of Rs. 22175100 under matching grant sanctioned by the state government, the highest amount of Rs. 6,80,000 was distributed in Mudigubba Mandal and the lowest is of Rs. 84,000 in Gandlpenta Mandal.

Table-4.19 : Caste Wise Distribution of Members in Anantapur District Up to 31-1-2001

S. No.	*Mandal*	*Caste Wise Distribution of Members*						
		Total No. of Group	*SC*	*STs*	*BCs*	*OCs*	*Minorities*	*Total*
1	*2*	*3*	*4*	*5*	*6*	*7*	*8*	*9*
1.	D. Herehal	122	576	31	806	140	0	1553
2.	Bommanahal	230	620	87	1340	697	28	2772
3.	Vidapanakal	189	631	28	1467	407	11	2544
4.	Vajrakarur	261	515	297	1199	312	34	2357
5.	Guntakal	246	597	317	1989	573	19	3495
6.	Gooty	239	1069	256	1648	199	18	3190
7.	Peddavadagur	193	902	17	1235	412	13	2579
8.	Yadiki	160	533	109	331	394	10	1377
9.	Tadipatri	169	690	69	897	659	0	2315
10.	Singanamala	177	692	184	973	564	28	2441
11.	Pamidi	212	707	216	1354	333	122	2732
12.	Garladinne	184	707	62	971	371	95	2206
13.	Kudair	265	947	273	1872	542	44	3678
14.	Uravakonda	281	836	216	1871	432	60	3415
15.	Kanekal	289	714	283	594	2229	0	3820
16.	Rayadurg	180	877	199	1141	254	30	2501
17.	Gummaghata	221	1013	91	1665	126	0	2895
18.	Brahmasamudram	244	869	176	2140	108	0	3293
19	Settur	234	1026	115	1899	323	3	3366
20.	Kudurpi	348	1962	878	1754	21	185	4800
21.	Kalyandurga	477	2316	1083	937	1430	91	5857
22.	Atmakur	257	747	452	2026	453	16	3694
23.	Anantapur	339	1231	215	2035	979	228	4688
24.	Bukkarayasamudram	303	1084	329	2332	524	2	4271
25.	Narpala	208	804	23	1608	400	15	2850
26.	Putlur	125	506	0	312	424	5	1247
27.	Yellanur	106	437	3	658	334	3	1435
28.	Tadimarri	250	826	76	1947	534	0	3383
29.	Bathalapalli	278	712	138	1477	740	60	3127
31.	Kanaganapalli	267	788	117	2729	214	20	3838
32.	Kamabadur	380	777	351	1484	596	313	3521

(Contd.)

(Table Contd.)

1	2	3	4	5	6	7	8	9
33.	Ramagiri	254	800	236	1867	510	9	3422
34.	Chennekothapalli	293	445	222	1997	1141	20	3825
35.	Dharmavaram	288	517	53	1215	434	15	2234
36.	Mudugubba	332	700	790	2008	793	128	4419
37.	Talapala	277	482	184	1504	1671	0	3841
38.	N.P. Kunta	201	399	256	1232	598	88	2573
39.	Tanakal	219	351	264	1409	435	653	3112
40.	Nallacheruvu	229	359	126	1097	1410	46	3038
41.	Gandlapenta	167	305	202	639	910	299	2355
42.	Kadiri	247	187	608	1771	794	0	3360
43.	Amadagur	160	256	89	889	637	16	1887
44.	Obuladevacheruvu	213	440	199	1572	446	75	2732
45.	Nallamada	188	480	508	910	327	30	2255
46.	Gorantala	299	523	518	1808	873	209	3931
47.	Puttaparthi	360	1461	402	1514	989	331	4697
48.	Bukkapathnam	216	318	355	1232	883	56	2844
49.	Kothacheruvu	291	400	214	1521	929	172	3236
50.	Penukonda	333	612	440	1407	775	752	3986
51.	Roddam	229	658	52	1944	271	32	2957
52.	Somandepalli	276	754	128	2252	332	0	3466
53.	Chilamatthur	220	396	50	1015	493	29	1985
54.	Lepakshi	78	107	1	540	341	3	992
55.	Hindupur	277	905	60	1574	849	115	3503
56.	Pargi	290	664	48	2306	722	2	3742
57.	Madakasira	309	1307	186	1534	941	223	4191
58.	Gudibanda	157	794	75	923	370	36	2198
60.	Amarapuram	167	694	25	848	768	83	2418
61.	Agali	187	544	17	871	1000	13	2445
62.	Rolla	196	384	78	801	1462	42	2767
	Total	14792	44402	13353	87403	38608	5258	189024

Source: Compelled from The Major Constraints of DRDA Anantapur, 2002.

Note: Peddapappur mandal was not included due to non availability of data by DRDA.

Table 4.19 intends to analyse the Mandal &Castewise distribution of member in mandals of Groups in Anantapur district as on 31-12-2001. It is evident from the table that there are 14792 groups covering all the 63 mandals. The caste wise distribution of members enables us to describe the involvement of castes in the working of SHGs. In total there are as many as 189024 members in the district. In total there are 44402 members belongs to Scheduled Castes. Out of which the highest number of 2316 is found in Kalyandurgam mandal. Kalyandurgam mandal is dominated by Scheduled Castes and Scheduled Tribe people. For of this reasons, the MLA constituency has been reserved of Scheduled Castes.[18] The lowest number of 107 members belonging to Scheduled Caste are found in Lepakshi mandal. the total number of Scheduled Tribe members is 13353, out of which the highest number 1083 members are found in Kalyandurgam and the lowest 0 (zero) in 3 mandals. The total number of 87403 members belonging to backward castes, which is the highest number in the district. Out of the total 2229 and 1410 members found in Kanekal and Nallacheruvu mandals respectively. And the lowest numbers of 140 are found in D. Hirihall mandal. the members belonging to OC caste are 38608 in total, out of which the highest 2229 members found

Table-4.20 : Caste Wise Distribution of Members with percentage to Total Number of Members

S. No.	*Caste*	*No. of Members*	*% to Total Number of Members*
1.	SC	44402	23.49
2.	ST	13353	7.06
3.	BC	87403	46.24
4.	OC	38608	20.42
5.	Minority	5258	2.79
	Total	189024	100.00

Source: Compelled form The Major Constraints of DRDA Anantapur, 2002.

in Kanekal mandal and the lowest 140 members in D. Hirehall mandal. The Minorities consists of 5258 members in total. Out of which the highest 752 is found in Penukoda mandal followed by 331 members in Puttaparthi mandal. Nearly in 9 mandals the minorities have not come forward. The lowest number 2 and 3 members found in Bukkaraya Samudram and Settur mandals respectively.

Table 4.20 reveals that the caste wise distribution of members in Anantapur District as on 31-12-2001 in terms of percentage to total number of members. The total members consists of 189024, out of which the highest member belonging to Backward castes 87403 (23.49%) followed by Scheduled Castes 44402 (23.49%) followed by Ocs 38608 (20.42%) Scheduled Tribes 13353 (7.06%) and the lowest number of 5258 (2.79%) members belonging to minorities.

Table-4.21 : Achievement of SGSY (Swaran Jayanti Gram Swarojga Yojana) for the Year 1999-2000 (Rs. in Lakhs)

S. No.	*Item*	*Physical Achievement*	*Financial Achievement*	*% of Financial Achievement*
1.	Individuals	1860	64.68	17.63
2.	Youth Groups	453	113.25	21.08
3.	Other Groups	206	134.53	25.05
4.	Revolving Fund to women Groups	1181	52.38	9.75
5.	Training and Capacity Building	-	27.71	5.16
6.	Infrastructure	-	114.60	21.33
	Total	3700	537.15	100.00

Source: Annual Action Plan DRDA Anantapur for the year 1999-2000.

Table-4.22 : Achievement of SGSY (for the Year 1999-2000 (Rs. in Lakhs)

S. No.	Item	Physical Achievement	Financial Achievement	% of Financial Achievement
1.	Individuals	998	74.58	17.16
2.	Youth Groups	174	43.50	10.01
3.	Other Groups	108	81.13	18.67
4.	Revolving Fund to women Groups	3105	111.97	25.77
5.	Training and Capacity Building	-	25.20	5.80
6.	Infrastructure	-	98.21	22.59
7.	Total	4385	434.59	100.00

Source: Annual Action Plan DRDA Anantapur for the year 2000-2001.

The above table reveals that the achievement of SGSY (Swaran Jayanti Gram Swarojga Yojana) for the year 1999-2000 and 2000-2001 in terms of physical and financial achievements. During the year 1999-2000 under physical achievement 1860 individuals are assisted.[19] And 1181 women groups individual was 94.68 lakhs with 17.63 per cent to the total financial achievement. In addition, the revolving fund to women groups was 52.38 lakhs with 9.75 per cent. for the year 2000-2001, 998 individuals were assisted under physical achievement with the financial achievement of Rs. 74.58 lakhs (17.16 per cent). For training and capacity building under physical achievement 3105 groups were assisted with Rs. 111.93 lakhs (25.77 per cent)[20].

The table below reveals that the action plan for the year 20001-2002, Under physical achievement the highest target was given to individuals, i.e., 567 followed by revolving fund to 236 women groups. Whereas the highest financial achievement was 42.53 lakhs for individual (19.72 per cent) followed by 39.39 lakhs (18.25 per cent) for youth groups and other groups respectively[21].

Table-4.23 : Action Plan for the Year 2001-2002

S. No.	Item	Physical Achievement	Financial Achievement	% of Financial Achievement
1.	Individuals	567	42.53	19.72
2.	Youth Groups	158	39.39	18.25
3.	Other Groups	53	39.39	18.25
4.	Revolving Fund to women Groups	236	23.63	10.94
5.	Training and Capacity Building	-	23.63	10.94
6.	Infrastructure	-	47.27	21.90
	Total	1014	215.84	100.00

Source: Annual Action Plan DRDA Anantapur for the Year 2001-2002.

Self Help Programmes in Selected Mandals

Here an attempt has been made to review the progress of SHGs in selected mandals, i.e., (1) Gorantala (2)Kalyan-

Table-4.24 : Distribution of Groups and Members in Gorantala Mandal from 1991-2001

Sl. No.	Year	No. of Groups	Total No. of Members	Average Member Per Group
1.	1990	1	15	6.27
2.	1992	2	30	8.29
3.	1993	0	0	0
4.	1994	20	279	8.95
5.	1995	39	556	14.26
6.	1996	21	287	13.67
7.	1997	20	264	13.2
8.	1998	33	436	13.30
9.	1998	88	1209	13.74
10.	2000	21	275	13.1
11.	2001	35	467	13.34
	Total	280	3818	13.64

Source: Collected form the documents of DRDA Anantapur for Gorantla mandal.

durgam and (3) Anantapur Rural Mandals. Data has been collected from the documents of DRDA Anantapur, Mandal Development Offices (MDO) and Mandal Revenue offices (MRO) or the selected mandals. The tables below have been compiled from the above information and conclusion are also drawn with the help of percentages, average, overall average and mean deviation.

The above table shows the distribution of groups and members with average member per group from 1990 to 2001 in Gorantla Mandal. An analysis of table shows that by the end of 2001 there are as many as 280 groups of SHG with

Table: 4.25 : Village and Urban Wise Distribution of Members in Gorantla Mandal from 1990-2001

S. No.	*Year*	*Groups in Villa-ges*	*Groups in Urban Area*	*Caste of Members* *SC*	*ST*	*BC*	*OC*	*Minority*	*Total*
1.	1990	1	-	8	6	0	1	0	15
2.	1991	-	-	-	-	-	-0	-	-
3.	1992	1	1	-	-	30	-	0	30
4.	1193	-	-	-	-	-		-	-
5.	1994	15	5	65	58	110	22	24	279
6.	1995	37	2	143	92	225	68	28	556
7.	1996	20	1	68	64	110	34	11	287
8.	1997	17	3	50	44	99	71	0	264
9.	1998	29	4	85	78	158	101	14	436
10.	1999	72	16	46	68	640	441	14	1209
11.	2000	17	4	43	62	83	79	8	275
12.	2001	15	20	32	20	218	91	106	467
	Total	224	56	540	492	1673	908	205	3818

Source: Collected form the document of DRDA Anantapur for Gorantal mandal.

3818 members registered in the mandal. Starting with 1 group with 15 members in 1990, the number of groups and the strength of the members went on adding each year. The highest number of groups formed was 88 in 1999, followed by 39 groups in 95 and 35 in 2001. The highest number of members joined as SHG members was 1209 in the year 1999, followed by 556 in 1995, 467 member in the year 2001 and 436 in 1998. The lowest number of members joined in 1990 with 15 members. The average number of members per group in each year ranged from 15.00 to 8.95 from 1990 to 2001. The height average was 15 for 2 years, i.e., 1990 and 1992. And the lowest average was 8.95 in 1994. On the whole, the average was 13.64.

The above table reveals the distribution of groups in villages and urban areas along with the caste composition of members in Gorantala mandal from 1990-2001.

It is evident from the table that there are as many as 280 groups in total among the total 224 are working in villages. The groups in villages started to work with 1 group in the year 1990 and 92 and the strength of the groups went on increasing to the maximum number of 72 groups in 1999. Followed by 37 groups in 1995. In Urban areas in total 56 groups have been working. It has started with 1 group in 92 and went on increasing to the maximum number of 20 groups in 2001. Followed by 16 groups in 1999.

As per the caste composition of members, it has started with 15 members of which 8 from Scheduled Caste[22], Six members from Scheduled Tribe and 1 from other caste. Over the period of time the maximum members belonging to Scheduled Castes are found in 1995 with 143 members followed by 85 member in 98, The total members of STs consisting of 492. The highest number of 92 found in 95 followed by 78 in 98 and 68 in 99. In this mandal the heights number of 1673 members belongs to BCs are found comparatively. The strength started with 1 member in 90 and went on increasing up to the maximum number of 640 members in 1999. Followed by 225 members in 1995 and 218 members in 2001. The total strength of other caste members is 908. Out of which 101 is the heights in 98 and the lowest number of 1 members is found in 1990, followed by 22 members in 1994. On the other hand there are only 205 members belonging to minorities which is relatively less than other castes. The highest number of 106 members are found in 2001 and the lowest number of 0 and 11 members are found in 97 and 96 respectively.

Table-4.26 : Distribution of Banks Participation in Gorantla Mandal

Sl. No.	*Year*	*A total No.of Groups*	*Name of the Bank and No. of Branches*					
			SAGB	*Andhra*	*SBI*	*Syndi-cate*	*ADC/ Others*	*Total*
1.	1990	1	1	-	-	-	-	1
2.	1991	-	-	-	-	-	-	-
3.	1992	2	-	-	-	-	-	2
4.	1193	-	-	-	-	-	-	-
5.	1994	20	16	2	2	-	-	20
6.	1995	39	27	5	7	-	-	39
7.	1996	21	14	2	5	-	-	21
8.	1997	20	13	1	2	4	-	20
9.	1998	33	12	4	5	12	-	33
10.	1999	88	78	-	6	4	-	88
11.	2000	21	8	5	6	2	-	21
12.	2001	35	19	-	6	4	6	35
13.	Total	280	190	19	39	26	6	280
			(67.86)	(6.79)	(13.93)	(9.28)	(2014)	(100.00)

Source: Collected from the document of DRDA Anantapur for Gorantla mandal.

The above table gives details about banks participation in SHG programmes in Gorantla mandal 1990-2001. It reveals that more than 5 banks are involved in SHGs activities in the mands. Which consists of both Nationalised, Regional Rural Banks and Agricultural Banks Nationalised

Banks like Andhra Bank, State Bank of India, Syndicate Bank and Canara Bank. The Regional Rural Bank like Sri Anatha Grameen bank and rural Agricultural bank like Agricultural Development and Co-operative bank. It is revealed from the table that Sri Anantha Grameen bank has financed the highest number of 190 (67.86 per cent) groups in the mandal. Followed by State bank of India 39 (13.93 per cent) and Syndicate Bank 26 (9.28 per cent) groups during period.

Table-4.27 : Yearwise Distribution of Revolving Fund in Gorantala Mandal from 1990-2001

S. No.	*Year*	*Total Amount of Revolving Fund*	*No.of Groups*	*No.of Members*	*% of Groups Received R.F. to Total No. of Groups*	*% of Members to Total No. of Members*
1.	1990	-	-	-	-	-
2.	1991	-	-	-	-	-
3.	1992	-	-	-	-	-
4.	1193	-	-	-	-	-
5.	1994	-	-	-	-	-
6.	1995	46000	4	60	10.81	12.47
7.	1996	-	-	-	-	-
8.	1997	16000	3	34	15.78	14.59
9.	1998	50000	5	61	17.24	17.43
10.	1999	48000	5	67	5.55	5.43
11.	2000	2500	2	26	11.11	11.11
12.	2001	-	-	-	-	-
13.	Total	162500	19	248	-	-

Source: Collected form the document of DRDA Anantapur for Gorantla mandal.

The above table reveals that the distribution of revolving fund to a number of groups and number of members. It is observed from the table that the total amount of Rs. 1,62,500 has been distributed as revolving fund. Out of which the highest amount of Rs. 48,000 distributed in 98 to 5 (17.24 per cent) groups with 61 (17.43 per cent) members. Followed by Rs. 46,000 to total number of 4 (16.8 per cent) groups with 60 (12.47 per cent) members. The lowest amount of revolving fund of Rs. 2,500 to the total number of 2 (11.11 per cent) groups with 26 (11.11 per cent) of members in the year 2000.

Table-4.28 : Caste Wise Distribution of Members in Gorantala Mandal from 1992-2001

S. No.	*Caste*	*Total No. of Members*	*% to Total Numbers*
1.	SC	540	13.97
2.	ST	462	12.81
3.	BC	1673	45.97
4.	OC	908	21.93
5.	Minority	205	5.32
6.		3818	100.00

Source : Collected form the document of DRDA Anantapur for Gorantla mandal.

The above table reveals that the distribution of members on caste base in terms of percentages. In total the members covering all the castes consists of 3818 members in total. Out of which Scheduled Castes are 540 with (13.97 per cent), Scheduled Tribe are 492 with (12.81 per cent), Backward Caste are 1673 with (45.97 per cent) other caste member are 908 with (21.93 per cent) and Minorities are 205 with (5.32 per cent). It is evident from the table that the highest number of 1673 (45.97 per cent) members belongs to BCs, followed by Ocs 908 (21.93 per cent). The lowest number of 205 (5.32 per cent) belongs to Minorities.

Table: 4.29 : Distribution of Group's Savings with Deviation from Mean and Average Mean Deviation of Each Group from 1999-2001 in Gorantala Mandal

S. No.	*Year*	*No. of Groups*	*No. of Members*	*Savings per Month*	*Savings per Year*	*Deviation for Mean*	*Average Mean Deviation of Each Group*
1.	1990	1	15	225	2700	-5106	-5106
2.	1991	-	-	-	-	-	-
3.	1992	2	30	450	5400	-2406	1203
4.	1193	-	-	-	-	-	-
5.	1994	20	279	5580	66960	59154	295.77
6.	1995	39	556	21684	260208	252402	6471.85
7.	1996	21	287	6027	72324	64518	3072.29
8.	1997	20	264	5280	63360	55554	2777.7
9.	1998	33	436	14388	172656	164850	4995.45
10.	1999	88	1209	106392	1276704	1268898	14419.3
11.	2000	21	275	5775	69300	61494	2928.29
12.	2001	35	467	16345	196140	188334	5380.97
13.	Total	280	3818	182146	2185782	2177976	36694.55

Over All Average = 7806.

Source: Collected fρrm the document of DRDA Anantapur for Gorantala mandal.

Above table reveals the distribution of savings by the members per month and per year in terms of deviation from mean and average mean deviation of each group. It is evident from the table that the overall average of savings per year is Rs. 7806, out of the total savings of Rs. 2185782. Saving of the members started with Rs. 2700 in 90 and went on increasing to maximum of Rs. 12,765,704 in 99 with 88 groups and 1209 members. The deviation from mean started with Rs. 5106 and Rs. 2406 in 90 and 92 respectively. And went on increasing to Rs. 12.68,898 in 1999. The average mean deviation of each group started with Rs. 5106 and Rs. 1203 in 90 and 92 and went on increasing to Rs. 14419.3 in 99, followed by Rs. 5380.97 in 2001.

Table-4.30 : Distribution of Groups and Members in Kalyandurgam Mandal from 1992-2001

S. No.	*Year*	*No.of Groups*	*Total No. of Members*	*Average Member Per Group*
1.	1992	2	20	10.00
2.	1993	2	34	17.00
3.	1194	71	1067	15.03
4.	1995	38	528	13.89
5.	1996	49	741	15.12
6.	1997	36	526	14.61
7.	1998	83	1195	14.4
8.	1998	113	1498	13.26
9.	2000	14	205	14.64
10.	2001	7	86	12.29
	Total	415	5900	14.22

Source: Collected form the document of DRDA Anantapur.

The above table intends to reveal that the distribution of groups and members with average member per group from 1992 to 2001 in Kalyandurgam mandal. in total there are 415 SHG groups with 59000 members registered in the mandal. Started with 2 groups in the year 1992 with 15 members. Further, the number of groups and the strength of the members went on adding each year. The highest number of groups formed was 113 in 1999, followed by 83 in 1998, 71 in 94, 38 in 95 and 36 in 97. The highest number of members who joined as SHG members was 1498 in the year 1999, followed by 1195 members in the year 98 and 1067 in 1994. The average number of members per group in each year ranged from 17.00 to 10.00 in 94 and 92 respectively. The highest average was 17.00 in 93 followed by 15.12 in 94 and 15.03 in 94. Moreover, the lowest average was 10.00 in 1992. Overall, the average was 14.22.

Table-4.31 : Village and Urbanwise Distribution of Members in Kalyandurgam Mandal from 1992-2001

S. No.	*Year*	*Groups in Villages*	*Groups in Urban Area*	*Caste of Members*					
				SC	*ST*	*BC*	*OC*	*Mino-rity*	*Total*
1.	1992	2	-	10	5	5	-	-	20
2.	1193	2	-	10	5	10	9	-	34
3.	1994	67	4	420	203	181	241	22	1067
4.	1995	37	1	255	81	78	104	10	528
5	1996	46	3	304	156	77	200	4	741
6.	1997	28	8	186	72	117	151	-	526
7.	1998	62	21	447	162	193	388	5	1195
8.	1999	70	43	478	315	325	333	47	1498
9.	2000	9	5	82	35	36	50	2	205
10.	2001	1	6	23	14	38	11	-	86
	Total	324	91	2215	1048	1060	1487	90	5900

Source: Collected form the document of DRDA Anantapur.

The above table shows the distribution of groups in villages and urban areas along with the caste composition of members in Kalyanadurgam mandal from 1992-2001.

It is evident from the table that there are as many as 415 groups in total. Out of the total, 324 groups are working in villages and 91 groups in Urban/semi Urban areas. the groups in villages started to work with 2 groups in the year 1990 and 92 the strength of the groups went on increasing to the maximum number of 70 groups in 1999. Followed by 67 groups in 1994, 62 in 98 and 46 in 96. Whereas in Urban areas the groups started to work a little bit later than in villages. Though it has started with 4 groups in 94 the strength decreased to 1 and 3 groups in 95 and 96 respectively. The maximum number of 43 groups are found in 1999, during the year 2000 and 2001 the strength has goan down to 5 and 6 groups.

As for as the caste composition of members, it has started with 20 members in 1992 and reached to the strength of 5900 in total up to the year 2001. It is evident from the table that there are as many as 2215 members belonging to Scheduled Castes, of which the highest of 478 members formed in 98 followed by 447 members in 98 and 420 in 94. The lowest number of 10 is found in the starting years, i.e., 92 and 93. Scheduled Tribe consists of 1048 in total. Out of which the highest number of 315 members are found in 99, followed by 162 in 98 and156 in 96. The lowest number of 5 members belonging to STs are found in 92 and 93 followed by 14 members in 2001. In total there are 1060 members belonging to Backward Castes. Out of which the highest number of 325 members are found in 99 followed by 193, 181 in 94, 117 in 97, 78 in 95, and 77 in 96. The lowest number of Backward Caste members are found in92 with 5 members. The total strength of other castes (OC) members is 1487. Out of which the highest number of 388 members are found in 98, followed by 333 in 99, 241 in 94 and 200 in 96. Though the (Ocs) caste members did not come forward in the beginning years, later on it has started with 9 members in 93, it has reached the maximum number of 388 members in 98. Again in 2001 the strength of Ocs members went down to 11 members. The total strength of minorities is 90 for 4 years. There are as many as 90 members belonging to minorities. For 4 years. Its strength was 0, i.e., 92,93,97 and 2001.

Overall comparison of the table shows that Kalyan-durgam mandal consists of more SC & ST members in SHGs groups.

Table-4.32 : Banks Participation for Groups Working in Kalyandurgam Mandal from 1992-2001

S. No.	Year	A total No.of Groups	Name of the Bank and No. of Branches SAGB	Andhra	SBI	Syndi-cate	ADC/ Others	Total
1.	1992	2	-	2	-	-	-	2
2.	1193	2	2	-	-	-	-	2
3.	1994	71	60	-	6	5	-	71
4.	1995	38	31	1	4	2	-	38
5.	1996	49	38	7	1	3	-	49
6.	1997	36	27	3	3	3	-	36
7.	1998	83	67	5	4	7	-	83
8.	1999	113	46	23	36	8	-	113
9.	2000	14	8	-	2	2	2	14
10.	2001	7	3	1	-	3	-	7
	Total	415	282 (67.95)	42 (10.12)	56 (13.5)	33 (7.95)	2 (0.48)	415 (100.00)

Source: Collected form the document of DRDA Anantapur.

Table 4.32 gives details about Bank's participation in SHGs programmes in Kalyandurgam mandal 1992-2001. It reveals that more than 5 Banks are involved in SHGs activities in the mandal. Which consists of both Nationalaised, Regional Rural Banks and Agricultural Banks. Nationalised Banks like State Bank of India and Syndicate Bank The Regional Rural Banklike Sri Anatha Grameen Bank and Agricultural Development Bank. It is revealed from the table that Sri Anantha Grameen Bank has financed the highest number of 282 (67.75 per cent) groups in the mandal. followed by State Bank of India 56 (13.5 per cent) of roups Andhra Bank 42 (10.12 per cent) of groups and Syndicate Bank 33 (7.95 per cent) of groups during the study period. The lowest number of 2 (0.48 per cent) of groups financed by Agricultural Bank (ADC) in the mandal.

Table-4.33 : Distribution of Revolving Fund in Kalyanadurgam Mandal from 1920-2001

S. No.	Year	Total Amount of Revolving Fund	No.of Groups	No.of Members	% of Groups Recei-ved R.F. to Total No. of Groups	% of Members to Total No. of Members
1.	1992	-	-	-	-	-
2.	1993	-	-	-	-	-
3.	1994	2	30	2000	0.49	0.53
4.	1995	1	10	1000	0.25	0.17
5.	1996	-	-	-	-	-
6.	1997	1	15	1000	0.25	0.26
7.	1998	-	-	-	-	-
8.	1999	53	479	68000	13.02	8.31
9.	2000	-	-	-	-	-
10.	2001	-	-	-	-	-
	Total	57	534	72000	14.00	9.26

Source: Collected form the document of DRDA Anantapur.

The table reveals the distribution of revolving fund to number of groups and number of members. It is observed from the table that the total amount of Rs. 72,000 has been distributed as revolving fund. Out of which the highest amount of Rs. 68,000 was distributed in 99 this amount was distributed to 53 groups. The percentage of groups getting revolving fund to the total number of groups is 13.02 and the percentage of members getting revolving fund to total number of members is (8.31 per cent). The lowest amount of revolving fund of Rs. 1000 has been distributed in two years., i.e., 95 and in 97.1 group (0.25 per cent) with of 10 (0.17 per cent) members. Whereas in 97 (0.25 per cent) group with 15 (0.26 per cent) members 2000.

Table-4.34 : Castewise Distribution of Members in Kalyandurgam Mandal from 1992-2001

S. No.	*Caste*	*Total No. of Members*	*% to Total Numbers*
1.	SC	2215	37.54
2.	ST	1048	17.76
3.	BC	1060	17.98
4.	OC	1487	25.20
5.	Minority	90	1.52
6.		5900	100.00

Source: Collected form the document of DRDA Anantapur.

The table intends to reveal castewise distribution of members with percentage in Kalyandurgam mandal from

Table: 4.35 : Distribution of Group's Savings with Deviation from Mean and Average Mean Deviation of Each Groups from 1992-2001 in Kalyandurgam Mandal

S. No.	*Year*	*No. of Groups*	*No. of Members*	*Savings per Month*	*Savings per Year*	*Deviation form Mean*	*Average Mean Deviation of each Group*
1.	1992	2	20	400	4800	677	338.5
2.	1193	2	34	680	8160	4037	2018.5
3.	1994	71	1067	25280	303360	299237	421.65
4.	1995	38	528	11940	143280	139157	3662.03
5.	1996	49	741	10830	129960	125837	2568.10
6.	1997	36	526	10720	128640	124517	3458.81
7.	1998	83	1195	25330	303960	299837	3612.49
8.	1999	113	1498	46910	562920	558797	4945.11
9.	2000	14	205	7750	93000	88877	6348.36
10.	2001	7	86	2780	33360	2923	4176.71
	Total	415	5900	142620	171140	1670210	31550.26

Source: Collected form the document of DRDA Anantapur.

92-2001 in terms of percentages. The member covering all the castes consists of 5900 members in total. As discussed earlier (Table. 4.19) Kalyandurgam Mandal has a large population of SC &STs. The highest number of 2215 with (37.54 per cent) members belonging to Scheduled Castes. Scheduled Tribe members are 1048 with (17.76 per cent), Backwardcaste members are 1060 with (17.98 per cent) other castes members are 1487 with (25.20 per cent). And there are only 90 with (1.52 per cent) members belonging to minorities.

The above table reveals the distribution of savings by the members per month pear year in terms of deviation from mean and average mean deviation of each group. It is evident from the table that the overall average of savings per year is Rs. 4123.95 out of the total savings of Rs. 17,11,440 per year.

Table-4.36 : Distribution of Groups and Members in Anantapur Rural Mandal from 1992-2001

S. No.	*Year*	*No.of Groups*	*Total No. of Members*	*Average Member Per Group*
1.	1992	1	12	12.00
2.	1993	4	62	15.5
3.	1194	35	499	14.26
4.	1995	38	552	14.53
5.	1996	50	687	13.74
6.	1997	55	747	13.58
7.	1998	44	615	13.98
8.	1998	57	891	15.63
9.	2000	33	454	13.76
10.	2001	3	45	15.0
	Total	320	4564	14.26

Source: Collected form the document of DRDA Anantapur.

Saving of the members started with Rs. 4800 with the mean deviation of 677 in 92 went on increasing to maximum amount of Rs. 5,62,7920 in 99 with 558797 mean deviation. The average mean deviation of each group started with Rs. 338.5 in 92 and went on increasing to Rs. 6348.36 in 2000, followed by Rs. 4945.11 in 99, 176.71 in 2001 and 3662.03 in 95.

The above table reveals that the distribution of groups and members with average member per group from 1992 to 2001 in Anantapur Rural mandal. in total, there are 320 SHG groups with 4564 members in the mandal. Started with 1 group in the year 1992 with 12 members. Further, the number of groups and the strength of members went on adding each year. The highest number of groups formed was 57 with 891 members in 1999, followed by 55 groups with

Table: 4.37 : Village, Urbanwise Distribution of Members in Anantapur Rural Mandal from 1992-2001

S. No.	*Year*	*Groups in Villages*	*Groups in Urban Area*	*AreaCaste of Members*					
				SC	*ST*	*BC*	*OC*	*Minority*	*Total*
1.	1992	1	-	1	-	10	1	-	12
2.	1193	3	1	42	-	15	5	-	62
3.	1994	33	2	256	10	188	42	3	499
4.	1995	24	14	166	34	228	111	13	552
5.	1996	29	21	205	16	348	85	33	687
6.	1997	49	6	114	51	351	130	101	747
7.	1998	27	17	104	7	261	197	46	615
8.	1999	54	3	193	40	402	248	8	891
9.	2000	26	7	83	35	239	89	8	454
10.	2001	3	-	20	-	15	10	-	45
	Total	249	71	1184	193	2057	918	212	4564
				(25.94)	(4.23)	(45.07)	(20.11)	(4.65)	(100)

Source: Collected from the document of DRDA Anantapur.

747 member in 1997. The lowest number of 0 is found at the starting year. Other than the starting year, 3 groups with 45 members are found in 2001. Followed by 4 groups with 62 members in 1993. The average number of members per group in each year ranged from 12.00 to 15.63 in 92 and 99 respectively. The highest average was 15.63 in 99 followed by 15.5 in 93 and 15.00 in 2001. Moreover, the lowest average was 12.00 in 1992. Overall the average was 14.26 and in any year, the average touched the maximum strength of 16.

The above table reveals the distribution of groups in villages and urban areas along with the caste composition of members in Anantapur Rural mandal from 1992-2001.

It is evident from the table that there are as many as 320 groups in total out of this total, 249 groups are working in villages and 71 groups in Urban/semi Urban areas. The groups in villages started to work with 1 group in the year 1992. And the strength of the groups went on increasing to the maximum number of 54 in 1999. Whereas in Urban areas the groups started to work a little bit later than villages, i.e., 1 group in 93 the maximum number of 21 groups are found in 1996, followed by 17 groups in 98.

As per as the caste composition of members, it has started with 12 members in 1992 and reached the strength of 4564 in total up to the year 2001. It is evident from the table that there are as many as 1184 with (25.94 per cent) members belonging to Scheduled Castes, of which the highest number of 256 members formed in 94 followed by 205 members in 96 and 193 with (4.23 per cent) in 99. The lowest number of 1 and 20 members are found in 92 and 2001 respectively. Scheduled Tribes consist of 193 with (4.23 per cent) in total, out of which the highest number of 51 members are found in 97, followed by 40 in 99 35 in 2001 and 34 in 95. It is clear from the table that nearly in 3 years, i.e., 92,93 and in 2001 members belonging to ST community wetre not found. In total, there are 2057 with (45.07 per cent) a member belonging to Backward castes. Out of which the highest number of 402 members are found in 99 followed by 348 in 96. The lowest numbers of backward caste members are found in 92 with 10 members, followed by 15 in 93 and in 2001. The total strength of other castes (OC) members is 918 with (20.11 per cent). Out of which the highest number of 248 members are formed in 99, and the lowest number of 1 in 92 followed by 5 in 93 and 10 in 2001. The total strength of minorities is 212 with (4.65 per cent). The highest numbers of 101 members are formed in 97. The lowest number of 0 (zero) members are found in 92,93 and in 2001, followed by 3 member in 94.

Table: 4.38 : Table Banks Participation for Groups Working in Anatapur Rural Mandal from 1992-2001

S. No.	*Year*	*A total No. of of Groups*	*Name of the Bank and No. of Branches*					
			SAGB	*Andhra*	*SBI*	*Syndi-cate*	*ADC/ Others*	*Total*
1.	1992	1	-	-	-	1	-	1
2.	1193	4	1	-	2	-	-	1
3.	1994	35	11	2	17	5	-	35
4.	1995	38	19	2	8	9	-	38
5.	1996	50	11	7	25	4	3	50
6.	1997	55	13	5	30	7	-	55
7.	1998	44	3	4	31	6	-	44
8.	1999	57	9	9	24	15	-	57
9.	2000	33	5	6	19	3	-	33
10.	2001	3	1	-	2	-	-	3
	Total	320	73 (22.81)	35 (10.94)	158 (49.37)	50 (15.63)	4 (1.25)	320 (100.00)

Source: Collected form the document of DRDA Anantapur.

The above table gives details about the bank participation in SHGs programmes in Antapur Ryural mandal 1992-2001. An analysis of table 4.38 reveals that more than 6 Banks are involved in SHGs activities in this mandal. Which consists of Nationalaised, Regional Rural Banks and Agricultural Banks.. out of which 4 are Nationaised Banks and 2 are Rural Banks. Nationalised Banks like State Bank of India and Syndicate Bank, Andhra Bank and Canra Bank. The regional Rural Bank like Sri Anatha Grameen Bank and Agricultural Development Bank. It is revealed from the table that SBI has financed the highest number of 158 (49.37 per cent) groups in the mandal. Followed by Sri Ananta Grameen bank 73 with (22.8 per cent) The lowest number of 4 (1.25 per cent) groups financed by Canara and other.

Table: 4.39 : Distribution of Revolving Fund in Anatapur Rural Mandal from 1920-2001

S. No.	*Year*	*Total Amount of Revolving Fund*	*No. of Groups*	*No. of Members*	*% of Groups Received R.F. to Total No. of Groups*	*% of Members to Total No. of Members*
1.	1992	-	-	-	-	-
2.	1193	-	-	-	-	-
3.	1994	-	-	-	-	-
4.	1995	-	-	-	-	-
5.	1996	6	75	18000	1.88	1.64
6.	1997	-	-	-	-	-
7.	1998	7	88	7000	2.19	1.93
8.	1999	23	324	60000	7.19	7.1
9.	2000	23	324	88000	4.60	3.99
10.	2001	-	-	-	-	-
	Total	49	669	173000	15.31	14.66

Source: Collected form the document of DRDA Anantapur.

The above table reveals that the distribution of revolving fund to number of groups and number of members. It is observed from the table that the total amount of Rs. 1,73,000 has been distributed as revolving fund to 49 groups with 669 members in the mandal. Out of which the highest amount Rs. 88,000 distributed in 2000. This amount was distributed to 13 groups with 182 members. The percentage of groups received revolving fund to the total number of groups is 4.06 per cent and the percentage of members got revolving fund was total number of members is (3.99 per cent). In 2 years, i.e., 97 and 2001 the fund did not received by any group.

Table: 4.40 : Caste Wise Distribution of Members in Anantapur Rural Mandal from 1992-2001

S. No.	*Caste*	*Total No. of Members*	*% to Total Numbers*
1.	SC	1184	25.94
2.	ST	193	4.25
3.	BC	2057	45.07
4.	OC	918	20.11
5.	Minority	212	4.45
6.		4564	100.00

Source: Collected from the document of DRDA Anantapur.

The above table reveals the castewise distribution of members with percentage in Kalyandurgam mandal from 92-2001 in terms of percentages. The member covering all the castes consists of 4564 members in total. The highest number of 2057 with (45.07 per cent) members belonging to backward castes. Followed by 1184 with (25.94 per cent) a member belonging to Scheduled Castes. From Ocs there are as many as 918 with (4.45 per cent). Minorities are 211 with (4.45) the lowest number of 193 with (4.25 per cent) belongs to Scheduled Tribes.

Table: 4.41 : Distribution of Group's Savings with Deviation from Mean and Average Mean Deviation of Each Group from 1992-2001 in Anantapur Rural Mandal

S. No.	*Year*	*No. of Groups*	*No. of Members*	*Savings per Month*	*Savings Year Per Year*	*Deviation form Mean*	*Average Mean Deviation of Each Group*
1.	1992	1	12	360	4320	-6224	-6224
2.	1193	4	62	1240	14880	4336	1084
3.	1994	35	499	162550	1950600	1642256	55430.17
4.	1995	38	552	17400	208800	198256	5217.26
5.	1996	50	687	20640	247680	237136	4742.72
6.	1997	55	747	11235	134820	124276	2259.56
7.	1998	44	615	17820	213840	203296	4620.36
8.	1999	57	891	27935	335220	324676	5696.07
9.	2000	33	454	20360	244320	233776	7084.12
10.	2001	3	45	1650	19800	9256	3085.33
	Total	320	4564	281190	3374280	3268840	82995.59

Over All Average = 10544.63.
Source: Collected form the document of DRDA Anantapur.

The table reveals the distribution of savings by the members per monthly and per year in terms of deviation from mean and average mean deviation of each group. It is evident from the table that the overall average of savings per year is Rs. 10544.63. out of the total savings of Rs. 3268840 per year. Saving of the members started with Rs. 4320 with the mean deviation of–6224 in 92 and went on increasing to the maximum amount of Rs. 3,35,220 in 99 with mean deviation of Rs. 3,24,676. The average mean deviation of each group started with Rs. 6224 in 92 and went on increasing to Rs. 55430.17 in 94 followed by Rs. 7084.12 in 2000 and 5696.07 in 98.

References

1. Government of Andhra Pradesh, District Gazetters, Anantapur, 1970. Chapter I. pp. 1-2.
2. Epigraphically Reports of 1906 and Epigraphica carnatica Vol. X.
3. www.manage-disaster.org p. 1.
4. *Ibid.*
5. AP year Book 2000. Hyderabad, Data News Features Publication, 2000, p. 149.
6. District Collectorate, Rural Works Programmes, Anantapur Distrit, Anantapur, 1974, pp. 2-3.
7. Eenadu, Telugu Daily,Tirupathi, 13th January, 1987, p. 1.
8. www.manage-dister.org, p. 2.
9. Govt. of Andhra Pradesh, Planning and Development of Backward regions, Vol. I, (Hyderabad: Govt. Central Press, 1987) p. 113.
10. www.manage-dister.org p. 2.
11. www.manage-dister.org p. 4.
12. Provisional Population, Paper 2 AP, Census of India. pp. 244-251.
13. *Ibid.*, p. 2.
14. *Ibid.*, pp. 244-251.
15. Collected from DRDA Anantapur.
16. *Ibid.*
17. *Ibid.*
18. AP Year Book 1990, Data News Features, Hyderabad, pp. 713 and 723.
19. Annual Action Plan DRDA, Anantapur, 1999-2000.
20. Action Plan for the year DRDA, Anantapur, 1999-2000.
21. DRDA, Anantpur.
22. *Ibid.*

5

Socio-Economic Background of the Sample Respondents

An attempt is made in this chapter to elaborate portray the opinion, socio-economic back ground on women beneficiaries concerning Self Help Groups.

The researcher has administered a well-formulated questionnaire[1] streching over 70 questions (open ended and close ended as well as main ended questions to elicit their views on different dimensions[2]. These respondents are spread over three revenue divisions, viz, Anantapur, Dharmavaram and Penukonda. From each revenue division one mandal

Table-5.1 : Mandal-Wise Distribution of Respondents

S. No.	*Name of the Mandal*	*Frequency*	*Percentage*
1.	Kalyandurgam	150	33.3
2.	Gorantla	150	33.3
3.	Anantapur Rural	150	33.3
4.	Total	450	100

Source: Compiled from the data collected from field survey in selected Mandalas.

Note: Figures in parentheses represent column wise percentage.

was selected and from one mandal 150 beneficiaries of self Help Groups were covered. Thus, in all 450 beneficiaries were covered.

It is revealed from the above table that in all the three mandals 150 of respondents consisting 33.3 per cent have been taken. The researcher has chosen the respondents from these mandals by keeping the nature of the places

Table-5.2 : Place-Wise Distribution of Respondents in Kalyandurgam Mandals

S. No.	*Place*	*Frequency*	*Percentage*
1.	Urban/Semiurban	54	36.0
2.	Village	87	57.0
3.	Hamlet	9	6.0
4.	Total	150	100

Source: Compiled from the data collected from field survey in selected Mandalas.

Note: Figures in parentheses represent column wise percentage.

Respondents have been drawn from three places, i.e., Urban/Semi-urban, Villages and hamlets. It is found in the table that the highest number of 87 respondents accounting

Table-5.3 : Place-Wise Distribution of Respondents in Gorantla Mandals

S. No.	*Place*	*Frequency*	*Percentage*
1.	Urban/Semi-urban	60	40.0
2.	Village	75	50.0
3.	Hamlet	15	10.0
4.	Total	150	100

Source: Compiled from the data collected from field survey in selected Mandalas.

Note: Figures in parentheses represent column wise percentage.

for 57.0 per cent are found in villages, 54 respondents accounting 36.0 per cent are in Urban or in Semi-urban places, and 9 respondents accounting for 6.0 per cent are found in hamlets. It is held that self-help groups as a public policy have been implementing both in urban areas and villages, thanks to the commitment of the government and other agencies. It observed that, the Self-Groups have not been entered into the hamlets. In fact, where these groups are essential.

It is found in the table that, in Gorantala Mandal the highest number of 75 respondents accounting 50.0 per cent are found in villages, and 60 respondents accounting for 40.0 per cent are in urban areas or in semi-urban areas, and only 15 respondents with 10.0 per cent are found in hamlets.

Table-5.4 : Place-Wise Distribution of Respondents in Anantapur Rural Mandals

S. No.	*Place*	*Frequency*	*Percentage*
1.	Urban/Semi-urban	7	4.7
2.	Village	133	87.7
3.	Hamlet	10	6.7
4.	Total	150	100

Source: Compiled from the data collected from field survey in selected Mandalas.

Note: Figures in parentheses represent column wise percentage.

It is found from the above table that the highest number of 133 respondents accounting for 87.3 per cent are found in villages, followed by 10 respondents accounting 6.7 per cent are found in hamlets. But, the lowest number of 7 respondents accounting for 46.0 per cent are found in urban or in semi urban areas. It is observed that, the Anantapur Rural Mandal is truely representing the rural character.

The overall observation of the above tables are that, except in Anantapur rural mandal the second highest number of respondents are found in urban or in semi urban places. The lowest numbers of respondents are drawn from the hamlets.

Table-5.5 : Distance-Wise Distribution of Respondents

S. No.	Distance	*Kalyandurgam*		*Gorantla*		*Anantapur Rural*	
		Fre-quency	*% age*	*Fre-quency*	*% age*	*Fre-quency*	*% age*
1.	0-2 km.	84	56.0	60	40.0	150	100
2.	3-5 km.	66	44.0	90	60.0	-	-
3.	6-7 km.	-	-	-	-	-	-
4.	7 km. and Above	-	-	-	-	-	-
5.	Total	150	100	150	100	150	100

Source: Compiled from the data collected from field survey in selected Mandalas.

Note: Figures in parentheses represent column wise percentage.

The above table explains the distribution of members working in SHG Programmes with the distance from mandal head-quarters. In Kalyandurgam mandal the majority of members are from 3-5 kms. of distance from the mandal head quarter. Out of the total, 66 respondents accounting for 44.0 per cent. It is observed from the above table that, as the distance from mandal head-quarters goes on increasing the number of members in SHG are decreasing. It is because of the other factors such as transport facilities, work at houses, traditional families does not allow women to visit offices, banks, and other places. Therefore, self help groups have been farming around are nearby places of mandal head quarters.

It is found in Gorantala mandal, that out of 150 respondents 60 respondents are working within the range of 0-2 kms. Accounting 40.0 per cent. It is also evident from the table that the 73 respondents accounting for 47.7 per cent distance between 7 kms and above. This is because of non-availability of transport and bank facilities in the rural areas.

In Anantapur rural mandal, the highest number of 123 respondents accounting for 82.0 per cent are working distance between 3-5 kms.

The overall observation of the table is that, in all the three mandals self-help groups are working nearby mandal head-quarters. Thus, distance as a variable has influence on the working of public policies in different places.

Table-5.6 : Distance from Road Wise Distribution of Respondents

S. No.	*Distance*	*Kalyandurgam Fre-quency*	*%age*	*Gorantla Fre-quency*	*%age*	*Anantapur Rural Fre-quency*	*%age*
1.	0-2 km.	84	56.0	60	40.0	150	100
2.	3-5 km.	66	44.0	90	60.0	-	-
3.	6-7 km.	-	-	-	-	-	-
4.	7 km. and Above	-	-	-	-	-	-
5.	Total	150	100	150	100	150	100

Source: Compiled from the data collected from field survey in selected Mandalas.

Note: Figures in parentheses represent column wise percentage.

The above table reveals that the distribution of members working in self-help groups with different distances from road transport. The Road transport facility is one of the important factors which facilitates for members to engage in developmental activities. Since self-help programmes need transport facilities for fetching, raw material and for market to sell the produced products. The Groups also are in need of good transport facilities for visiting offices and banks.

In Kalyandurgam mandal the highest number of 84 respondents consisting of 56.0 per cent are found distance from road transport between 0-2 kms of distance. In Gorantla mandal 90 respondents consisting of 60.0 per cent are found at a distance between 3-5 kms. In Anantapur rural mandal all the respondents of 150 accounting for 100 per cent are found at a distance between 0-2 kms.

The overall observation of the table is that, distance from road transport has significance in the working of self-help groups particularly in rural places of Anantapur district.

Table 5.7 : Transport Facilities-Wise Distribution of Respondents

S. No.	*Distance*	*Kalyandurgam*		*Gorantla*		*Anantapur Rural*	
		Fre-quency	*% age*	*Fre-quency*	*% age*	*Fre-quency*	*% age*
1.	Yes	131	86.3	60	40.0	149	99.3
2.	No	19	12.7	90	60.0	1	.7
3.	Total	150	100	150	100	150	100

Source: Compiled from the data collected from field survey in selected Mandalas.

Note: Figures in parentheses represent column wise percentage.

The above table intends to explain that whether self-help groups working with transport facilities or not. As discussed in the earlier table, transport facilities are very important for the working of self help groups in rural areas. It is found from the table that, in Kalyandurgam mandal out of the total the highest number 131 respondents accounting 86.3 per cent expressed that, they have transport facilities. Only 19 respondents accounting for 2.7 per cent expressed that, they don't have transport facilities. It is an assumption and also a fact that, with good transport facilities, groups can perform very effectively. Otherwise groups have to face a number of difficulties.

It is also true in case of Anantapur mandal that the highest number 149 respondents accounitng 99.3 per cent are working with transport faciltieis and only one respondent account 0.7 per cent is working without only transport facilities.

It is evident from the above table that, in Gorantala mandal 90 respondents accounting 60.0 per cent are working without only transport facilities.

Table-5.8 : Distance Wise Distribution of Respondents on the Basis of distance from Banks

Sl. No.	*Distance*	*Kalyandurgam*		*Gorantla*		*Anantapur Rural*	
		Fre-quency	*% age*	*Fre-quency*	*% age*	*Fre-quency*	*% age*
1.	0-2 km	54	36.0	60	40.0	27	17.0
2.	3-5 km	66	44.0	15	10.0	26	16.3
3.	6-7 km	30	20.0	75	50.0	97	64.7
4.	7 km and Above	-	-	-	-	-	-
5.	Total	150	100	150	100	150	100

Source: Compiled from the data collected from field survey in selected Mandalas.

Note: Figures in parentheses represent column wise percentage.

For the working of Self-Help Groups, the Bank's role is essential. The distance from the Bank to the place of SHG has its influence for the success or failure of groups. It is found in Kalyan Durg Mandal that the distance is longer from the Bank. There exists the less number of respondents between 6-7 kilometers. There are only 30 respondents accounting 20.0 per cent.

In Gorantala Mandal the less number of 15 respondents accounting 10.0 per cent are found at a distance between 3-5 km. and in Anantapur Rural Mandal 26 respondents accounting 16.3 per cent are found with distance between 3-5 km.

The overall observation is that, if the distance from the bank to SHG is longer there exists less number of members in groups and vice-versa.

Table-5.9 : Other Facilities-Wise Distribution of Respondents in Selected Mandals

S. No.	Distance	Kalyandurgam		Gorantla		Anantapur Rural	
		Fre-quency	% age	Fre-quency	% age	Fre-quency	% age
1.	School	9	7.0	88	57.7	-	-
2.	Politicians	20	13.3	-	-	-	-
3.	Social worker	66	44.0	-	-	-	-
4.	Anganwadi	-	-	-	-	-	-
5.	All	55	36.7	62	41.3	150	100
6.	Total	150	100	150	100	150	100

Source: Compiled from the data collected from field survey in selected Mandalas.

Note: Figures in parentheses represent column wise percentage.

The above table is about SHG's working with the services such as School, Politicians, Social Worker, Anganwadi Centre. These facilities will help the successful of implementation of any governmental programmes, in India in general and in rural areas in particular. Due to low literacy rate, lack of awareness and ignorance, several governmental programmes did not achieve their goals. Hence, the other above mentioned facilities create awareness among the group members in order to utilise facilities from government policies. Politicians will also create political awareness among the members. Social worker create social awareness and Anganwadi workers will help the illiterate group members for the formation of groups and for maintenance of records and for conducting.

It is evident from the above table that in Kalyan Durgam Mandal 55 respondents accounting for 36.7 per cent are working with all facilities, followed by 66 respondents accounting for 44.0 per cent with facilities of social worker.

In Gorantala Mandal the highest number of 88 respondents accounting for 57.7 per cent are working with school facilities, followed by 62 respondents accounting for 41.3 per cent with all facilities.

In Anantapur rural Mandal all the respondents (150) accounting for 100 per cent are working with all facilities.

The overall observation of the Table is that a greater number of SHG's are working with other facilities. In Anantapur Rural Mandal SHG's are working with all facilities. In Gorantala mandal SHG's are not working with the agencies such as Politicians, Social Worker and Anganwadi Workers. In Kalyan Durgam Mandal groups are working with only Anganwadi workers.

Table-5.10 : Age-Wise Distribution of Respondents

Sl. No.	*Distance*	*Kalyandurgam*		*Gorantla*		*Anantapur Rural*	
		Fre-quency	*% age*	*Fre-quency*	*% age*	*Fre-quency*	*% age*
1.	18-25	47	31.3	31	20.7	38	25.3
2.	26-35	80	53.3	100	66.7	87	57.0
3.	36-45	19	12.7	16	10.7	24	16.0
4.	46 & Above	4	2.7	3	2.0	1	7
5.	Total	150	100	150	100	150	100

Source: Compiled from the data collected from field survey in selected Mandalas.

Note: Figures in parentheses represent column wise percentage.

The above Table reveals the age-wise distribution of respondents working in SHG programmes.

In Kalyandurgam Mandal the highest number of 80 respondents accounting for 53.3 per cent are in the age group of 26-35 years. Which is the younger age group, is evincing interest in SHG activities.[3] The higher the age of the respondents, the less the number of respondents. The lowest number of 4 respondents accounting for 2.7 per cent are found between the age groups 46 and above.

In Gorantala Mandal the highest number of 100 respondents accounting for 66.7 per cent belong to younger age group that is between 26-35 years. And the lowest number of 3 respondents accounting for 2.0 per cent belong to the age group between 46 and above.

In Anantapur Rural Mandal more number 87 respondents who account for 57.0 per cent belong to the younger age group between 26-35. And only I respondent accounting for 0.7 per cent belong to the age group between 46 and above.

The overall observation of the Table is that the younger age group respondents are actively participating in SHG programmes. It is held by social scientists that age has a significance in the implementation of programmes.[4] Hence in the present work age has significance in the implementation of SHG programme as a public policy.

Table-5.11 : Caste-Wise Distribution of Respondents

Sl. No.	*Distance*	*Kalyandurgam*		*Gorantla*		*Anantapur Rural*	
		Fre-quency	*% age*	*Fre-quency*	*% age*	*Fre-quency*	*% age*
1.	SC	33	22.0	-	-	23	15.3
2.	ST	18	12.0	91	60.7	92	61.3
3.	OBC	82	54.7	59	39.3	22	14.7
4.	Others	17	11.3	-	-	13	7.7
5.	Total	150	100	150	100	150	100

Source: Compiled from the data collected from field survey in selected Mandalas.

Note: Figures in parentheses represent column wise percentage.

The above Table reveals the caste-wise distribution respondents in selected mandals.

In Kalyandurgam Mandal the highest number of 82 respondents accounting for 54.7 per cent belong to OBC's, followed by 33 respondents accounting for 22.0 per cent belonging to Scheduled Castes, Scheduled Tribes consisting of 18 respondents accounting for 12.0 per cent and the lowest number 17 respondents accounting for 11.3 per cent belong to other castes.

In Gorantala mandal, the highest number of 71 respondents accounting for 46.3 per cent belong to Scheduled Tribes. It is held that in Gorantala Mandal the population of Scheduled Tribes is relatively high. Therefore in Gorantala mandal there is a greater number of respondents belonging to Scheduled Tribes in SHG programmes. The second largest segment of respondents belong to OBCs, consisting of 59 respondents accounting for 39.3 per cent. In this mandal Scheduled Caste respondents are only 20 accounting for 13.3 per cent.

In Anantapur Rural Mandal the highest number of 92 respondents accounting 61.3 per cent belong to Scheduled Tribes, followed by 23 respondents accounting for 15.3 per cent belong to Scheduled Caste. It is found in the table that there are only 22 respondents accounting for 14.7 per cent belong to OBCs. The lowest number 13 respondents accounting for 7.7 per cent belong to other castes.

The overall observation of the table is that in all study mandals the representatives belonging to other castes are low. Only in Kalyandurgam mandal OBC respondents are more. Whereas in Gorantala and Anantapur Rural mandal, there are more respondents from the Scheduled Tribes. From the pattern of the distribution of caste groups, it may be maintained that the scheme of SHG largely meets the objectives of extending benefits to the weaker sections of the society who deserve such benefits more than others section of women groups.

Table-5.12 : Respondents Marital Status-Wise Distribution

Sl. No.	*Distance*	*Kalyandurgam*		*Gorantla*		*Anantapur Rural*	
		Fre-quency	*% age*	*Fre-quency*	*% age*	*Fre-quency*	*% age*
1.	Unmarried	12	7.0	5	3.3	6	4.0
2.	Married	137	91.3	141	94.0	130	86.7
3.	Widow	1	.2	4	2.7	13	7.7
4.	Divorced	-	-	-	-	1	.7
5.	Total	150	100	150	100	150	100

Source: Compiled from the data collected from field survey in selected Mandalas.

Note: Figures in parentheses represent column wise percentage.

The above table reveals the Marital status-wise distribution of respondents in selected mandals. In Kalyandurgam Mandal, it may be noted that among the 150 respondents just 01 respondent is widow consisting 0.2 per cent, followed by 12 repondents belonging to unmarried consisting of 80.0 per cent. While a predominant number 137 respondents aggregating 91.3 per cent are married.

Whereas in Gorantala Mandal the lowest number of 4 respondents consisting 2.7 per cent are widows, and the highest number 141 respondents consisting 94.0 per cent are married.

In Anantapur rural mandal the lowest number 1 respondent belong to divorced category accounting 0.7 per cent, followed by 6 respondents consisting 4.0 per cent belong to married category. While a predominant number 130 respondents consisting of 86.7 per cent belong to married category.

The overall observation of the table is that, in the study area majority of respondents belong to married category are found in SHG programmes.

Table-5.13 : Religion-Wise Distribution of Respondents

Sl. No.	*Distance*	*Kalyandurgam*		*Gorantla*		*Anantapur Rural*	
		Fre-quency	*% age*	*Fre-quency*	*% age*	*Fre-quency*	*% age*
1.	Hindus	141	94.0	119	79.3	149	99.3
2.	Muslims	9	6.0	29	19.3	1	.7
3.	Christians	-	-	2	1.3	-	-
4.	Others	-	-	-	-	-	-
5.	Total	150	100	150	100	150	100

Source: Compiled from the data collected from field survey in selected Mandalas.

Note: Figures in parentheses represent column wise percentage.

The above table reveals that Religion-wise Distribution of Members in selected Mandals. In Kalyandurgam Mandal a predominant number 137 respondents belong to Hindus consisting of 94.0 per cent and the lowest number 9 respondents belong to Muslims accounting for 6.0 per cent.

In Gorantala Mandal the lowest number 2 respondents belong to Christians consisting of 1.3 per cent. And the highest number 119 respondents consisting 79.3 per cent belong to Hindus.

In Anantapur Rural Mandal the lowest number 1 respondent consisitng 0.7 per cent is Muslim. The highest number 149 respondents consisting 99.3 per cent is Hindus.

The overall observation of the Table is that SHG programmes are reaching to each and every religion. It is proved that India being a secular country, the policies and programmes of the government have been reaching to each and every beneficiary irrespective of religion to whichever they may belong.

Table-5.14 : Education-Wise Distribution of Respondents

Sl. No.	*Distance*	*Kalyandurgam*		*Gorantla*		*Anantapur Rural*	
		Fre-quency	*% age*	*Fre-quency*	*% age*	*Fre-quency*	*% age*
1.	Illiterates	93	62.0	90	60.0	102	67.0
2.	Literates	57	37.0	57	37.0	44	29.3
3.	Graduates	-	-	3	2.0	4	2.7
4.	Others	-	-	-	-	-	-
5.	Total	150	100	150	100	150	150

Source: Compiled from the data collected from field survey in selected Mandalas.

Note: Figures in parentheses represent column wise percentage.

The above Table reveals the Education-wise Distribution of Members in selected Mandals. Education is supposed to be the most important factor influencing individual awareness. In this view, in the present study, information was gathered about educational status of individual group members.[5]

It is found in the Table that in Kalyandurgam mandal the highest number 93 respondents of consisting 62.0 per cent are illiterates, followed by 57 respondents consisting of 37.0 per cent belongs to literate. In this Mandal no respondent is graduates and no other education has not found.

In Gorantala Mandal the lowest number 3 respondents consisting of 2.0 per cent belong to graduates, followed by 57 respondents consisting 37.0 per cent belong to literates. The highest number 90 respondents consisting of 60.6 per cent belong to illiterates.

In Anantapur Rural mandal the highest number 102 respondents consisting of 67.0 per cent belong to illiterates, followed by 44 respondents consisting of 29.3 per cent belong to literates. And the lowest number 4 respondents consisting of 2.7 per cent belong to graduates.

The overall observation of the Table is that a majority of illiterate respondents are working in SHGs, whereas the Graduates are very meagre. It differs with the findings made in a study by Dr.D.K. Ghosh. He found in his study that there was a high relationship between the educational status and group cohesiveness[6]

Table 5.15 : Occupation-Wise Distribution of Respondents

Sl. No.	*Distance*	*Kalyandurgam*		*Gorantla*		*Anantapur Rural*	
		Fre-quency	*% age*	*Fre-quency*	*% age*	*Fre-quency*	*% age*
1.	Agriculture	24	16.0	-	-	23	15.3
2.	Cooli	126	84.0	91	60.7	92	61.3
3.	Business	-	-	59	39.3	22	14.7
4.	Others	-	-	-	-	13	7.7
5.	Total	150	100	150	100	150	100

Source: Compiled from the data collected from field survey in selected Mandalas.

Note: Figures in parentheses represent column wise percentage.

The above Table reveals the Occupation-wise distribution of Members in selected Mandals. It is evident from the table that in Kalyandurgam Mandal only 2 categories of respondents are found, i.e., agriculture and Cooli. The highest number 126 respondents consisting of 84.0 per cent belong to Cooli. While the lowest number 24 respondents consisting of 16.0 per cent belong to agriculture. It is held that the policies of the government should reach only the needy persons. In this connection, SHG programmes have been helpful only to the landless poor and agricultural labours. It is also right to argue that SHG as a public policy has aimed at the upliftment of families who are living below the poverty line (BPL).

In Gorantala Mandal no respondents was found from Agriculture category. Out of the total, the highest number 91 respondents consisting of 60.7 per cent belongs to cooli category and 59 respondents consisting of 39.3 per cent belong to small business category.

In Anantapur rural mandal, it is found that four categories of respondents are working in SHG programmes. The highest number 92 respondents consisting of 61.3 per cent belongs to Cooli category, followed by 23 respondents consisting of 15.3 per cent belong to agriculture and 22 respondents consisting of 14.7 per cent belong to small business category.

The overall observation of the table is that in all the three mandals the occupational background of respondents is mainly from Cooli, followed by Agriculture, and lastly petty business category. It is evident that the income derived from Agricultural activities and Cooli are not enough to meet the needs of family and so the women are also forced to seek opportunities for earning additional income.[7]

Table 5.16 : Nature of Family-Wise Distribution of Respondents

Sl. No.	*Type of Family*	*Kalyandurgam*		*Gorantla*		*Anantapur Rural*	
		Fre-quency	*% age*	*Fre-quency*	*% age*	*Fre-quency*	*% age*
1.	Joint	76	50.7	150	100	104	69.3
2.	Elementary	74	49.3	-	-	46	30.7
3.	Total	150	100	150	100	150	100

Source: Compiled from the data collected from field survey in selected Mandalas.

Note: Figures in parentheses represent column wise percentage.

The above Table reveals the Nature of Family wise Distribution of Members in selected Mandals. India is traditionally known for joint family system. The impact of elementary family system had been steadily penetrating in the Indian urban and rural parts. It is because, the benefits of small family in the new market mechanism has greatly influenced both the urban and rural sections considerably. It is therefore, observed in Kalyandurgam Mandal more or less equally the respondents have been divided between joint and elementary families. The highest number 76 respondents consisting of 50.7 per cent belong to joint family, and 74 respondents consisting of 49.3 per cent belong to elementary families.

Whereas in Gorantla mandal all the respondents belong to the joint family system.

In Anantapur Rural Mandal the highest number 104 respondents consisting of 69.3 per cent belong to joint family system and 46 respondents consisting of 30.7 per cent belong to elementary family system.

Table-5.17 : Income-Wise Distribution of Respondents

Sl. No.	*Income*	*Kalyandurgam*		*Gorantla*		*Anantapur Rural*	
		Fre-quency	*% age*	*Fre-quency*	*% age*	*Fre-quency*	*% age*
1.	2000	103	67.7	70	46.7	94	62.7
2.	2001-4000	31	20.7	60	40.0	42	27.0
3.	4001-6000	16	10.7	20	13.3	14	9.3
4.	Total	150	100	150	100	150	100

Source: Compiled from the data collected from field survey in selected Mandalas.

Note: Figures in parentheses represent column wise percentage.

The above Table reveals the Income-wise Distribution of Members in selected Mandals. It is evident from the table that in Kalyandurgam Mandal the highest 103 respondents consisting of 67.7 per cent have an annual Income below Rs. 2000.

In Gorantala Mandal the highest member 70 respondents consisting 46.7 per cent have annual income below Rs. 2000/-followed by 60 respondents consisting 40.0 per cent have annual income in between Rs. 2001 to 4000.

In Ananatapur Rural Mandal the highest number 94 respondents consisting of 62.7 per cent belong to annual Income below Rs. 2000, followed by 42 respondents consisting of 27.0 per cent belong to annual income between Rs. 2001-4000.

It is observed from the above table that in all the three Mandals the lowest number and percentage belong to annual income in between Rs. 4001–6000. From the table, it is quiet possible that the respondents in low and medium income group must avail the benefits of SHG.

Table-5.18 : Land-Wise Distribution of Respondents

Sl. No.	*Land*	*Kalyandurgam*		*Gorantla*		*Anantapur Rural*	
		Fre-quency	*% age*	*Fre-quency*	*% age*	*Fre-quency*	*% age*
1.	<5 Acres	41	26.3	54	36.0	59	39.3
2.	>5 Acres	78	52.0	87	57.0	62	41.3
3.	No Land	31	20.7	9	6.0	29	19.3
4.	Total	150	100	150	100	150	100

Source: Compiled from the data collected from field survey in selected Mandalas.

Note: Figures in parentheses represent column wise percentage.

The above Table reveals the Land-wise Distribution of Members in selected Mandals. In Kalyandurgam Mandal out of the Total respondents as many as 31 respondents consisting of 20.7 per cent had no land, 41 respondents consisting of 26.3 per cent had landed property of less than 5 acres. And 78 respondents consisting of 52.0 per cent had landed property more than 5 acres.

In Gorantala Mandal out of 150 respondents 9 respondents consisting 6.0 per cent had no landed property. 54 respondents consisting 36.0 per cent had landed property less than 5 acres. And 87 respondents consisting 57.0 per cent had landed property more than 5 acres.

In Anantapur rural Mandal out of 150 respondents 29 respondents consisting 19.3 per cent had no landed property. 59 respondents consisting 39.3 per cent had landed property less than 5 acres. And the highest number 62 respondents consisting 41.3 per cent had landed property more than 5 acres.

Table-5.19 : Total Value of All Assets Wise Distribution of Respondents

Sl. No.	*Value*	*Kalyandurgam*		*Gorantla*		*Anantapur Rural*	
		Fre-quency	*% age*	*Fre-quency*	*% age*	*Fre-quency*	*% age*
1.	<1000	29	19.3	35	23.3	35	23.3
2.	1000-5000	113	75.3	107	71.3	105	70.0
3.	5001& Above	8	5.3	8	5.3	10	6.7
4.	Total	150	100	150	100	150	100

Source: Compiled from the data collected from field survey in selected Mandalas.

Note: Figures in parentheses represent column wise percentage.

The above Table reveals the Total Value of All Assets wise Distribution of Members in Selected Mandals. It is evident from the table that in the Kalyandurgam Mandal the lowest number 8 respondents consisting of 5.3 per cent belong to total value of all assets (land, livestock and other assets), is ranged between Rs. 5000 and above, followed by

29 respondents consisting of 19.3 per cent belong to total value of all assets is less than Rs. 1000/-. The highest number 113 respondents consisting of 75.3 per cent belong to total values of all assets range between Rs. 1000-5000.

In Gorantala Mandal the lowest number 8 respondents consisting of 5.3 per cent is belong to total value of all assets Rs. 5001 and above. The highest number 107 respondents consisting 71.3 per cent belongs to total value of all assets ranged between Rs. 1001 to 5000.

In Anantapur rural mandal the highest number 105 respondents consisting of 70.0 per cent belong to total value of all assets ranged between Rs. 1001–5000 and the lowest number 10 respondents consisting of 6.7 per cent belong to total value of all assets ranged Rs. 5001 and above.

Table-5.20 : Nature of House-Wise Distribution of Respondents

Sl. No.	*Type of House*	*Kalyandurgam*		*Gorantla*		*Anantapur Rural*	
		Fre-quency	*% age*	*Fre-quency*	*% age*	*Fre-quency*	*% age*
1.	Owned	136	90.7	150	100	150	100
2.	Rented	14	9.3	-	-	-	-
3.	Pucca	-	-	-	-	-	-
4.	Kaccha	-	-	-	-	-	-
5.	Semi Pucca	-	-	-	-	-	-
6.	Total	150	100	150	100	150	100

Source: Compiled from the data collected from field survey in selected Mandalas.

Note: Figures in parentheses represent column wise percentage.

The above Table reveals the Nature of House wise Distribution of Members in selected Mandals. In Kalyandurgam Mandal, out the total 150 respondents the highest number 136 respondents consisting of 90.7 per cent have owned houses and 14 respondents consisting of 9.3 per cent have no houses. In Gorantala Mandal all 150 respondents have owned houses. In Anantapur rural mandal all the 150 respondents have owned houses. In these two mandals the respondents have expressed that they have benefited by the government schemes. Particularly the Government of Andhra Pradesh has been constructing pucca houses for houseless householders both in urban and rural areas.

Table-5.21 : Distribution of Respondents on the Basis, Whether they Borrowed Loan or Not

Sl. No.	*Opinion*	*Kalyandurgam*		*Gorantla*		*Anantapur Rural*	
		Fre-quency	*% age*	*Fre-quency*	*% age*	*Fre-quency*	*% age*
1.	Yes	100	66.7	150	100	150	100
2.	No	50	33.3	-	-	-	-
3.	Total	150	100	150	100	150	100

Source: Compiled from the data collected from field survey in selected Mandalas.

Note: Figures in parentheses represent column wise percentage.

The above Table reveals the Distribution of Members in Selected Mandals on the basis, whether they borrowed Loan or not. In Kalyandurgam Mandal out of 150 respondents the highest number 100 respondents consisting of 66.3 per cent have taken loan. 50 respondents consisting of 33.3 per cent have not availed loan. In Gorantala Mandal all the respondents (150) have availed loan. In Anantapur Rural Mandal 150 respondents have availed loan.

It is observed from the table that in a majority of mandals the respondents are in need of financial assistance.

Table-5.22 : Source of Loan-Wise Distribution of Respondents

Sl. No.	*Source*	*Kalyandurgam*		*Gorantla*		*Anantapur Rural*	
		Fre-quency	*% age*	*Fre-quency*	*% age*	*Fre-quency*	*% age*
1.	Cooperative agencies	14	9.3	8	5.3	27	17.0
2.	Regional Rural Banks	19	12.7	11	6.3	25	16.7
3.	Commercial banks	9	6.0	55	36.7	35	23.3
4.	Money Lenders	18	12.0	15	10.0	29	19.3
5.	Land Lords	21	14.0	33	22.0	12	7.0
6.	Others	10	6.7	28	17.7	22	14.7
7.	Total	150	100	150	100	150	100

Source: Compiled from the data collected from field survey in selected Mandalas.

Note: Figures in parentheses represent column wise percentage.

The above Table reveals the Source of Loan wise distribution of Members in Selected Mandals. In Kalyandurgam Mandal the respondents have borrowed loan from all the sources such as Cooperative agencies, Regional Rural Banks, Commercial Banks, Money Lenders, Land Lords and from other sources. It is evident from the table that the highest number 19 respondents consisting of 12.7 per cent have borrowed loan from regional rural bank. And the lowest number 10 respondents consisting of 6.7 per cent have borrowed loan from other than the above mentioned sources.

In Gorantala Mandal respondents have borrowed loan from all the sources, the highest number 55 respondents consisting of 36.7 per cent have borrowed loan from commercial banks and the lowest 8 respondents consisting of 5.3 per cent have borrowed loan from cooperation agencies such as, agricultural cooperative bank.

In Anantapur rural Mandal respondents have borrowed loan from all the sources. The lowest number 12 respondents consisting of 7.0 per cent have borrowed loan from landlords. And the highest number 35 respondents consisting of 23.3 per cent have borrowed loan from commercial banks.

Table-5.23 : Loan Purpose Wise Distribution of Respondents

Sl. No.	*Purpose*	*Kalyandurgam*		*Gorantla*		*Anantapur Rural*	
		Fre-quency	*% age*	*Fre-quency*	*% age*	*Fre-quency*	*% age*
1.	Purchase	59	39.3	45	30.0	42	27.0
2.	Religion	30	20.0	70	45.7	49	32.7
3.	Health	14	9.3	35	23.3	59	39.3
4.	Others	47	31.3	-	-	-	-
5.	Total	150	100	150	100	150	100

Source: Compiled from the data collected from field survey in selected Mandalas.

Note: Figures in parentheses represent column wise percentage.

The above Table reveals the Loan Purpose wise distribution of Members in selected Mandals. In Kalyandurgam mandal the respondents have borrowed loan for the purpose of purchase of property, religion, health and other purposes. The lowest number 14 respondents consisting of 31.3 per cent have borrowed loan for health purpose. And the lowest number 59 respondents consisting of 39.3 per cent have borrowed loan for purchase of property.

In Gorantala Mandal the respondents have borrowed loan for purchase, religion and health the highest number 70 respondents consisting 45.7 per cent have borrowed loan for religious purposes. And the lowest number 35 respondents consisting 23.3 per cent have borrowed loan for health purpose.

In Anantapur rural mandal the highest number 59 respondents consisting 39.3 per cent have bollowed loan for health purposes and 42 respondents accounting for 27.0 per cent have borrowed loan for purchase of property.

The overall observation of the table is that the respondents borrowed loan from various sources is to purchase of property such as houses, house sites, home appliances, etc. Followed by health purpose. In all the three mandals a good number of respondents have borrowed loan for health purpose.

References

1. See Appendix: questionnaire.
2. Introduction in regard to methodology adopted.
3. Hemalatha Prasad, "Development of Women and Children in Rural Areas : Successful Case Studies, Journal of Rural Development" Vol.14 (1), 1995, NIRD Hyderabad, p. 79.
4. Ramshray Roy, "The Uncertain Verdict", Orient Longman, Delhi, 1972.
5. K.Ghosh, "Group Cohesiveness in DWACRA Groups : An Application of Sociometric Approach, Kurukshetra", May-June, 1995, p. 69.
6. *Ibid.*, p. 62.
7. Dr. K.N.Ramanujan, "Women's Cooperatives and Economic Development", Kurukshetra, Nov. 1995, p. 13.

6

Problems and Perceptions of Beneficiaries of Self Help Groups

This chapter deals in detail with the problems and perceptions of beneficiaries of self help groups. Beneficiaries' problems and satisfaction are the acide test for the success or efficiency of any women development programme. The beneficiaries or "Member-Beneficiaries" of SHG groups are the key members of any rural development and women welfare network. The beneficiaries who are enrolled in SHG programmes as members possess rural base and who came to equip with the given financial potency to invest on their income generating activities in order to keep away from the exploitation of the rural money lenders. Even though the government of Indian has been launching various schemes and providing subsidies, due to poor socio-economic background, these rural women are not able to generate sufficient income from various programmes.

The working performance of DRDA in general and SHG administrative machinery in meeting the credit need of the member beneficiaries of the SHG has great importance as it has direct relationship with the member beneficiaries satisfaction. The SHG's operational performance vis-a-vis, the member beneficiaries' satisfaction depends on various aspects like the seasonal and timely credit provided by the government as well as various other financial institutions. The amount of subsidy, the quantum of revolving fund, the saving habit of the members, the attitude of the SHG organisers, the involvement of bank personnel, the skills of the members in utilising the loans, repayment habit of the borrowers and so on. Today the work performance because of the SHGs and the total involvement of government, the banks and other government machinery in bringing out effective output for the SHGs and providing satisfactory arrangements to make success of the income generating scheme grounded by the member beneficiaries has been objected to severe public security and criticism.

In view of the above sweeping remarks, it became necessary for the researcher to test their credibility and establish truth. The researcher tested the hypothesis from the angle from the member beneficiaries' problems and perceptions in the light of functioning of the SHG programmes in chapter VI (Problems and perception of self help groups).

Table 6.1. reveals the education-wise distribution of respondents, awareness of self help groups.

In Kalyandurga mandal respondents' educational level has been restricted to only two categories, i.e., illiterates and litterates. Out of the total, 98 respondents are aware self help programmes. And 5 respondents are not aware of self help programmes, which is mainly because of the efforts of by the government. As is known, the Government. of Andhra Pradesh has been conducting various rounds of Janmabhoomi programmes. Where officials of all departments have to visit each and every village and conduct grama sabhas. During these meetings, the officials have to announce various governmental programmes, which are being operated for the upliftment of the down trodden, weaker sections and

Table-6.1 : Education-wise Distribution of Respondents' Awareness of Self Help Groups

S. No.	Item	Kalyandurgam Mandal Education					Gorantla Mandal Education					Anantapur Rural Mandal Education				
		Illiterates	Literate	Graduates	Other	Total	Illiterates	Literate	Graduates	Other	Total	Illiterates	Literate	Graduates	Other	Total
	Yes	66	32	—	—	98	6	49	3	—	58	101	40	2	—	143
1.		(66.3)	(32.7)			(100)	(10.3)	(84.5)	(5.2)		(100)	(70.6)	(27.0)	(1.4)		(100)
	No	27	25	—	—	52	84	8	—	—	92	1	4	2	—	7
2.		(51.9)	(47.1)			(100)	(91.3)	(7.7)			(100)	(14.3)	(56.1)	(27.6)		(100)
	Total	93	57	—	—	150	90	57	3	—	150	102	44	4	—	150
3.		(62.0)	(37.0)			(100)	(60.0)	(37.0)	(100)		(100)	(67.0)	(29.3)	(2.7)		(100)

Source: Compiled from the data collected from field survey in selected Mandalas.
Note: Figures in parentheses represent column wise percentage.

for women (1) Another important feature of the Janmabhoomi is that, it had conducted a special programme exclusively for women 'Mahila Janma Bhoomi'. Thus, women are aware of governmental programmes Irrespective of educational status. Another important feature of above table is that, out of the total, 98 respondents consisting 66.3 per cent belonging to illiterates are aware of SHGs. And 32.7 per cent respondents belong to literate. On other hand 59 per cent respondents belong to illiterate and 47.1 per cent literate are not aware of SHGs.

In Gorantla mandal the educational level of respondents are from three categories, i.e., illiterate, literate and graduates. Out of 150 respondents, the lowest number 58 respondents are aware of SHG programmes. Among these, there are three graduates, 49 illiterates and six literates are six. The education is supposed to be the most important factor influencing individuals awareness[2]. It is found in the study that there exists a high relationship between educational status and awareness of SHG. Respondents who are not aware of SHG programmes comprise of both illiterates and literate. The lowest number 8 respondents are aware of SHG programmes. On the other hand 84 illiterate respondents are not aware of self help programmes.

In Anantapur rural mandal, out of the total, the lowest number Seven respondents are not aware of SHG programmes. Which comprises of One illiterate respondent, Four literate respondents, and Two graduate respondents. The highest number 143 respondents are aware of SHG programme. Among these 70.6 per cent respondents are illiterates, 27.0 per cent respondents are literate and 1.4 per cent are graduates.

The overall observation of the table is that, education as variable has its significance in creating awareness among the respondents regarding public policies.

Table: 6.2 : Caste-wise Distribution of Respondents' Awareness of Self Help Groups

S. No.	Item	*Kalyandurgam Mandcl* Caste					*Gorantala Mandal* Caste					*Anantapur Rural Mandal* Caste				
		SC	*ST*	*BC*	*Other*	*Total*	*SC*	*ST*	*BC*	*Other*	*Total*	*SC*	*ST*	*BC*	*Other*	*Total*
	Yes	20	9	56	13	98	3	—	18	37	58	39	—	60	44	143
1.		(20.4)	(9.2)	(56.1)	(13.3)	(100)	(5.2)		(31.0)	(63.8)	(100)	(26.3)		(42.0)	(30.8)	(100)
	No	13	9	26	4	52	33	14	24	21	92	—	7	—	—	7
2.		(25.0)	(16.3)	(50.0)	(6.7)	(100)	(35.9)	(15.2)	(26.1)	(22.8)	(100)		(100)			(100)
	Total	33	18	82	17	150	36	14	52	58	150	39	7	60	44	150
3.		(22.0)	(12.0)	(54.7)	(11.3)	(100)	(24.0)	(9.3)	(27.0)	(37.7)	(100)	(26.0)	(4.7)	(40.0)	(29.3)	(100)

Source: Compiled from the data collected from field survey in selected Mandalas.
Note: Figures in parentheses represent column wise percentage.

The Table 6.2. reveals that the caste-wise distribution of respondents regarding awareness of self help groups.

In Kalyandurga mandal, respondents have been distributed into four categories, i.e., SC, ST, BC and Other Castes. Out of the total, 98 respondents are aware of SHG programmes. The highest 56.1 per cent respondents belong to backward castes, and the lowest 9.2 per cent respondents belong to Scheduled Tribes. Moreover, 20.4 per cent respondents belong to Scheduled Castes. In Kalyandurga mandal the Second largest population after Scheduled Castes is occupied by backward castes[3] thus, SHG programmes are being utilised by backward castes. On the other hand, 52 respondents are not aware of SHG programmes. Out of which the highest 50.0 per cent respondents belong to backward castes and the lowest 6.7 per cent respondents belongs to other castes, 20.0 per cent respondents belong to Scheduled Castes and 16.3 per cent respondents belong to Scheduled Tribes.

In Gorantala mandal the highest number 92 respondents are not aware of SHG programmes. Out of which 35.9 per cent respondents belong to Scheduled Castes and 15.2 per cent respondents belong to Scheduled Tribes. 25.1 per cent respondents belong to both BCs.

In Anantapur rural mandal only Seven respondents are not aware of SHG programmes. Particularly, from Scheduled Tribes. On the other hand, 143 respondents are aware of SHG programmes. Except STs other caste respondents are aware of SHG programmes. The highest 42.0 per cent respondents belong BCs, followed by 30.8 per cent respondents belong to other castes and 26.3 per cent respondents belongs to SCs. In this mandal the awareness is high because they are close to the district headquarter, and are easily accessible to programmes of government and being aware of governmental programmes.

Table-6.3 : Education-Wise Distribution of Respondents by Type of Agencies Which Created Awareness Among the Members of SHG

S. No.	Item	*Kalyandurgam Mandal Education*					*Gorantla Mandal Education*					*Anantapur Rural Mandal Education*				
		Illite-rates	*Lite-rate*	*Gra-duates*	*Other*	*Total*	*Illite-rates*	*Lite-rate*	*Gra-duates*	*Other*	*Total*	*Illite-rates*	*Lite-rate*	*Gra-duates*	*Other*	*Total*
1.	VDO	22	15	—	—	37	90	54	3	—	147	102	44	4	—	150
		(59.5)	(40.5)			(100)	(61.2)	(36.7)	(2.0)		(100)	(67.0)	(29.3)	(2.7)		(100)
2.	Sarpanch	—	—	—	—	—	—	3	—	—	3	—	—	—	—	—
								(100)			(100)					
3.	Media	18	12	—	—	30	—	—	—	—	—	—	—	—	—	—
		(60.0)	(40.0)			(100)										
4.	Middle-men	—	—	—	—	—	—	—	—	—	—	—	—	—	—	—
5.	NGO	53	30	—	—	83	—	—	—	—	—	—	—	—	—	—
		(63.9)	(36.1)			(100)										
6.	**Total**	93	57	—	—	150	9	57	3	—	150	102	44	4	—	150
		(62.0)	(37.0)			(100)	(60.0)	(37.0)	(2.0)		(100)	(67.0)	(29.3)	(2.7)		(100)

Source: Compiled from the data collected from field survey in selected Mandalas.
Note: Figures in parentheses represent column wise percentage.

Overall observation of table is that, in all the mandals SCs and BCs respondents have been more awareness. In Anantapur rural mandal awareness is high among the respondents belonging to STs. Thus, caste as variable has significance in deciding the level of awareness among the respondents regarding SHG programmes. As majority respondents from various castes are aware of it.

The above Table 6.3 reveals that education–wise distribution of respondents, whether agencies created awareness among the members of SHG. Awareness regarding self help groups brought to respondent's notice mainly by VDOs, Sarpanchs, media particularly Radio, TV, Newspaper, middle men and NGO's (Non Government Organisations). In rural areas, still illiterate population is high and people are not aware of governmental programmes. Such being the case, people alone cannot be aware of various policies and programmes of the government. Therefore, the other agencies involvement is essential. Unless these agencies take part, any public policy or programme will not achieve its goal.

In Kalyandurga mandal, out of 150 respondents, the highest number 83 respondents are aware of SHG programmes through NGOs. In India the role of NGOs is very much needed, and NGOs have been taking part in the development of society at various level. In which 63.9 per cent respondents belong to illiterate and 36.1 per cent respondents belong to literate. 37 respondents are aware of SHG programmes through VDOs. As discussed earlier the Government of Andhra Pradesh has been conducting Janma Bhoomi programmes for spread of its programmes and policies. In Andhra Pradesh the role of VDO is being utilised for the implementation of all governmental prorgrammes. Thus, in this mandal 59.5 per cent respondents have been aware of SHG programmes through VDOs. And 40.5 per cent respondents are aware of SHG programmes through VDOs. And 13 respondents are aware of SHG programmes through media. Out of which 40.0 per cent are literate and 60.0 per cent are illiterate.

In Gorantala mandal, 147 respondents are aware of SHG programmes through VDOs. Out of which 61.2 respondents belong to illiterates and 36.7 per cent respondents belong to literate and only 2.0 per cent belong to graduates. On the other hand, only three respondents are aware of self help prgrommes through sarpanchs.

In Anantapur rural mandal, all the respondents are aware of self help programmes through VDOs. Out of which 67.0 per cent respondents belong to illiterates 29.3 per cent respondents belong to literate and 2.7 per cent respondents belong to graduates.

The overall observation of the table is that, most of the respondents belonging to illiterate got awareness of SHG programmes through VDOs, Secondly media and lastly through NGOs. Another important finding of the study is that, except in the Gorantala mandal in other two mandals Sarpanchs of village panchayats are not involving in the implementation of these self help programmes. Thus, education as a variable has no significance to decide the level of awareness among the respondents regarding the governmental programmes. As media has compansated this lacuna.

The Table 6.4. That caste-wise distribution of respondents whether agencies created awareness among the members of SHG. In the earlier table the researcher discussed the impact of various agencies which are influencing the level of awareness among respondents towards SHG programmes with reference to educational level was discussed. Here, an attempt is made to find the impact of various agencies for the creation of awareness among respondents belonging to various categories of caste.

Table-6.4 : Caste–Wise Distribution of Respondents by Type of Agencies Which Created Awareness

S. No.	Item	Kalyandurgam Mandal Caste					Gorantala Mandal Caste					Anantapur Rural Mandal Caste				
		SC	ST	BC	Other	Total	SC	ST	BC	Other	Total	SC	ST	BC	Other	Total
1.	VDO	9	9	16	3	37	36	14	41	56	147	39	7	60	44	150
		(24.3)	(24.3)	(43.2)	(7.1)	(100)	(24.5)	(9.5)	(26.9)	(37.1)	(100)	(26.0)	(4.7)	(40.0)	(29.3)	(100)
2.	Sarpanch	—	—	—	—	—	—	—	1	2	3	—	—	—	—	—
									(33.3)	(66.7)	(100)					
3.	Media	12	1	15	2	30	—	—	—	—	—	—	—	—	—	—
		(40.0)	(3.3)	(50.0)	(6.7)	(100)										
4.	Middle-Men	—	—	—	—	—	—	—	—	—	—	—	—	—	—	—
5.	NGO	12	8	51	12	83	—	—	—	—	—	—	—	1	2	3
		(14.5)	(9.6)	(61.4)	(14.5)	(100)										
6.	**Total**	33	18	82	17	150	36	24	42	58	150	39	7	60	44	150
		(22.0)	(12.0)	(54.2)	(11.3)	(100)	(24.5)	(9.3)	(27.0)	(37.7)	(100)	(26.0)	(4.7)	(40.0)	(29.3)	(100)

Source: Compiled from the data collected from field survey in selected Mandalas.
Note: Figures in parentheses represent column wise percentage.

In Kalyandurga mandal out of 150 respondents, the highest number 83 respondents got awareness through NGOs. Out of which 61.4 per cent respondents belong to BCs, 14.5 per cent respondents belong to SCs, 9.6 per cent respondents belong to STs and 14.0 per cent belong to other castes. 37 respondents got awareness through VDOs, out of which 43.2 per cent respondents belong to BCs, 24.3 per cent respondents belong to SCs respectively. 30 respondents got awareness through media.

In Gorantala mandal, the highest number 147 respondents are aware of SHG programmes through VDOs. Out of which 24.5 per cent belong to SCs, 9.5 per cent belong to STs, 26.9 per cent belong to BCs and 37.1 belong to other castes. And only Three respondents are aware of SHG programmes through sarpanchs of village panchayats. Which does not comprise of SCs and STs.

In Anantapur rural mandal, all the respondents are aware of SHG programmes only through VDOs. Out of which 26.0 per cent belong to SCs, 4.7 per cent belong to STs and 40.0 per cent belong to BCs.

The overall observation of the table is that, respondents from all castes are aware of SHG programmes mainly through VDOs, NGOs and media. Thus, caste as a variable has no significance in understanding the level of awareness created by various agencies among the respondents regarding SHG programmes.

In Gorantala mandal, the respondents have visited the offices and banks to get sanctioned either loan or revolving fund between 5-10 times. Out of the total, the highest number 92 respondents have visited offices and banks for 10 times. Which consists of the age group between 18-45 and above. Out of which 71.7 per cent respondents belong to age group between 26-35. Which is the younger middle age group. Followed by 15.2 per cent respondents belonging to younger age group between 18-26 years and the lowest 5.3 per cent respondents belonging to upper age group between 45 years and above. The respondents who visited offices and banks for Five times consist of 58 respondents. Out of which the highest number 34 belong to the age group between 26-35 and the lowest number Seven respondents belong to the age group between 36-45 years.

In Anantapur rural mandal, 143 respondents have visited the offices and banks for Five times. Included 57.7 per cent respondents belong to age group between 26-35 followed by 23.8 per cent respondents belonging to age group between 18-26 years and only Seven respondents have visited offices for 10 times. Out of which 56.1 per cent respondents belong to the age group between 18-26 and 42.9 per cent respondents belong to age group 26-35.

The overall observations of the table is that the younger age group respondents and younger middle aged respondents do not have patience to visit offices and banks more than 10 times. On the other hand, the upper age group respondents have patience to visit offices and banks for more than 10 times. The study made by Hemalata Prasad is quite relevant to the findings of the study. In her study she found that, number of visits made to the banks for the purpose of getting loan ranged between 4-10 times.[4] Thus, age as a variable has a significance to decide the number of visits made to the offices.

The above Table 6.6. reveals that, the castewise distribution of respondents on the basis of visits made by them to offices and banks to get revolving fund and loan.

In Kalyandurgam mandal, out of the total the highest number 78 respondents have visited offices for 10 times. Out of which 56.1 per cent belong to BCs, 23.1 per cent belong to SCs and 14.1 per cent belong to STs. On the other hand, 70 respondents have visited offices for Five times to get loan

Table-6.5 : Age-Wise Distribution of Respondents by Number of Visits to Offices and Banks to Get Revolving Fund and Loan

S. No.	Item	Kalyandurgam Mandal Age					Gorantla Mandal Age					Anantapur Rural Mandal Age				
		18-25	26-35	36-45	46 Above	Total	18-25	26-35	36-45	46 Above	Total	18-25	26-35	36-45	46 Aboves	Total
1.	5 Times	14	40	14	2	70	17	34	7	—	58	34	84	24	1	143
		(20.0)	(56.1)	(20.0)	(.9)	(100)	(29.3)	(57.6)	(1.1)		(100)	(23.8)	(57.7)	(16.8)	(.7)	(100)
2.	10 Times	33	40	4	1	78	14	66	9	3	92	4	3	—	—	7
		(42.3)	(51.3)	(5.1)	(1.3)	(100)	(15.2)	(71.7)	(9.8)	(5.3)	(100)	(56.1)	(42.9)			(100)
3.	15 Times	—	—	—	1	1	—	—	—	—	—	—	—	—	—	—
					(1.3)	(100)										
4.	20 Times	—	—	1	—	1	—	—	—	—	—	—	—	—	—	—
				(100)		(100)										
5.	**Total**	47	80	19	4	150	31	100	16	3	150	38	87	24	1	150
		(31.3)	(53.3)	(12.7)	(2.7)	(100)	(20.7)	(66.7)	(10.7)	(2.0)	(100)	(25.3)	(57.0)	(16.0)	(.7)	(100)

Source: Compiled from the data collected from field survey in selected Mandalas.
Note: Figures in parentheses represent column wise percentage.

sanctioned, which included the highest 52.9 per cent respondents belonging to BCs, and 21.4 per cent respondents belong SCs.

In Gorantla mandal, 92 respondents have visited 10 times, out of which 55.9 per cent respondents belong to SCs, 50.2 per cent respondents belong to STs and 25.1 per cent respondents belong to BCs. 58 respondents have visited for Five times. Which did not include SC representatives, 31.0 per cent respondents belong to STs and 53.8 per cent respondents belong to BCs.

In Anantapur rural mandal the highest number 143 respondents have visited for Five times. Out of which 26.3 per cent respondents belong to SCs, 42.0 per cent respondents belong to BCs and 30.8 per cent respondents belong Ocs. Only Seven respondents belonging to ST category visited offices for more than 10 times.

It is observed from the table that, in Anantapur rural mandal, the respondents are able to get loan within a short period. This is mainly because the officials have been disposing of the files quickly. It is felt that, Anantapur rural mandal has been surrounded by districthead quarter. Mandals in remote places like Kalyandurgam and Gorantala seem to face delay in disposal of files either in MDO offices or in banks. In these two mandals SCs and BCs have visit for 10 times. Thus, caste as a variable has significance in deciding the number of visits made by respondents to get loan and revolving fund.

The above Table 6.7 reveals that the caste-wise distribution of respondents regarding the expenditure made by them for having visited officials and banks to get loan and revolving fund.

In Kalyandurgam mandal, out of the sample 76 respondents have spent less than Rs. 200 among these 15.8

Table-6.6 : Caste-wise Distribution of Respondents by Number of Visits to Offices and Banks to Get Revolving

S. No.	Item	Kalyandurgam Mandal Caste					Gorantala Mandal Caste					Anantapur Rural Mandal Caste				
		SC	*ST*	*BC*	*Other*	*Total*	*SC*	*ST*	*BC*	*Other*	*Total*	*SC*	*ST*	*BC*	*Other*	*Total*
1.	5 Times	15	6	37	12	70	3	—	18	37	58	39	—	60	44	143
		(21.4)	(7.6)	(52.9)	(16.1)	(100)	(5.2)		(31.0)	(63.8)	(100)	(26.3)		(42.0)	(30.8)	(100)
2.	10 Times	18	11	45	4	78	33	14	24	21	92	—	7	—	—	7
		(23.1)	(14.1)	(56.7)	(5.1)	(100)	(55.9)	(50.2)	(26.1)	(22.8)	(100)		(100)			(100)
3.	15 Times	—	1	—	—	1	—	—	—	—	—	—	—	—	—	—
			(100)			(100)										
4.	20 Times	—	—	—	—	—	—	—	—	—	—	—	—	—	—	
5.	**Total**	—	—	—	1	1	—	—	—	—	—	—	—	—	—	
					(100)	(100)										
6.	**Total**	33	18	82	17	150	36	14	42	58	159	39	7	60	44	150
		(22)	(12.0)	(54.7)	(11.3)	(100)	(24.0)	(9.3)	(27.0)	(37.2)	(100)	(26.0)	(4.7)	(40.0)	(29.3)	(100)

Source: Compiled from the data collected from field survey in selected Mandalas.

Note: Figures in parentheses represent column wise percentage.

Table-6.7 : Caste-wise Distribution of Respondents by Expenditure for Visiting Offices and Banks

S. No.	Item	*Kalyandurgam Mandal* Caste					*Gorantala Mandal* Caste					*Anantapur Rural Mandal* Caste				
		SC	*ST*	*BC*	*Other*	*Total*	*SC*	*ST*	*BC*	*Other*	*Total*	*SC*	*ST*	*BC*	*Other*	*Total*
1.	Rs. <200	12 (15.8)	10 (13.2)	47 (61.8)	7 (9.2)	76 (100)	23 (24.2)	8 (7.4)	27 (27.4)	37 (37.9)	95 (100)	28 (32.2)	2 (2.3)	29 (33.3)	28 (32.2)	87 (100)
2.	Rs. 201-300	21 (27.4)	8 (10.8)	35 (46.3)	10 (13.5)	74 (100)	13 (23.6)	6 (10.9)	15 (26.3)	21 (37.2)	55 (100)	11 (16.5)	5 (75.9)	31 (49.2)	16 (25.4)	63 (100)
3.	Rs. 301-500	—	—	—	—	—	—	—	—	—	—	—	—	—	—	—
4.	**Total**	33 (22.0)	18 (12.0)	82 (54.7)	17 (11.3)	150 (100)	36 (24.0)	14 (9.3)	42 (27.0)	58 (37.7)	150 (100)	39 (26.0)	7 (4.7)	16 (40.0)	44 (29.3)	150 (100)

Source: Compiled from the data collected from field survey in selected Mandalas.
Note: Figures in parentheses represent column wise percentage.

per cent respondents belong to SCs, 13.2 per cent respondents belong to STs, 61.8 per cent respondents belong to BCs and 9.2 per cent respondents belong to OCs. The lowest number of 74 respondents have spent amount between Rs. 201-300. Among these 46.3 per cent belong to BCs, 27.4 per cent belong to SCs, 10.8 per cent STc, 13.5 per cent belong to Ocs.

In Gorantala mandal, out of the total the highest number 92 respondents have spent amount less than Rs. 200. Among these 72.8 per cent respondents belong to STs, 14.1 per cent respondents belong to SCs, 9.8 per cent respondents and 3.3 per cent respondents belong to BCs and other castes respectively.

In Anantapur rural mandal, outs of the sample, 94 respondents have spent amount less than Rs. 200. Which consists of 57.5 per cent respondents belonging to STs, 21.2 per cent respondents belong to SCs, and 20.2 per cent respondents belong to BCs. On the other hand, 50 respondents have spent amount between Rs. 201-300. Among these 56.1 per cent respondents belong to STs, 32.1 per cent respondent belong to SCs and other caste's respondents percentage is negligible.

The overall observation of the table is that, in all the three mandals respondents belonging to Scheduled Tribes have spent a large amount of money to visit offices and banks, followed by Scheduled Castes. It is found in the table that, respondents belonging to BC and other castes have spent only a meager amount. Hence, caste as a variable has a significance with regard to expenditure increased by respondents.

The above Table 6.8 reveals that the caste-wise distribution of respondents, and whether they have approached the officials directly or indirectly in relating to the issues of SHGs.

In Kalyandurgam mandal out of the total, 135 respondents have said that they have approached the officials directly, which indicated the awareness of the respondents. In a democratic country as is known,people should be awakened about their welfare. Otherwise, there will be apathy from bureaucrats. It is found that in kalyandurgam mandal a leading NGO has been orgnising programmes, street dramas, and awareness camps for rural poor.[5] As for the caste composition of respondents, who have direct access to the officers consists of the highest percentage 53.3 is belonging to BCs, followed by 21.5 per cent belonging to SCs, 13.3 per cent STs and 11.9 per cent belonging to other castes.

In Gorantala mandal the highest number 92 respondents have visited officers directly. Includeding 35.9 per cent belonging to SCs, 26.1 per cent belonging to BCs and 15.2 per cent belonging to STs.

In Anantapur rural mandal, the highest number 94 respondents have visited officers directly and 56 respondents have visited indirectly. As far as caste composition,53.6 per cent met indirectly and 9.6 per cent met directly belonging to Scheduled Caste. STs have direct access. The highest number 60 respondents belong to BCs consisting 50.0 per cent have directly and 23.2 per cent indirectly approached the officials.

The overall observation of the table is that greater the number of respondents belonging to SCs and BCs having direct approach, other caste respondents are more for indirect approach. Therefore, caste as a variable has a significance to decide the type of approach of respondents towards officers.

Perception of Beneficiaries

The Table 6.9 reveals that the age-wise distribution of respondents regarding the awareness of development programmes.

Table-6.8 : Caste–Wise Distribution of Respondents by Type of Approach to meet Officials

S. No.	Item	Kalyandurgam Mandal Caste					Gorantala Mandal Caste					Anantapur Rural Mandal Caste				
		SC	ST	BC	Other	Total	SC	ST	BC	Other	Total	SC	ST	BC	Other	Total
1.	Direct	29	18	72	16	135	33	14	24	21	92	9	7	47	31	94
		(21.5)	(13.3)	(53.3)	(11.9)	(100)	(35.9)	(15.2)	(26.1)	(22.8)	(100)	(9.6)	(6.4)	(50.0)	(33.)	(100)
2.	Indirect	4	—	10	1	15	3	—	18	37	58	30	—	13	13	56
		(26.7)		(66.7)	(66.7)	(100)	(5.2)		(31.0)	(63.8)	(100)	(53.6)		(23.2)	(23.2)	(100)
3.	**Total**	33	18	82	17	150	36	14	42	58	150	39	7	60	44	150
		(22)	(12.0)	(54.7)	(11.3)	(100)	(24.0)	(9.3)	(27.0)	(37.7)	(100)	(26.0)	(4.7)	(40.0)	(29.3)	(100)

Source: Compiled from the data collected from field survey in selected Mandalas.
Note: Figures in parentheses represent column wise percentage.

Table-6.9 : Age-Wise Distribution of Respondents by Awareness of Self Help Groups

S. No.	Item	Kalyandurgam Mandal Age 18-25	26-35	36-45	46 Above	Total	Gorantla Mandal Age 18-25	26-35	36-45	46 Above	Total	Anantapur Rural Mandal Age 18-25	26-35	36-45	46 Aboves	Total
1.	Yes	42	69	19	4	134	13	65	9	3	90	38	87	24	1	150
		(31.3)	(51.5)	(14.2)	(3.0)	(100)	(14.4)	(72.2)	(10.0)	(3.3)	(100)	(25.3)	(57.0)	(16.7)	(.7)	(100)
2.	No	5	11			16	18	35	7		60					
		(31.3)	(67.8)			(100)	(30.0)	(57.3)	(11.7)		(100)					
3.	**Total**	47	80	19	4	150	31	100	16	3	150	38	87	24	1	150
		(31.3)	(53.3)	(12.7)	(2.7)	(100)	(20.7)	(66.7)	(10.7)	(2.0)	(100)	(25.3)	(57.0)	(16.7)	(.7)	(100)

Source: Compiled from the data collected from field survey in selected Mandalas.
Note: Figures in parentheses represent column wise percentage.

There is greater need to study the perception of regarding the various governmental programmes is very more needed in the study. One of the objectives of this study is to known the awareness of the people regarding the development programmes, which are being implemented both by the central and state governments. Specifically for the upliftment of women who intend to assist the below poverty (BPL) families.[6]

In Kalyandurga mandal out of 150 respondents, the highest number of 134 respondents is aware of governmental programmes, which consist of 51.5 per cent belonging to the age group of 26-35, 31.3 per cent belonging to the age group of 18-25 and 14.2 per cent belonging to the age group of 36-45. The percentage of age group of 45 and above is negligible. Only 16 respondents are not aware of developmental programmes. The lower age group and younger middle age group respondents are fully aware of governmental programme aimed there upliftment.

In Gorantla mandal 90 respondents are aware of governmental programmes, out of which, the highest 72.2 per cent belong to the age group of 26-35, followed by 14.4 per cent belong to the age group of 18-26. The percentage of other age group is negligible. In this mandal, 60 respondents are not aware of governmental programmes. Among these, 57.3 per cent belong to the age group of 26-35, followed by 30.0 per cent belonging to the age group of 18-26.

In Anantapuram rural mandal out of 150 respondents, all respondents are aware of developmental programmes. 57.0 per cent belong to the age group of 26-35 and 25.3 per cent belong to the age group of 18-26.

The overall observation of the table is that the respondents working in SHG programes in and around the district headquarters are fully aware of the governmental programes. The respondents in remote mandals are partially aware of governmental programmes. Another observation of the table is that in all the three mandals the lower younger age groups (18-25) and the upper younger age group respondents have high awareness. Thus, age as a variable has significant in identifying the level of awareness of respondents regarding various governmental programmes.

The Table 6.5 reveals that, the age-wise distribution of respondents on the basis of visits made by them to offices and banks to get revolving fund and loan. In Kalyandurgam mandal out of 150 respondents, 70 respondents have traveled Five times. Out of which, the younger middle age group has occupied the highest number, i.e., 40 respondents accounting 56.1 per cent and the lowest number Two respondents accounting 0.9 per cent between the age group of 45 and above. 78 respondents have traveled nearly 10 times, which consists of 50.3 per cent respondents belong to age group of 26-35, and the lowest number One respondent belong to the age group of 45 and above has visited nearly 15 time The above Table 6.10 reveals that the education-wise distribution of respondents regarding the awareness of development programmes.

In the earlier table, awareness of respondents with reference to the age was discussed in this table awareness with reference to education is being analysed.

In Kalyandurgam mandal out of 150 respondents, 134 respondents are aware of governmental programmes. Among these 59.7 per cent belong to illiterate and 40.3 per cent belong to literate. On the other hand 60 respondents are not aware of governmental programmes out of which 81.3 per cent belong to illiterate, 17.8 per cent belong to literate.

In Gorantla mandal out of the total, 90 respondents are aware of developmental programmes. The highest 93.3 per cent belong to illiterate and 6.7 per cent belong to literate. 60 respondents are not aware of governmental programmes. The

Table: 6.10 : Education-Wise Distribution of Respondents by Awareness of Self Help Groups

S. No.	Item	Kalyandurgam Mandal Education					Gorantla Mandal Education					Anantapur Rural Mandal Education				
		Illite-rates	Lite-rates	Gradu-ates	Other	Total	Illite-rates	Lite-rates	Gradu-ates	Other	Total	Illite-rates	Lite-rates	Gradu-ates	Other	Total
1.	Yes	80	54			134	84	6			90	102	44	4		150
		(59.7)	(40.3)			(100)	(93.3)	(6.70			(100)	(67.0)	(29.3)	(2.7)		(100)
2.	No	13	3			60	6	51	3		60					
		(81.3)	(17.8)			(100)	(10.0)	(85.8)	(50.0)		(100)					
3.	**Total**	93	93	3		150	90	57	3		150	44	4		150	150
		(62.0)	(62.0)	(17.8)		(100)	(60.0)	(37.0)	(2.08)		(100)	(29.3)	(2.7)		(100)	(100)

Source: Compiled from the data collected from field survey in selected Mandalas.

Note: Figures in parentheses represent column wise percentage.

Table-6.11 : Education-Wise Distributions of Respondents by Awareness of the Purpose of Public Policies

S. No.	Item	Kalyandurgam Mandal Education					Gorantla Mandal Education					Anantapur Rural Mandal Education				
		Illiterates	Literates	Graduates	Other	Total	Illiterates	Literates	Graduates	Other	Total	Illiterates	Literates	Graduates	Other	Total
1.	Yes	86	55	—	—	141	90	54	3	—	147	102	44	4	—	150
		(61.0)	(39.0)			(100)	(61.2)	(36.7)	(2.0)		(100)	(67.0)	(29.3)	(2.7)		(100)
2.	No	72	—	—	—	9	—	3	—	—	3		—	—	—	—
		(1.0)	(22.2)			(100)		(100)			(100)					
3.	**Total**	93	57	—	—	150	90	57	3	—	150	102	44	4	—	150
		(62.0)	(37.0)			(100)	(60.0)	(37.0)	(2.0)		(100)	(67.0)	(29.3)	(2.7)		(100)

Source: Compiled from the data collected from field survey in selected Mandalas.
Note: Figures in parentheses represent column wise percentage.

lowest 4.2 per cent belong to graduates and the highest 85.8 per cent belong to illiterate.

In Anantapur rural mandal, all the respondents are aware of governmental programmes. Among these 67.0 per cent belong to illiterate, 29.3 per cent belong to literate and 2.7 per cent belong to graduates.

The overall observation of the table is that there is a high awareness among illiterates and less awareness among the literate respondents. Thus, education as a variable has no significance in deciding the level of awareness regarding governmental programmes, as other means are significant.

The Table 6.11 Shows that the education-wise distributions of respondents whether they are aware of the purpose of public policies or not.

Education is supposed to be the most important factor influencing individual awareness.[7] The assumption of the study is that "due to the illiteracy and ignorance among the rural women,several public policies aimed at their development are not administered by the district administration".

This table also analyses main objective of various public policies aimed at the upliftment of weaker sections.

In Kalyandurgam mandal out of 150 respondents, the highest number 141 respondents are aware of the self help groups for the upliftment of the poor, particularly families below the poverty line. (BPL)[8] out of which, the highest 61.0 per cent belong to illiterate and 39.0 per cent belong to literate. Only Nine respondents are not aware that SHGs as a public policy is for the welfare of the poor.

In Gorantala mandal, out of 150 respondents 141 are aware that public policies are for the welfare of the poor.

Table-6.12 : Distribution of Respondents Castewise and by their Awareness of their Purpose of Public Policies

S. No.	Item	Kalyandurgam Mandal Caste					Gorantala Mandal Caste					Anantapur Rural Mandal Caste				
		SC	*ST*	*BC*	*Other*	*Total*	*SC*	*ST*	*BC*	*Other*	*Total*	*SC*	*ST*	*BC*	*Other*	*Total*
1.	Yes	39	7	60	44	150	36	14	41	56	147	39	7	60	44	150
		(26.0)	(4.7)	(40.0)	(29.3)	(100)	(24.5)	(9.5)	(26.9)	(37.1)	(100)	(26.0)	(4.7)	(40.0)	(29.3)	(100)
2.	No	—	—	—	—	—	—	—	1	2	3	—	—	—	—	—
									(33.3)	(66.7)	(100)					
3.	**Total**	39	7	60	44	150	36	14	42	58	150	39	7	60	44	150
		(26.7)	(4.7)	(40.0)	(29.3)	(100)	(24.0)	(9.3)	(27.0)	(37.7)	(100)	(26.0)	(4.7)	(40.0)	(29.3)	(100)

Source: Compiled from the data collected from field survey in selected Mandalas.
Note: Figures in parentheses represent column wise percentage.

Among these, 61.2 per cent belong to illiterate and 36.7 per cent belong to literate and 2.0 per cent belong to graduate.

In Anantapur rural mandal out of the total, 150 respondents are aware that public policies are for the uplifment of the poor. Among these the highest 67.0 per cent respondents belong to illiterates and 29.3 per cent respondents belong to literate.

The overall observation of the table is that in all the three mandals illiterate respondents have high awareness compared to literate respondents. Thus, education as a variable has no significance in understanding the objectives and purposes of various governmental programmes. Hence the said hypotheses 'has been rejected. This is a significant observation which is useful for policy implications.

The Table 6.12. reveals the Caste-wise distribution of respondents as to whether they aware of the purpose of public policies.

The table is analysaed with an objective to 'find out various public policies aimed at the upliftment of weaker sections particularly women'. It is also ananlysed with an assumption of the study is that 'all the rural development programmes including the Self Help Programmes have helped more the rural rich, middle class peasant women than the poor.

In Kalyandurga mandal all of 150 respondents, are aware of public policies that are meant for welfare of weaker sections. Among these the highest, 40.0 per cent of respondents belong to BCs, followed by 26.0 per cent of respondents belong to SCs, 29.3 per cent belong to other castes and 4.7 per cent of respondents belong to STs.

In Gorandala mandal out of the total, the lowest number three respondents are not aware that public policies are meant

Table-6.13 : SES-Wise Distribution of Respondents by Aware of Purpose of Public Policies

S. No.	Item	Kalyandurgam Mandal SES				Gorantala Mandal SES				Anantapur Rural Mandal SES			
		Medium	*Low*	*High*	*Total*	*Medium*	*Low*	*High*	*Total*	*Medium*	*Low*	*High*	*Total*
1.	Yes	98	28	15	141	70	58	19	147	94	42	14	150
		(69.5)	(19.9)	(10.6)	(100)	(46.6)	(39.5)	(12.9)	(100)	(62.7)	(27.0)	(9.3)	(100)
2.	No	5	3	1	9	—	2	1	3	—	—	—	—
		(55.6)	(33.3)	(11.1)	(100)		(66.7)	(33.3)	(100)				
3.	**Total**	103	31	16	150	70	60	20	150	94	42	14	150
		(67.7)	(20.7)	(10.7)	(100)	(46.7)	(40.0)	(13.3)	(100)	(62.7)	(27.0)	(9.3)	(100)

Source: Compiled from the data collected from field survey in selected Mandalas.
Note: Figures in parentheses represent column wise percentage.

for upliftment of weaker sections. Among these 33.3 per cent of respondents belong to BCs, 66.7 per cent of respondents belong to other castes. Out of the total 147 respondents are aware about the purpose of public policies. Among these, the highest 37.1 per cent of respondents belong to other castes. Followed by 26.9 per cent of respondents belong to BCs, 24.5 per cent of respondents belong to SCs and 9.5 per cent of respondents belong to STs. In this mandal the upper caste respondents have greater awareness of public policies.

In Anatapur rural mandal out of the sample (150) all are aware of the purpose of public policies. Among these 40.0 per cent of respondents belong to BCs, 29.3 per cent of respondents belong to the other castes, 26.0 per cent of respondents belong to SCs and 4.7 per cent of respondents belong to STs.

The overall observation of the table is that upper caste people have greater awareness towards the purpose and objectives of public policies. Lower caste people such as SCs and STs have less awareness towards the purpose and objectives of public policies. Hence, caste as a variable is significant in deciding the level of awareness of respondents relating to governmental policies. Therefore, the said hypothesis has been accepted.

The Table 6.13 reveals the SES-wise distribution of respondents and whether they aware of the purpose of public policies or not.

This table is analysed with the main objective to find out various public policies aimed at the upliftment of weaker sections.

In Kalyanadurga mandal the highest number 141 respondents are aware of the purpose of public policies. Out of which 69.5 per cent of respondents belong to medium socio-economic status, 19.9 per cent respondents belong to low socio-economic status. And only Nine respondents are not aware. Among these 33.3 per cent of respondents belong to low socio-economic status.

In Gorantala mandal out of 150 respondents, 147 respondents are aware that public policies are meant for the upliftment of the poor. Among these, the highest 46.6 per cent respondents belong to the medium socio-economic status. 12.9 per cent of the respondents belong to high socio-economic status. Only three respondents are not aware of the purpose and objectives of public policies.

In Anantapur rural mandal all the respondents are aware of public policies that are meant for welfare of the weaker section. The highest 62.7 per cent of respondents belong to medium socio-economic status and the lowest 9.3 per cent of respondents belong to high socio-economic status.

The overall observation of the table is that the respondents belong to medium socio-economic status have greater awareness regarding the purpose, objective of public policies. And low and high SES respondents have less awareness.Hence, SES as a variable has no significance in deciding the level of awareness of respondents relating to the purpose and objectives of public policies.

The Table 6.14.reveals that the SES-wise distribution of respondents and whether they were benefited by public policies or not.

The objective was to examine the relationship between SHGs and women's economic empowerment (production, consumption, and economic status).

It is also ananlysed with an assumption of the study that 'all the rural development programmes including the Self Help Programmes have helped the rural rich, middle class peasant women more than the poor.'

In Kalyandurga mandal all the respondents have expressed that they are benefited by public policies. Among these, the highest 67.7 per cent of respondents belong to the medium socio-economic status and the lowest 10.7 per cent of respondents belong to high socio-economic status.

In Gorantala mandal out of 150 respondents, 130 respondents have expressed that they have benefited by public policies. Among these, the highest 49.2 per cent respondents belong to medium socio-economic status and the lowest 12.3 per cent respondents belong to the high socio-economic status.

In Anantapur rural mandal only Nine respondents have expresed that they are benefited by SHG programmes as public policies. Among these 50.0 per cent respondents belong to low SES, 25.0 per cent respondents belong to medium and high SES. On the other hand, 142 respondents have expressed that they have not benefited by public policies. Among these 64.6 per cent respondents belong to medium SES and 7.5 per cent respondents belong to high SES.

The overall observation of the table is that except Anatapur rural mandal in the remaining two mandals high percentage of respondents have expressed that they have benefited by public policies. Which comprise of all SES categories. Thus, SES as a variable has no significance in deciding the impact of public policies for the eradication of poverty. In addition, the said hypothesis has been rejected.

The Table 6.15.reveals that the Caste-wise distribution of respondents on the basis of for not having benefited through public policies.

This table is analysed with the main objective to find out various public policies aimed at the upliftment of weaker sections.

Table-6.14 : Caste-Wise Distribution of Respondents by Type of Satisfaction from the Services of MDO,VDO and Banks

S. No.	Item	Kalyandurgam Mandal Caste					Gorantala Mandal Caste					Anantapur Rural Mandal Caste				
		SC	ST	BC	Other	Total	SC	ST	BC	Other	Total	SC	ST	BC	Other	Total
1.	Satisfied	33 (24.6)	70 (12.7)	67 (50.0)	17 (12.7)	134 (100)	36 (24.7)	14 (9.6)	40 (26.4)	56 (37.4)	146 (100)	9 (9.5)	7 (6.4)	48 (50.5)	31 (32.6)	95 (100)
2.	Not Satisfied	—	1 (6.3)	15 (93.8)	—	16 (100)	—	—	2 (50.0)	2 (50.0)	4 (100)	30 (54.5)	—	12 (21.8)	13 (23.6)	55 (100)
3.	**Total**	33	71	82	17	150	36 (24.0)	14 (9.3)	42 (27.0)	58 (37.7)	150 (100)	39 (26.0)	7 (4.7)	60 (40.0)	44 (29.3)	150 (100)

Source: Compiled from the data collected from field survey in selected Mandalas.

Note: Figures in parentheses represent column wise percentage.

In Kalyanadurga mandal out of 150 respondents,all the respondents expressed the opinion that they have not benefited through public policies not because of any of this reason. In their opinion there are other reasons which might have affected from the benefit of these public policies. Among these, the highest 54.7 per cent belong to BCs, and the lowest 11.3 per cent belong to other castes. percentages of respondents belong to SCs and STs is medium.

In Gorantala mandal out of 150 respondents, the highest number 125 respondents have faced problems due to other reasons. Out of which 88.0 per cent respondents belong to ST and 10.8 per cent respondents belong to BCs.

In Anatapur rural mandal out of 150 respondents,the highest number of 37 respondents have expressed the reason, because of wrong guidance by middle men. This shows that middlemen have their own roll in the implementation of any public policies. The lowest number of one respondent has expressed the opinion that VDO is not co-operative, followed by Three respondents have express that VDO is not helpful. out of which 47.6 per cent belong to BCs and 29.7 per cent belong to other castes.

The Table 6.16 reveals that the Caste-wise distribution of respondents whether they are satisfied with the service rendered by MDO,VDO and Bank Officials.

It is ananlysed with an assumption of the study is that 'all the rural development programmes including the Self Help Programmes have helped the rural rich, middle class peasant women than the poor.'

In Kalyanadurga mandal out of 150 respondents, the highest number 134 respondents have expressed that the services rendered by MDO/VDO and Bank officers is satisfactory. Among these 50.0 per cent respondents belong to BCs, 24.6 per cent respondents belong to SCs. Only 16 respondents are of the opinion that the officers are not co-operative. This opinion was expressed by respondents

Table-6.15 : Caste-Wise Distribution of Respondents by Problems Faced from MDO, VDO and Bank Officials

S. No.	Item	Kalyandurgam Mandal Caste					Gorantala Mandal Caste					Anantapur Rural Mandal Caste				
		SC	ST	BC	Other	Total	SC	ST	BC	Other	Total	SC	ST	BC	Other	Total
1.	MDO	13 (25.0)	9 (16.3)	26 (50.0)	4 (6.7)	52 (100)	36 (24.5)	14 (9.5)	41 (26.9)	56 (37.1)	147 (100)	39 (26.2)	7 (4.7)	59 (39.6)	44 (29.5)	149 (100)
2.	VDO	13 (32.5)	2 (5.0)	24 (60.0)	1 (2.5)	40 (100)	—	—	1 (33.3)	2 (66.7)	3 (100)	—	—	1 (100)	—	1 (100)
3.	Bank Officers	7 (12.3)	6 (10.5)	32 (56.1)	12 (21.1)	57 (100)	—	—	—	—	—	—	—	—	—	—
4.	**Total**	33 (22.0)	18 (12.0)	82 (54.7)	17 (11.3)	150 (100)	36 (24.0)	14 (9.3)	42 (27.0)	58 (37.7)	150 (100)	39 (26.0)	7 (4.7)	60 (40.0)	44 (29.3)	150 (100)

Source: Compiled from the data collected from field survey in selected Mandalas.
Note: Figures in parentheses represent column wise percentage.

belonging to BCs and STc,which dose not comprises of SCs and other caste people.

In Gorantala mandal out of 150 respondents, the highest number 146 respondents have positive opinion about the services made by MDO/VDO and Bank officials. Among these, 37.4 per cent belong to other caste, 26.4 per cent respondents belong to BCs and 24.7 per cent respondents belong to SCs.

In Anantapur rural mandal 95 respondents have positive opinion regarding the services made by MDO/VDO and Bank officials. Among these 50.5 per cent belong to BCs, 32.6 per cent belong to other castes. And the percentage from SCs and STs is negligible. On the other hand, 55 respondents have in the negative opinion.

The over all observation of the table is that the high percentages of respondents belonging to SCs and STs has positive opinion of service rendered by MDO/VDO and Bank officials. Thus, caste as a variable has no bearing on rendering of the services by MDO/VDO and Bank official a process of implementing of the self help groups programmes. The said hypothesis has been rejected.

The Table 6.17 reveals that the Caste-wise distribution of respondents whether they faced problems from MDO,VDO and Bank Officials

The objective was to examine the relationship between SHGs and women economic empowerment (production, consumption, and economic status).

In Kalyanadurga mandal out of 150 respondents, 57 respondents have expressed that they have faced difficulties with bank officials. Among these 56.1 per cent respondents belong to BCs and 21.1 per cent respondents belong to other castes. The opinion of SCs and STs is negligible, followed by 52 respondents who have faced problems with MDOs and 40 respondents with VDOs.

In Gorantla mandal out of 150 respondents,the highest number 147 respondents have expressed that they faced difficulties with MDOs. Among these 37.1 per cent respondents belong to other caste and 24.5 per cent respondents belong to SCs. The percentage of other caste respondents is very negligible.

In Anantapur rural mandal out of 150 respondents, 149 respondents have faced problems with MDOs. Among these 39.5 per cent respondents belong to BCs, 29.5 per cent respondents belong to other castes and 26.2 per cent respondents belong to SCs. In this mandal only one respondent belongs to BC, who expressed that he has faced problem with VDO.

The overall observation of the table is that the majority of respondents have faced the problems with MDOs. Secondly with Bank officials. As far as caste composition, high percentage of respondents belong to SCs and STs have difficulties with MDOs. Therefore caste as a variable has a significance in deciding the amount of problems caused by the services of officials in the process of implementing self help programmes. The said hypothesis has been rejected.

References

1. WWW.Andhra Pradesh.com.
2. Dr.D.K.Ghosh, *op. cit.*
3. Opinion of Respondents.
4. Hemalatha Prasad, *op. cit.*
5. NGO.
6. Harjet Ahluwalia Empowerment of Women: An economic Agenda Yojana, Aug. 2000. p. 33.
7. Dr. D.K.Ghosh, *op. cit.*
8. Harjet Ahluwalia, *op. cit.*

7

Performance of Self Help Groups

The government has initiated the action but how far it is successful in achieving the given objectives mainly eradication poverty and empowerment of the weaker groups is essential to underlined. The SHGs were adopted as a viable alternative to the individual approach focused in earlier programmes. It is expected that group approach will deliver the desired results. Therefore, one has to evaluate the performance of groups. Therefore, in this chapter, the performance of self help groups has been analysed. With reference to cross sectional analysis such as Caste, education, Age and SES of the respondents in three mandals.

Placewise distribution of respondents in relation to type of groups formed by different agencies has been discussed in table 7.1.

In India Self Help Groups are being formed by three agencies. First category of groups formed by government, second groups formed by NGO, third groups formed by NABARD[1] the government of India has been implementing self help programmes under the scheme known as (SGSY) Swaran Jayanthi Swarojgar Yojna[2.] In India the role of NGO is essential for the implementation of various developmental programmes of government. The NGOs, which economist

Table-7.1 : Placewise Distribution of Respondents by Type of Groups

S. No.	Item	Kalyandurgam Mandal Place				Gorantala Mandal Place				Anantapur Rural Mandal Place			
		Urban	Village	Hamlet	Total	Urban	Village	Hamlet	Total	Urban	Village	Hamlet	Total
1.	Government	—	53	9	62	58	75	15	148	7	132	10	149
			(85.5)	(14.5)	(100)	(39.2)	(50.7)	(10.1)	(100)	(4.7)	(87.6)	(6.7)	(100)
2.	NGO	26	15	—	41	2	—	—	2	—	—	—	—
		(63.4)	(36.6)		(100)	(10.0)			(100)				
3.	NABARD	28	19	—	47	—	—	—	—	—	1	—	1
		(59.6)	(40.4)		(100)						(100)		(100)
3.	**Total**	54	87	9	150	60	75	15	150	7	133	10	150
		(36.0)	(57.0)	(6.0)	(100)	(40.0)	(50.0)	(10.0)	(100)	(4.7)	(87.7)	(6.7)	(100)

Source: Compiled from the data collected from field survey in selected Mandalas.
Note: Figures in parentheses represent column wise percentage.

have called the "Third sector", receive importance in this context.[3] Since the state (the first sector) is reprehended immensely for its hierarchical, bureaucratic, rigid as well as faulty functions, the role of the third sector assumes special significance.[4]

Another important aspect in the formation of self help groups is through NABARD. The National Bank for Agriculture and Rural Development (NABARAD) is the primary agency in the rural credit system. This agency has involved in direct financing through the assistance extended to various self help groups in India.[5]

The analysis of the table 7.1 explains that in Kalyandurgam mandal out of 150 respondents 62 respondents are formed by government initiation. Among these 85.5 per cent respondents belong to rural areas and 14.5 per cent respondents belong to Hamlets. 47 respondents are formed by NABARD. Among these 59.6 per cent respondents belong to urban or semi urban places and 40.4 per cent respondents belong to villages. 41 respondents are formed with the help of NGOs. Among these 63.4 per cent respondents in urban and semi urban and 36.6 per cent respondents belong to villages.

In Gorantala mandal, out of 150 respondents,the highest number 148 respondents are formed by the government. Among these 50.7 per cent respondents belong to villages and 39.2 per cent respondents belong to urban and semi urban areas. Only Two respondents are formed by NGOs in urban areas.

In Anantapur rural mandal out of 150 respondents 149 respondents, are formed by government. Among these 87.6 per cent respondents belong to villages, 6.7 per cent respondents belong to hamlets. In addition, 4.7 per cent respondents belong to urban areas. Only one respondents has formed by NABARD belong to urban area.

Table 7.2 : Placewise Distribution of Respondents by Services of Banks

S. No.	Item	Kalyandurgam Mandal Place				Gorantala Mandal Place				Anantapur Rural Mandal Place			
		Urban	Village	Hamlet	Total	Urban	Village	Hamlet	Total	Urban	Village	Hamlet	Total
1.	Grameena Bank	10 (40.3)	13 (56.5)	—	23 (100)	13 (12.6)	75 (72.8)	15 (14.6)	103 (100)	7 (10.0)	—	—	7 (100)
2.	SBI	—	—	—	—	47 (10.0)	—	—	47 (100)	—	15 (100)	—	15 (100)
3.	Andhra Bank	—	—	—	—	—	—	—	—	—	29 (100)	—	29 (100)
4.	Corporation	—	—	—	—	—	—	—	—	—	—	—	—
5.	Co-operative	—	—	—	—	—	—	—	—	—	29 (100)	—	29 (100)
6.	Vysya Bank	—	—	—	—	—	—	—	—	—	—	—	—
7.	ADB	—	—	—	—	—	—	—	—	—	54 (100)	—	54 (100)
8.	Syndicate Bank	44 (34.6)	74 (57.3)	9 (6.1)	127 (100)	—	—	—	—	—	—	—	—
9.	Others Bank	—	—	—	—	—	—	—	—	—	—	—	—
10.	**Total**	54 (36.0)	87 (57.0)	9 (6.0)	150 (100)	60 (40.0)	75 (55.0)	15 (10.0)	150 (100)	7 (4.7)	133 (87.7)	10 (6.7)	150 (100)

Source: Compiled from the data collected from field survey in selected Mandalas.
Note: Figures in parentheses represent column wise percentage.

The overall observation of the table is that, in Kalyanadurgam mandal respondents are formed by government, NGO and NABARD. In Gorantala and Anantapur rural mandals respondents are being formed by government only.

Placewise distribution of respondents in relation to the services of Bank's is ananlysed in table 7.2.

For the implementation of Self Help Group's programmes banks role is very essential. In this process the operation of banks, particularly commercial banks have to be restructured and streamlined. Usually banks do not like to involve themselves in risk oriented ventures.[6]

In Kalyanadurgam, mandal out of 150 respondents,the highest number 127 respondents have the services of Syndicate Bank. Among these 57.3 per cent respondents belong to villages, 34.6 per cent respondents belong to urban areas. Only 6.1 per cent respondents belong to Hamlets. 23 respondents have the services from grameen bank.

In Gorantala mandal out of 150 respondents, the highest number 103 respondents have the services from Grameena bank. Among these 72.8 per cent respondents belong to villages, 14.6 per cent respondent belong to Hamlets and 12.6 per cent in urban areas.

In Anantapur rural mandal out of 150 respondents, the highest number 54 respondents have services from Agricultural Development Bank. Among these all respondents belong to villages. Followed by 29 respondents belonging to the villages have the services from Andhra Bank and Co-operative bank respectively. The lowest Seven respondents have services from Grameen banks. They all belong to urban areas.

The overall observation of the table is that in Kalyanadurgam and Gorantala mandal the services of

Table-7.3 : Placewise Distribution of Respondents on the Basis of Revolving Fund Received

S. No.	Item	Kalyandurgam Mandal Place				Gorantala Mandal Place				Anantapur Rural Mandal Place			
		Urban	*Village*	*Hamlet*	*Total*	*Urban*	*Village*	*Hamlet*	*Total*	*Urban*	*Village*	*Hamlet*	*Total*
1.	8000-	54	87	—	141	14	75	15	104	7	76	10	93
	10000	(37.3)	(61.7)		(100)	(23.46)	(72.12)	(14.42)	(100)	(6.53)	(81.72)	(10.75)	(100)
2.	10001	9	—	—	9	13	—	—	13	—	29	—	29
	14000	(100)			(100)	(100)			(100)		(100)		(100)
3.	14001	—	—	—	—	11	—	—	11		28	—	28
	18000					(100)			(100)		(100)		(100)
4.	18001	—	—	—	—	22	—	—	22	—	—	—	—
	20000					(100)			(100)				
5.	**Total**	63	87	—	150	60	75	15	150	7	133	10	150
		(42.0)	(57.0)		(100)	(40.0)	(55.0)	(10.0)	(100)	(4.67)	(87.67)	(6.66)	

Source: Compiled from the data collected from field survey in selected Mandalas.
Note: Figures in parentheses represent column wise percentage.

Grameen bank is predominant. And in Anantapur rural mandal the services of the banks such as Andhra Bank, co-operative and Agricultural development bank are extending service for the activities of self help programmes.

Placewise distribution of respondents in relation to revolving fund received is ananlysed in table 7.3.

The government through DRDA has been encouraging the group activities by providing revolving fund to group members. Revolving fund has been distributed after careful observations of the group's activities. Particularly the continuity in savings and thrift activities.

In Kalyandurgam mandal out of the total, the highest number 141 respondents have received revolving fund between Rs. 8000-10000. Among these 61.7 respondents belong to villages and 37.3 respondents belong to urban areas. Only Nine respondents belonging to villages received revolving fund of Rs. 10001-14000.

In Gorantala mandal out of 150 respondents, the highest number 104 respondents have received revolving fund between Rs. 8000-10000. Among these 72.12 respondents belong to villages, 14.42 respondents belong to Hamlets and 13.46 respondents belong to urban areas. Only 11 respondents belonging to urban areas received revolving fund between Rs. 14,001 to 18,000.

In Anantapur rural mandal out of the total, the highest number 93 respondents have received revolving fund between Rs. 8,000 to 10,000. Among these 81.72 respondents from villages and 6.53 respondents from urban areas. Only 29 respondents have received revolving fund between Rs. 10,001-14,000 belonging to villages.

The overall observation of the table is that in all the three mandals the highest number of respondents have received revolving fund between Rs. 8,000-10,000 only.

Table-7.4 : Placewise Distribution of Respondents by the Type of Activities Taken

S. No.	Item	Kalyandurgam Mandal Place				Gorantala Mandal Place				Anantapur Rural Mandal Place			
		Urban	Village	Hamlet	Total	Urban	Village	Hamlet	Total	Urban	Village	Hamlet	Total
1.	Flower Business	11 (46.8)	8 (34.8)	4 (16.4)	23 (100)	12 (41.4)	14 (47.3)	3 (10.3)	29 (100)	—	21 (100)	—	21 (100)
2.	Weighable Business	10 (36.0)	17 (63.0)	—	27 (100)	15 (42.9)	18 (51.4)	2 (5.7)	35 (100)	—	33 (100)	—	33 (100)
3.	Fruits Business	2 (9.5)	19 (90.5)	—	21 (100)	4 (50.0)	1 (12.5)	3 (36.5)	8 (100)	—	5 (100)	—	5 (100)
4.	Kirana Shop	5 (26.3)	14 (26.7)	—	19 (100)	7 (46.7)	4 (26.7)	4 (26.7)	15 (100)	—	11 (100)	—	11 (100)
5.	Milk Activity	7 (26.9)	14 (53.8)	5 (19.2)	26 (100)	3 (16.6)	12 (70.6)	2 (11.8)	17 (100)	—	25 (92.6)	2 (6.4)	27 (100)
6.	Tailoring	12 (22.2)	5 (29.4)	—	17 (100)	8 (37.1)	18 (56.1)	1 (4.8)	21 (100)	—	17 (67.0)	8 (32.0)	25 (100)
7.	Hand Work	7 (41.2)	10 (57.8)	—	17 (100)	11 (44.0)	14 (56.0)	—	25 (100)	7 (25.0)	21 (75.0)	—	28 (100)
8.	Bakery	—	—	—	—	—	—	—	—	—	—	—	—
9.	Others Activities	—	—	—	—	—	—	—	—	—	—	—	—
10.	**Total**	54 (36.0)	87 (57.0)	9 (6.0)	150 (100)	60 (40.0)	75 (55.0)	15 (10.0)	150 (100)	7 (4.7)	133 (87.7)	10 (6.7)	150 (100)

Source: Compiled from the data collected from field survey in selected Mandalas.
Note: Figures in parentheses represent column wise percentage.

Placewise distribution of respondents in relation to the activities taken up is analysed in table 7.4. This table has been interpreted to test one of the objectives of the study, that is to examine the relationship between SHGs and women's economic empowerment (production, consumption and economic status).

In Kalyandurgam mandal, respondents in SHG have taken activities such as flower business, vegetable and fruits business, Kirana Shop, milk business, tailoring and hand works. Out of 150 respondents, the highest number 27 respondents have taken vegetable business. Among these 63.0 per cent belong to villages and 36.0 per cent belong to urban areas, followed by 23 respondents who have taken up flower business. Among these, 46.8 per cent belong to urban and semiurban areas and 34.8 per cent belong to villages. The lowest number 17 respondents have taken up hand works.

In Gorantala mandal, respondents have taken up activities on par with Kalyanadurga mandal out of 150 respondents, the highest number 35 respondents have taken vegetable business. Among these 51.4 per cent belong to villages and 42.9 per cent belong to urban areas, followed by 29 respondents who have taken up flower business. Among these 47.3 per cent belong to the villages and 41.4 per cent belong to urban areas. The lowest number 8 respondents have taken up fruits business. Among these 50.0 per cent belong to urban areas and 12.5 per cent belong to villages.

In Anantapur rural mandal the highest number 33 respondents have taken up vegetable business. All these respondents belong to villages, followed by 25 respondents who have taken up tailoring. Among these 67.0 per cent belong to villages and 32.0 per cent belong to hamlet. The lowest number Five respondents have taken up fruits and they belong to villages.

It is observed from the above table that in all the three mandals respondents belonging to villages have taken up vegetable, flower and froot business. Since a greater number of respondents belonging to villages have taken up various economic activities comparatively to urban respondents, place as a variable has no significance in identifying the activities of respondents.

Placewise distribution of respondents in relation to their involvement in SHG is analysed in table 7.5.

In Kalyanadurgam mandal out of 150 respondents the highest number 81 respondents are involved in SHG activities partially. Among these 54.3 per cent respondents belonging to villages. Followed by 36.0 per cent respondents belonging to urban areas and 7.6 per cent respondents belong to Hamlets on the other hand 63 respondents involved fully in the activities of SHG. Among these 54.0 per cent respondents belong to villages and 45.0 per cent respondents belong to urban areas.

In Gorantala mandal out of 150 respondents,75 respondents are involved fully and 75 respondents involved partially. Among these two categories, the highest percentage of respondents belong to villages and the lowest percentage of respondents and belong to hamlets.

In Anantapur rural mandal, 75 respondents involve partially and 75 respondents are involved fully in the activities of SHG. Among these, respondents who are partially involved consisting of 92,0 per cent belong to villages. And 85.3 per cent respondents belong to the villages have been fully involved.

The over all observation of the table is that respondents belonging to villages has been fully engaged in SHG activities. Thus, place, as a variable has no significance in deciding the level of involvement of respondents in the programmes of SHG.

Table-7.5 : Placewise Distribution of Respondents by Type of Involvement

S. No.	Item	*Kalyandurgam Mandal Place*				*Gorantala Mandal Place*				*Anantapur Rural Mandal Place*			
		Urban	*Village*	*Hamlet*	*Total*	*Urban*	*Village*	*Hamlet*	*Total*	*Urban*	*Village*	*Hamlet*	*Total*
1.	Partially	30	44	7	81	30	40	5	75	3	69	3	75
		(36.0)	(54.3)	(7.6)	(100)	(40.0)	(53.3)	(6.7)	(100)	(4.0)	(92.0)	(4.0)	(100)
2.	Fully	29	34	—	63	30	35	10	75	4	64	7	75
		(46.0)	(54.0)		(100)	(40.0)	(46.7)	(13.3)	(100)	(5.3)	(85.3)	(9.3)	(100)
3.	**Total**	54	87	9	150	60	75	15	150	7	133	10	150
		(36.0)	(57.0)	(6.0)	(100)	(40.0)	(50.0)	(10.0)	(100)	(4.7)	(87.7)	(6.7)	(100)

Source: Compiled from the data collected from field survey in selected Mandalas.
Note: Figures in parentheses represent column wise percentage.

Table 7.6 : Placewise Distribution of Respondents by Nature of Savings

S. No.	Item	Kalyandurgam Mandal Place				Gorantala Mandal Place				Anantapur Rural Mandal Place			
		Urban	Village	Hamlet	Total	Urban	Village	Hamlet	Total	Urban	Village	Hamlet	Total
1.	Rs. 150	44	44	—	88	—	—	—	—	—	65	—	65
		(40.0)	(50.0)		(100)						(100)		(100)
2.	Rs. 51-100	10	30	—	4	35	40	15	90	7	—	—	7
		(25.0)	(75.0)		(100)	(37.89)	(44.44)	(16.67)	(100)	(100)			(100)
3.	Rs. 101-150	—	13	9	22	20	40	—	60	8	70	—	78
			(59.1)	(40.9)	(100)	(33.33)	(66.67)		(100)	(10.26)	(89.74)		(100)
4.	Rs. 151-200	—	—	—	—	—	—	—	—	—	—	—	—
5.	**Total**	54	87	9	150	60	75	15	150	15	135	—	150
		(36.0)	(57.0)	(6.0)	(100)	(40.0)	(55.0)	(10.0)	(100)	(10)	(90.0)		(100)

Source: Compiled from the data collected from field survey in selected Mandalas.
Note: Figures in parentheses represent column wise percentage.

Placewise distribution of respondents in relation to saving is analysed in table 7.6.

In Kalyanadurgam mandal out of 150 respondents, the highest number 88 respondents have saving between Rs. 1.00-50.00, Among them 50.0 respondents from urban and 50.0 respondents from rural areas. The lowest number 22 respondents have savings between Rs. 101–150 belong to villages and Hamlets consisting of 59.1 per cent and 40.9 per cent respectively.

In Gorantla mandal out of the total 90 respondents, have savings between Rs. 51-100. Among these the highest number 44.44 respondents belong to villages, 38.89 respondents belong to urban areas. And 16.67 respondents belonging to hamlets.

In Anantapur rural mandal out of the total the highest number 78 respondents belonging to the villages have savings between 101-150. Among these 89.74 per cent respondents belong to villages and 10.26 per cent respondents belong to urban areas. The lowest number Seven respondents have savings between Rs. 51-100 belong to urban areas.

The overall observation of the table is that the more number of respondents belong to rural areas have more saving than respondents belong to urban areas. Therefore, in deciding the pattern of savings in SHG place as a variable has no significance.

Placewise distribution of respondents in relation to quantity of products produced monthly is analysed in table 7.7.

In Kalyandurga mandal out of the total, the highest number 80 respondents have produced 200 products for a month. Among these 51.3 per cent belong to the villages, 36.5 per cent belong to urban areas and 11.3 per cent belong

Table 7.7 : Placewise Distribution of Respondents by Quantity of Products Produced Monthly

S. No.	Item	Kalyandurgam Mandal Place				Gorantala Mandal Place				Anantapur Rural Mandal Place			
		Urban	Village	Hamlet	Total	Urban	Village	Hamlet	Total	Urban	Village	Hamlet	Total
1.	50	—	1 (100)	—	1 (100)	—	—	—	—	3 (7.8)	26 (76.5)	5 (14.7)	34 (100)
2.	100	10 (66.7)	5 (33.3)	—	15 (100)	7 (50.0)	7 (50.0)	—	14 (100)	4 (9.1)	35 (79.5)	5 (11.4)	44 (100)
3.	150	14 (25.9)	40 (74.1)	—	54 (100)	25 (50.0)	25 (50.0)	—	50 (100)	—	72 (100)	—	72 (100)
4.	200	30 (36.5)	41 (51.3)	9 (11.3)	80 (100)	28 (32.6)	43 (50.0)	15 (16.4)	86 (100)	—	—	—	—
5.	**Total**	54 (36.0)	87 (57.0)	9 (6.0)	150 (100)	60 (40.0)	75 (55.0)	15 (10.0)	150 (100)	7 (4.7)	133 (87.7)	10 (6.7)	150 (100)

Source: Compiled from the data collected from field survey in selected Mandalas.
Note: Figures in parentheses represent column wise percentage.

to Hamlets. The lowest number one respondent from a village produced 50 products.

In Gorantla mandal out of the total, 86 respondents produced 200 products. Among these 51.3 per cent belong to villages, 36.5 per cent belong to urban areas and 11.3 per cent belong to Hamlet. The lowest number 14 respondents produced 100 products for a month. Among these, 50.0 per cent respondents belong to villages and urban areas respectively.

In Anantapur rural mandal out of 150 respondents, 72 respondents have produced 150 products and they belong to villages. The lowest number 34 respondents produced 50 products. Among these 76.5 per cent belong to villages and 7.8 per cent respondents belong to urban areas.

The overall observation of the table is that greater the number of respondents belonging to villages more the produced, more products, thanks to the availability of raw-materials in villages. Thus, place as a variable has a significance to identify the capability of respondents for producing products in SHG activities.

SES wise distribution of respondents in relation to the opinion whether they need training or not is analysed in table 7.8.

In Kalyanadurga, mandal out of 150 respondents 108 respondents have expressed that they need training regarding the activities of SHG programmes. Out of which 70.4 per cent respondents belong to medium Socio-economic status. And 13.0 per cent respondents belong to high socio-economic status. And 14 respondents said they don't need any training.

In Gorantala mandal out of 150 respondents 99 respondents are in favour of training regarding SHG activities. Among these 51.4 per cent belong to medium socio-

Table 7.8 : SES-wise Distribution of Respondents by Opinion Towards Training

S. No.	Item	Kalyandurgam Mandal SES				Gorantala Mandal SES				Anantapur Rural Mandal SES			
		Medium	*Low*	*High*	*Total*	*Medium*	*Low*	*High*	*Total*	*Medium*	*Low*	*High*	*Total*
1.	Yes	76	18	14	108	51	34	14	99	56	33	7	96
		(70.4)	(16.7)	(13.0)	(100)	(51.5)	(34.3)	(14.1)	(100)	(57.3)	(34.4)	(6.3)	(100)
2.	No	26	13	2	42	19	26	6	51	38	9	7	54
		(63.4)	(31.7)	(4.9)	(100)	(36.3)	(51.0)	(11.8)	(100)	(70.4)	(16.7)	(13.0)	(100)
3.	**Total**	102	31	16	150	70	60	20	150	94	42	14	150
		(67.5)	(20.8)	(10.7)	(100)	(46.7)	(40.0)	(13.3)	(100)	(62.7)	(27.0)	(9.3)	(100)

Source: Compiled from the data collected from field survey in selected Mandalas.
Note: Figures in parentheses represent column wise percentage.

economic status and 14.1 per cent respondents belong to high socio-economic status. 51 respondents are of the opinion that they do not need any training.

In Anantapur rural mandal out of 150 respondents,the highest number 96 respondents are in need of training. Among these 57.3 per cent belong to medium socio-economic status, 34.4 per cent respondents belong to low socio-economic status and 6.3 per cent respondents belong to high socio-economic status. 54 respondents are not in need of training. Among these 70.4 per cent respondents belong to medium soci-economic status, 13.0 per cent respondents belong to high socio-economic status.

The overall observation of the table is that the respondents who belong to medium socio-economic status is a need of training for SHG programmes. Therefore, SES as a variable has significance to identify the opinion of respondents.

SES wise distribution of respondents in relation to opinion regarding the visit made by VDO to identify the problems of the groups is analysed in table 7.9.

In Kalyandurgam mandal out of 150 respondents the highest number 139 respondents have expressed that the VDO visits SHG regularly and enquires about its functioning. Among these the highest 66.9 per cent respondents belong to medium SES and the lowest 10.8 per cent respondents belong to high SES.

In Gorantala mandal, out of the total, the highest number 147 respondents are of the positive opinion regarding the visits made by VDO. Among these the highest 46.9 per cent belong to medium SES, and the lowest 12.9 per cent respondents belong to high SES. And only three respondents from each SES category are of the negative opinion regarding the visits made by the VDO.

Table-7.9 : SES-wise Distribution of Respondents by Opinion of Visits Made by VDO

S. No.	Item	*Kalyandurgam Mandal SES*				*Gorantala Mandal SES*				*Anantapur Rural Mandal SES*			
		Medium	*Low*	*High*	*Total*	*Medium*	*Low*	*High*	*Total*	*Medium*	*Low*	*High*	*Total*
1.	Yes	93	31	15	139	69	59	19	147	94	42	14	150
		(66.9)	(22.3)	(10)	(100)	(46.9)	(40.1)	(12.9)	(100)	(62.7)	(27.0)	(9.3)	(100)
2.	No	10	—	1	11	1	1	1	3	—	—	—	—
		(90.9)		(9.1)	(100)	(33.3)	(33.3)	(33.3)	(100)				
3.	**Total**	103	31	16	150	70	60	20	150	94	42	14	150
		(67.7)	(20.7)	(10.7)	(100)	(46.7)	(40.0)	(13.3)	(100)	(62.7)	(27.0)	(9.3)	(100)

Source: Compiled from the data collected from field survey in selected Mandalas.
Note: Figures in parentheses represent column wise percentage.

In Anantapur rural mandal all the respondents have a positive opinion regarding the visits made by VDO. Among these the highest 62.7 per cent respondents belong to medium SES. And the lowest 9.3 per cent respondents belong to high SES.

The overall observation of the table is that a greater number of respondents belong to medium and high SES have positive opinion regarding the visits made by VDO. Thus, SES as a variable has significance in deciding the level of awareness of respondents towards services offered by officers of the governments.

Educationwise distribution of respondents in relation to the opinion expressed about whether they need training or not is analysed in table 7.10.

In Kalyanadurga mandal, out of 150 respondents, the highest number 125 respondents are in favour of training. Among these 72.0 per cent respondents belong to illiterate and 28.0 per cent respondents belong to literate. Only 25 respondents are not in favour of training among these 92.0 belonging literates and 8.0 per cent belonging to illiterate.

In Gorantala mandal out of the total, the highest number 99 respondents are in need of training. Among these 62.9 per cent respondents are illiterate 35.4 per cent respondents are literate. The percentage of graduate respondents is negligible. 51 respondents are not in favour of training.

In Anantapur rural mandal, 96 respondents are in favour of training. Among these 63.3 per cent respondents are illiterate and 33.3 per cent respondents are literate. 54 respondents are of the opinion that they don't need any training.

The overall observation of the table is that most of the respondents whoare to illiterate and a few respondents who

Table-7.10 : Educationwise Distribution of Respondents by the Opinion Expressed Towards Training

S. No.	Item	Kalyandurgam Mandal Education					Gorantla Mandal Education					Anantapur Rural Mandal Education				
		Illiterates	Literates	Graduates	Other	Total	Illiterates	Literates	Graduates	Other	Total	Illiterates	Literates	Graduates	Other	Total
1.	Yes	90	35	—	—	125	62	35	2	—	99	61	32	3	—	96
		(72.0)	(27.0)			(100)	(62.9)	(35.4)	(2.0)		(100)	(63.5)	(33.3)	(3.1)		(100)
2.	No	2	23	—	—	25	28	22	1	—	51	41	12	1	—	54
		(7.0)	(92.0)			(100)	(54.9)	(43.1)	(2.0)		(100)	(75.9)	(22.2)	(1.9)		(100)
3.	**Total**		52	—	—	149	90	57	3	—	150	102	44	4	—	150
		(61.3)	(37.67)			(100)	(60.0)	(37.0)	(2.0)		(100)	(67.0)	(29.3)	(2.7)		(100)

Source: Compiled from the data collected from field survey in selected Mandalas.
Note: Figures in parentheses represent column wise percentage.

Table 7.11 : Educationwise Distribution of Respondents by the Opinion of Visits Made by VDO

S. No.	Item	Kalyandurgam Mandal Education					Gorantla Mandal Education					Anantapur Rural Mandal Education				
		Illite-rates	Lite-rates	Gradu-ates	Other	Total	Illite-rates	Lite-rates	Gradu-ates	Other	Total	Illite-rates	Lite-rates	Gradu-ates	Other	Total
1.	Yes	86	53	—	—	139	90	54	3	—	147	102	44	4	—	150
		(61.9)	(37.1)			(100)	(61.2)	(36.70)	(2.0)		(100)	(67.0)	(29.3)	(2.7)		(100)
2.	No	7	4	—	—	11	—	3	—	—	3	—	—	—	—	—
		(63.6)	(36.4)			(100)		(100)			(100)					
3.	**Total**	93	57	—	—	150	90	57	3	—	150	102	44	4	—	150
		(62.0)	(37.0)			(100)	(60.0)	(37.0)	(2.0)		(100)	(67.0)	(29.3)	(2.7)		(100)

Source: Compiled from the data collected from field survey in selected Mandalas.
Note: Figures in parentheses represent column wise percentage.

are literate are in favour of training. Therefore, it is assumed that education as a variable has no significance in deciding the opinion of respondents towards training.

Education-wise distribution of respondents in relation to the opinion whether the visits made by VDO is regular or not is ananlysed in table 7.11.

In Kalyandurga mandal the highest number 139 respondents have possitive opinion, among these 61.9 per cent respondents are illiterate and 37.1 per cent respondents are literate. Only 11 respondents have negative opinion regarding the visits made by the VDO.

In Gorantala mandal out of total, the highest number 147 respondents have possitive opinion. Among these 61.2 per cent respondents belong to illiterate, 36.7 per cent belong to literate. Moreover, the percentage of graduate is negligible. Only three respondents have negative opinion.

In Anantapur rural mandal, out of the total, all the respondents have positive opinion. Out of these 67.0 per cent respondents are illiterate and 29.3 per cent respondents are literate. And the percentage of graduates is negligibale.

The overall observation of the table is that in all the three mandals the majority of the respondents who are illiterate and literate have a positive opinion. Therefore, education as a variable has no significance in deciding the level of awareness regarding the services provided by VDO.

SESwise distribution of respondents in relation to the employment before the implementation of SHG programmes is analysed in table 7.12.

In Kalyanadurga mandal, out of the total, 60 respondents were engaged in agriculture, among these 60.0 per cent respondents belong to medium SES and 27.3 per

Table-7.12 : SESwise Distribution of Respondents by Nature of Employment Before SHG Programmes

S. No.	Item	Kalyandurgam Mandal SES				Gorantala Mandal SES				Anantapur Rural Mandal SES			
		Medium	*Low*	*High*	*Total*	*Medium*	*Low*	*High*	*Total*	*Medium*	*Low*	*High*	*Total*
1.	Coolly	35	9	6	50	19	18	8	45	29	10	3	42
		(70.0)	(18.0)	(12.0)	(100)	(42.2)	(40.0)	(16.8)	(100)	(69.0)	(23.8)	(6.1)	(100)
2.	Agriculture	36	17	7	60	22	24	7	53	32	15	5	52
		(60.0)	(27.3)	(11.7)	(100)	(41.5)	(45.3)	(13.2)	(100)	(61.5)	(27.8)	(9.6)	(100)
3.	House works	32	5	3	40	29	18	5	52	33	17	6	56
		(80.0)	(12.5)	(6.5)	(100)	(55.8)	(34.6)	(9.6)	(100)	(57.9)	(30.4)	(10.7)	(100)
4.	**Total**	130	31	16	150	70	60	20	150	94	42	14	150
		(67.7)	(20.7)	(10.7)	(100)	(46.7)	(40.0)	(13.3)	(100)	(62.7)	(27.0)	(9.3)	(100)

Source: Compiled from the data collected from field survey in selected Mandalas.
Note: Figures in parentheses represent column wise percentage.

Table-7.13 : SESwise Distribution of Respondents by Satisfaction with Income Earned from SHG Activities

S. No.	Item	*Kalyandurgam Mandal* SES				*Gorantala Mandal* SES				*Anantapur Rural Mandal* SES			
		Medium	*Low*	*High*	*Total*	*Medium*	*Low*	*High*	*Total*	*Medium*	*Low*	*High*	*Total*
1.	Yes	93	31	16	140	63	15	12	90	41	17	5	63
		(66.4)	(22.1)	(11.4)	(100)	(70.0)	(16.7)	(13.3)	(100)	(65.1)	(26.0)	(6.9)	(100)
2.	No	10	—	—	10	7	45	8	60	53	25	9	87
		(100)			(100)	(11.7)	(75.0)	(13.3)	(100)	(60.9)	(57.7)	(10.3)	(100)
3.	**Total**	103	31	16	150	70	60	20	150	94	42	14	150
		(67.3)	(20.7)	(10.7)	(100)	(46.7)	(40.0)	(13.3)	(100)	(62.7)	(27.0)	(9.3)	(100)

Source: Compiled from the data collected from field survey in selected Mandalas.

Note: Figures in parentheses represent column wise percentage.

cent respondents belong to low SES and 11.7 per cent respondents belong to high SES. Followed by 50 respondents were engaged in paid labour. Among these 70.0 per cent respondents belong to medium SES and 17.0 per cent belong to low SES. 40 repondents were engaged in house work.

In Gorantala mandal, 53 respondents were engaged in agricultural work. Among these 45.3 per cent respondents belong to low SES, 41.5 respondents belong to medium SES and 13.2 respondent belong to high SES. 52 respondents were engaged in housework. Among these 55.8 per cent respondents belong to medium SES 34.6 per cent respondents belong to low SES and 9.6 per cent respondents belong to high SES. 45 respondents were engaged in casual labour.

In Anantapur rural mandal the respondents engaged in three activities, i.e., casual labour, agricultural and house work. The highest number 56 respondents were engaged in house works, among these 57.9 per cent respondents belong to medium SES, 30.4 per cent respondents belong to low SES, 10.7 respondents belong to high SES.

The overall observation of the table is that higher the number of respondents belonging to medium and low SES categories the higher the number engaged in all kinds of work. There fore, SES as a variable has no significance in identify the nature of work engaged by respondents belonging to various SES categories.

SESwise distribution of respondents in relation to the satisfaction with income earnd from SHG is analysed in table 7.13

In Kalyanadurga mandal, out of the total, the highest number 140 respondents have expressed positive satisfaction with the income earned from SHG activities. Among these 66.4 per cent respondents belong to medium SES, 22.1 per cent respondents belong to low SES and 11.4 per cent respondents belong to high SES. Only 10 respondents are not satisfied with the income earned from SHG activities.

In Gorantala mandal out of the total, 90 respondents have positive satisfaction from the income earned from SHG activities. Among these 70.0 per cent respondents belong to medium SES, 16.7 per cent respondents belong to low SES and 13.3 per cent respondents belong to high SES. On the other, hand 60 respondents have negative satisfaction with income earned from SHG activities. Among these 75.0 per cent respondents belong to low SES, 13.3 per cent respondents belong to high SES and 11.7 per cent respondents belong to medium SES.

In Anatapur rural mandal 87 respondents have negative satisfation. Among these 60.9 per cent respondents belong to medium SES, 57.7 per cent respondents belong to low SES. 63 respondents have positive satisfaction consisting 65.1 per cent respondents belonging to medium SES, 26.0 per cent respondents belonging to low SES.

The overall observation of the table is that in Kalyanadurgam and Gorantala mandals respondents belonging to medium and low SES have greater satisfaction with the income earned from SHG activities. Thus, SES as a varible has a significance to understand the level of satisfaction of respondents in SHG activities.

SES wise distribution of respondents in relation to range of income earned from SHG is analyssed in the table 7.14

In Kalyanadurga mandal out of total, the highest number 118 respondents have earning Rs. 1000 for a month. Among these, 72.0 per cent respondents belong to medium SES, 16.8 per cent respondents belong to low SES and 10.2 per cent respondents belong to high SES. Only 32 respondents have earning Rs. 500 for month.

Table-7.14 : SESwise Distribution of Respondents by Range of Income Earned From SHG Activities

S. No.	Item	Kalyandurgam Mandal SES				Gorantala Mandal SES				Anantapur Rural Mandal SES			
		Medium	*Low*	*High*	*Total*	*Medium*	*Low*	*High*	*Total*	*Medium*	*Low*	*High*	*Total*
1.	Rs. 500	18	10	4	32	16	19	7	42	26	16	6	48
		(56.3)	(31.3)	(12.5)	(100)	(37.1)	(45.20)	(16.7)	(100)	(54.2)	(33.3)	(12.5)	(100)
2.	Rs. 1000	85	21	12	118	54	41	13	108	68	26	8	102
		(72.0)	(16.80)	(10.2)	(100)	(50.0)	(37.0)	(12.0)	(100)	(66.7)	(25.5)	(6.8)	(100)
3.	Rs. 1500	—	—	—	—	—	—	—	—	—	—	—	—
4.	**Total**	103	31	16	150	70	60	20	150	94	42	14	150
		(67.7)	(20.7)	(10.7)	(100)	(46.7)	(40.0)	(13.3)	(100)	(62.7)	(27.0)	(9.3)	(100)

Source: Compiled from the data collected from field survey in selected Mandalas.
Note: Figures in parentheses represent column wise percentage.

In Gorantala mandal out of the total, the highest number 108 respondents have earning Rs. 1000 per month. Among these 54.0 per cent respondents belong to medium SES, 37.0 per cent respondents belong to low SES and 12.0 per cent respondents belong to high SES. Only 42 respondents earn Rs. 500 per month.

In Anantapur rural mandal out of the total, 102 respondents earn Rs. 1000 per month. Among these 66.7 per cent respondents belong to medium SES, 25.5 per cent respondents belong to low SES and 6.8 per cent respondents belong to high SES. 48 respondents earn rupees 500 per month.

The overall observation of the table is that in all the three mandals respondents have not crossed monthly earnings from SHGs beyond Rs. 1000. Medium and low SES respondents have less earning from SHG activities. Therefore SES as a variable has significance in identifying the level of earnings of respondents from SHG activities.

SES-wise distribution of respondents in relation to the amount spent for children's education is analysed in table 7.15

In Kalyanadurgam mandal, out of the total, the highest number 118 respondents have spent their earning from SHG Rs. 200 for the education of their children. Among these, 72.0 per cent respondents belong to medium SES, 16.8 per cent respondents belong to low SES and 10.2 per cent respondents belong to high SES. Only 32 respondents have spent earnings from SHG of Rs. 100 for the children's education.

In Gorantala mandal out of the total, 106 respondents have spent Rs. 200 for their children's education. Among these 50.0 per cent respondents belong to medium SES, 37.0 per cent respondents belong to low SES and only 12.0 per cent

Table-7.15 : SESwise Distribution of Respondents by the Amount Spent for Children's Education

S. No.	Item	*Kalyandurgam Mandal SES*				*Gorantala Mandal SES*				*Anantapur Rural Mandal SES*			
		Medium	*Low*	*High*	*Total*	*Medium*	*Low*	*High*	*Total*	*Medium*	*Low*	*High*	*Total*
1.	Rs. 100	18	10	4	32	16	19	7	42	26	16	6	48
		(56.3)	(31.3)	(12.5)	(100)	(37.1)	(45.2)	(16.7)	(100)	(56.2)	(33.3)	(12.5)	(100)
2.	Rs. 200	85	21	12	118	54	41	13	108	68	26	8	102
		(72.0)	(16.8)	(10.2)	(100)	(50.0)	(37.0)	(12.0)	(100)	(66.7)	(25.5)	(6.8)	(100)
3.	Rs. 300	—	—	—	—	—	—	—	—	—	—	—	—
4.	**Total**	103	34	16	150	70	60	20	150	94	42	14	150
		(67.7)	(20.7)	(10.7)	(100)	(46.7)	(40.0)	(13.3)	(100)	(62.7)	(27.0)	(9.3)	(100)

Source: Compiled from the data collected from field survey in selected Mandalas.
Note: Figures in parentheses represent column wise percentage.

respondents belong to high SES. On the other hand, 42 respondents have spent Rs. 100 for their children's education. Among these, 45.2 per cent respondents belong to low SES, 37.1 per cent respondents belong to medium SES and 16.7 per cent respondents belong to high SES.

In Anantapur rural mandal, out of the total, 102 respondents have spent Rs. 200 for their children's education. Among these 66.7 per cent respondents belong to medium SES, 25.5 per cent respondents belong to low SES and 6.8 per cent respondents belong to high SES. Only 48 respondents have spent Rs. 100 for their children's education.

The overall observation of the table is that greater the number of respondents belonging to medium SES, the greater their earnings from SHG spent for the children's education. The respondents belong to low SES have been spending only a meagre amount earned from SHG activities for their children's education.

Castewise distribution of respondents in relation to the income earned from SHGs is sufficient or not is analysed in table 7.16.

In Kalyandurga mandal out of the total, the highest number 140 respondents have expressed that earnings from SHG activities is sufficient. Among these 55.0 per cent respondents belong to BCs, 22.1 per cent respondents belong to SCs, 12.1 per cent respondents belong to STs, and 10.7 per cent belong to other castes. Only 10 respondents have expressed that earnings from SHG activities are not sufficient.

In Gorantala mandal out of the total, 90 respondents have positive satisfaction. Among these 36.7 per cent respondents belong to SCs, 25.6 per cent respondents belong to BCs, 22.2 per cent belong to other castes and 15.0 per cent belong to STs. 60 respondents have negative satisfaction.

In Anantapur rural mandal, out of the total, 143 respondents have positive satisfaction. Among these 42.0 per cent respondents belong to BCs, 36.3 per cent respondents belong to SCs and 30.8 per cent respondents belong to Other castes.

The overall observation of the table is that the respondents belong to BC and Other castes in greater number have positive satisfaction. And SCs and STs in greater number have negative satisfaction. Thus, caste as a varible has a significance in identifying the satisfaction of respondents earnings earned from SHG activities.

Castewise distribution of respondents in relation to social status is analysed in table 7.17.

The above table was analysed to test the following objective in order to find out the role of Government in formulation of public policies and its impact on socio-economic development of nation.

In Kalyanadurga mandal out of the total, the highest number 113 respondents are of the opinion that after becoming members of SHG their social status has not improved. Among these 57.4 per cent respondents belong to BCs, 21.2 per cent respondents belong to SCs and 12.4 per cent respondents belong to Other castes. On the other hand, 37 respondents are of the opinion that their status has improved from the activities of SHG. Among these 43.2 per cent respondents belong to BCs, 24.3 per cent respondents belong to SCs, 24.3 per cent respondents belong to STs and 7.1 respondents belong to Other castes.

In Gorantala mandal out of the total, the highest number 146 respondents are of the opinion that their social status has improved after becoming members of SHG. Among these, 39.0 per cent repondents belong to Other castes, 27.0 per cent respondents belong to BCs, 22.0 per cent respondents

Table-7.15 : SESwise Distribution of Respondents by the Amount Spent for Children's Education

S. No.	Item	Kalyandurgam Mandal SES				Gorantala Mandal SES				Anantapur Rural Mandal SES			
		Medium	*Low*	*High*	*Total*	*Medium*	*Low*	*High*	*Total*	*Medium*	*Low*	*High*	*Total*
1.	Rs. 100	18	10	4	32	16	19	7	42	26	16	6	48
		(56.3)	(31.3)	(12.5)	(100)	(37.1)	(45.2)	(16.7)	(100)	(56.2)	(33.3)	(12.5)	(100)
2.	Rs. 200	85	21	12	118	54	41	13	108	68	26	8	102
		(72.0)	(16.8)	(10.2)	(100)	(50.0)	(37.0)	(12.0)	(100)	(66.7)	(25.5)	(6.8)	(100)
3.	Rs. 300	—	—	—	—	—	—	—	—	—	—	—	—
4.	**Total**	103	34	16	150	70	60	20	150	94	42	14	150
		(67.7)	(20.7)	(10.7)	(100)	(46.7)	(40.0)	(13.3)	(100)	(62.7)	(27.0)	(9.3)	(100)

Source: Compiled from the data collected from field survey in selected Mandalas.

Note: Figures in parentheses represent column wise percentage.

Table 7.17 : Castewise Distribution of Respondents by Social Status

S. No.	Item	Kalyandurgam Mandal Caste					Gorantala Mandal Caste					Anantapur Rural Mandal Caste				
		SC	ST	BC	Other	Total	SC	ST	BC	Other	Total	SC	ST	BC	Other	Total
1.	Low	24	9	66	14	113	3	—	—	1	4	9	—	47	31	87
		(21.2)	(7.0)	(57.4)	(12.4)	(100)	(75.0)			(25.0)	(100)	(10.3)		(54.0)	(35.6)	(100)
2.	Improved	9	9	16	3	37	33	14	42	57	146	30	7	13	13	63
		(24.3)	(24.3)	(43.2)	(7.1)	(100)	(22.0)	(9.6)	(27.8)	(39.0)	(100)	(46.6)	(11.1)	(20.6)	(20.6)	(100)
3.	**Total**	33	18	82	17	150	36	14	42	58	150	39	7	60	44	150
		(22.0)	(12.0)	(54.7)	(11.3)	(100)	(24.0)	(9.3)	(27.0)	(37.7)	(100)	(26.0)	(4.7)	(40.0)	(29.3)	(100)

Source: Compiled from the data collected from field survey in selected Mandalas.

Note: Figures in parentheses represent column wise percentage.

belong to SCs and 9.6 per cent repondents belong to STs. Only four respondents expressed that their social status is still low.

In Anantapur rural mandal out of the total, 87 respondents expressed that their social status is low even after becoming members of SHG. Among these 54.0 per cent respondents belong to BCs, 35.6 per cent respondents belong to Other castes and 10.3 per cent respondents belong to SC.

The overall observation of the table is that in Gorantala and Anantapur rural mandals a greater number of respondents belonging to all caste have expressed that their social status has increased. Only in Kalyanadurgam mandal, the respondents belonging to BCs and SCs have expressed that their social status is still low. Therefore caste as a varible has no significance in identifying the level of social status of respondents in SHG activities.

Castewise distribution of respondents in relation to the status enjoyed is analysed in table 7.18.

It has been ananlysed to test one of the objectives of the study in order to find out various public policies aimed at the upliftment of weaker sections particularly women.

In Kalyanaduragm mandal out of total, 125 respondents have equal status on par with men. Among these 54.4 per cent respondents belong to BCs, 19.2 per cent respondents belong to SCs, 12.8 per cent respondents belong to Other castes and 13.6 per cent respondents belong to STs. Only 25 respondents have not enjoyed equal status on par with men.

In Gorantala mandal, 103 respondents have equal status on par with men. Among these 36.7 per cent respondents belong to Other castes and 12.84 per cent respondents belonging to STs. 41 respondents have not enjoyed equal status on par with men.

Table 7.18 : Castewise Distribution of Respondents by Status Enjoyed on Par with Men

S. No. Item	Kalyandurgam Mandal Caste					Gorantala Mandal Caste					Anantapur Rural Mandal Caste				
	SC	ST	BC	Other	Total	SC	ST	BC	Other	Total	SC	ST	BC	Other	Total
1. Yes	24	17	68	16	125	31	14	24	40	109	7	—	—	—	7
	(19.2)	(13.6)	(54.4)	(12.8)	(100)	(27.44)	(12.8)	(22.02)	(36.7)	(100)	(100)				(100)
2. No	9	1	14	1	25	5	—	18	18	41	39	7	60	44	143
	(36.0)	(4.0)	(56.0)	(4.0)	(100)	(7.8)		(43.42)	(43.90)	(100)	(26.0)	(4.7)	(40.0)	(29.3)	(100)
3. **Total**	33	18	82	17	150	36	14	42	58	150	39	7	60	44	150
	(22.0)	(12.0)	(54.67)	(11.33)	(100)	(24.0)	(9.33)	(27.0)	(37.67)	(100)	(26.0)	(4.7)	(40.0)	(29.3)	(100)

Source: Compiled from the data collected from field survey in selected Mandalas.
Note: Figures in parentheses represent column wise percentage.

Table 7.19 : Castewise Distribution of Respondents by Nature of Contest for Elections

S. No.	*Item*	*Kalyandurgam Mandal Caste*					*Gorantala Mandal Caste*					*Anantapur Rural Mandal Caste*				
		SC	*ST*	*BC*	*Other*	*Total*	*SC*	*ST*	*BC*	*Other*	*Total*	*SC*	*ST*	*BC*	*Other*	*Total*
1.	Yes	24	9	66	14	113	3	—	2	6	11	—	—	—	—	—
		(21.2)	(7.0)	(57.4)	(12.4)	(100)	(26.3)		(17.2)	(54.5)	(100)					
2.	No	9	9	16	3	37	33	14	40	52	139	39	7	60	44	150
		(24.3)	(24.3)	(43.2)	(7.1)	(100)	(23.7)	(10.1)	(27.8)	(36.4)	(100)	(26.0)	(4.7)	(40.0)	(29.3)	(100)
3.	**Total**	33	18	82	17	150	36	14	42	58	150	39	7	60	44	150
		(22.0)	(12.0)	(54.7)	(11.3)	(100)	(24.0)	(9.3)	(27.0)	(37.7)	(100)	(26.0)	(4.7)	(40.0)	(29.3)	(100)

Source: Compiled from the data collected from field survey in selected Mandalas.
Note: Figures in parentheses represent column wise percentage.

In Anantapur rural mandal out of the total, the highest number 143 respondents have not enjoyed equal status on par with men. Among these 40.0 per cent respondents belong to BCs, 26.0 per cent respondents belong to SC, 29.3 per cent respondents belong to Other castes. Moreover, 4.7 per cent respondents belong to STs.

The overall observation of the table is that in Kalyanadurgam and Gorantala mandal a greater number of respondents belonging to BCs and Other castes have equal status on par with men. Thus caste as a variable has significance in deciding the level of social status enjoyed by the respondents.

Castewise distribution of respondents on the basis whether they contested for election or not is ananlysed in table 7.18.

It was analysed to test the objective, namely, 'to examine the relationship between SHGs and women's political empowerment (improvement in the capacity or ability of women to demand or raise their voice regarding entitlements and rights in various public forums, as well as their participation of members, president in Panchayat Raj institutions (ZP/MPP/VP/Gramama Sabha) and other local organisations like village forest, educational and health committees.)'

In Kalyanadurga mandal, out of the total, 150 respondents, 113 respondents have contested for election such as village panchayat, taluk panchayat and Zilla Panchayat. Among these 57.4 per cent respondents belong to BCs, 21.2 per cent respondents belong to SCs, 12.4 per cent respondents belong to other castes and 7.0 per cent respondents belong to STs. Only 37 respondents did not contest in any election.

In Gorantala mandal out of the total, the highest number 139 respondents have not contested in any election.

Among these 36.4 per cent respondents belong to Other castes, 27.8 per cent respondents belong to BCs, 23.7 per cent respondents belong to SCs and 10.1 per cent respondents belong to STs. Only 11 respondents have contested in election.

In Anatapur rural mandal, all the respondents did not contest in any elections. Among these 40.0 per cent respondents belong to BCs, 29.3 per cent respondents belong to Other castes, 25.0 per cent respondents belong to SCs and 4.7 per cent respondents belong to STs.

The overall observation of the table is that in one mandal, i.e., Kalyanadurga mandal a greater number of respondents have contested in elections. In the remaining two mandals, the majority of respondents did not contest in any election.

Educationwise distribution of respondents in relation to interest in contesting elections is analysed in table 7.19.

In Kalyandurga mandal, out of the total, the highest number 94 respondents are in favour of contesting elections. Among these, 65.0 per cent respondents are to illitetrate, 34.0 per cent respondents are to literate. 56 respondents are not have interested in to contesting the elections. Among these 55.4 per cent respondents are illiterate and 44.5 per cent respondents are literate.

In Gorantala mandal out of the total, 85 respondents are of the opinion of contesting the election. Among these 50.6 per cent respondents are literate, 45.9 per cent respondents belong to illiterate and 3.5 per cent respondents are graduate. 65 respondents are not in favour of contesting elections. Among these 77.5 per cent respondents are illiterate and 21.5 per cent respondents are literate.

In Anantapur rural mandal out of the total, the highest number 85 respondents are not in favour of contesting elections. Among these 65.9 per cent respondents are

Table-7.20 : Educationwise Distribution of Respondents by Interest of Contesting Elections

S. No.	Item	Kalyandurgam Mandal Education					Gorantla Mandal Education					Anantapur Rural Mandal Education				
		Illiterates	Literates	Graduates	Other	Total	Illiterates	Literates	Graduates	Other	Total	Illiterates	Literates	Graduates	Other	Total
1.	Yes	24	7	50	13	94	5	—	18	33	56	—	—	2	1	3
		(25.5)	(6.4)	(53.2)	(13.8)	(100)	(86.9)		(32.1)	(57.9)	(100)			(66.7)	(33.3)	(100)
2.	No	9	11	32	4	56	31	14	24	25	94	39	7	58	43	147
		(16.1)	(19.6)	(56.1)	(6.3)	(100)	(33.0)	(14.9)	(25.5)	(26.6)	(100)	(26.5)	(4.8)	(39.5)	(29.3)	(100)
3.	**Total**	33	18	82	17	150	36	14	42	58	150	39	7	60	44	150
		(22.0)	(12.0)	(54.7)	(11.3)	(100)	(24.0)	(9.3)	(27.0)	(37.7)	(100)	(26.0)	(4.7)	(40.0)	(29.3)	(100)

Source: Compiled from the data collected from field survey in selected Mandalas.
Note: Figures in parentheses represent column wise percentage.

Table-7.21 : Educationwise Distribution of Respondents by Opinion of Franchise

S. No.	Item	Kalyandurgam Mandal Education					Gorantla Mandal Education					Anantapur Rural Mandal Education				
		Illiterates	Literates	Graduates	Other	Total	Illiterates	Literates	Graduates	Other	Total	Illiterates	Literates	Graduates	Other	Total
1.	Yes	77	44	—	—	121	57	49	3	—	109	99	39	2	—	140
		(63.6)	(36.4)			(100)	(52.3)	(45.0)	(2.8)		(100)	(70.7)	(26.9)	(1.4)		(100)
2.	No	16	13	—	—	29	33	8	—	—	41	3	5	2	—	10
		(55.2)	(44.8)			(100)	(80.5)	(19.5)			(100)	(30.0)	(50.0)	(20.0)		(100)
3.	**Total**	93	57	—	—	150	90	57	3	—	150	102	44	4	—	150
		(62.0)	(37.0)			(100)	(60.0)	(37.0)	(2.0)		(100)	(67.0)	(29.3)	(2.7)		(100)

Source: Compiled from the data collected from field survey in selected Mandalas.
Note: Figures in parentheses represent column wise percentage.

illiterates, 32.9 per cent respondents are literate and 1.2 per cent respondents are graduate.

The overall observation of the table is that a high percentage of respondents are interested in contesting elections. On the other hand literate and graduate respondents are less interested of contesting election. Therefore it is said that these respondents are aware of the difficulties and problems to be faced in contesting elections. Thus, education as a variable has a significance in determining the level of interest of respondents to contest in elections.

Educationwise distribution of respondents in relation to franchise has been analysed in table 7.20.

In Kalyandurgam mandal out of the total, the highest number 121 respondents have been exercising franchises in various elections. Among these 63.6 per cent respondents belong to illiterate and 36.4 per cent respondents belong to literate. Only 29 respondents are for not exercising franchise.

In Gorantala mandal out of the total, 109 respondents have been exercising franchise. Among these 52.3 per cent respondents belong to illiterate, 45.0 per cent respondents belong to literate and 2.6 per cent respondents belong to graduate. 41 respondents have not been exercising franchise. Among these 80.9 per cent belong to illiterate and 19.5 per cent belong to literate.

In Anantapur rural mandal out of total, 140 respondents have been exercising franchise. Among these 70.7 per cent are illiterate, 26.9 per cent belong to literate and 1.4 per cent are graduate. In this mandal only 10 respondents have not been exercising franchise.

The overall observation of the table is that a greater number of illiterate respondents have been exercising

Table-7.22 : Educationwise Distribution of the Respondents by Nature of Discussion of Politics and Administration

S. No.	Item	Kalyandurgam Mandal Education					Gorantla Mandal Education					Anantapur Rural Mandal Education				
		Illiterates	Literates	Graduates	Other	Total	Illiterates	Literates	Graduates	Other	Total	Illiterates	Literates	Graduates	Other	Total
1.	Yes	87	54	—	—	141	80	13	—	—	93	100	42	4	—	146
		(61.7)	(37.3)			(100)	(86.0)	(14.0)			(100)	(67.5)	(27.8)	(2.7)		(100)
2.	No	6	3	—	—	9	10	44	3	—	57	2	2	—	—	4
		(66.7)	(33.3)			(100)	(16.5)	(76.2)	(5.3)		(100)	(50.0)	(50.0)			(100)
3.	**Total**	93	57	—	—	150	90	57	3	—	150	102	44	4	—	150
		(62.0)	(37.0)			(100)	(60.0)	(37.0)	(2.0)		(100)	(67.0)	(29.3)	(2.7)		(100)

Source: Compiled from the data collected from field survey in selected Mandalas.

Note: Figures in parentheses represent column wise percentage.

franchise. However, the percentage of respondents belonging to literate and graduate is very medium. Because educated people are aware of the consequences and they don't want to take risk. Therefore, education as a variable has significance in deciding the level of franchise of respondents.

Educationwise distribution of the respondents whether they discus politics and administration during group meetings is analysed in table 7.21.

Political processes are the devices which offer citizens the opportunity to choose from among political party's candidates and authorities to rule the nation. According to a political scientist, a political process is an educative opportunity.[6] According to the document on women's development (1985) women's role in political structure has virtually remained unchanged.[8] Thus, this table is analysed with the objective of 'to examining the relationship between SHGs and women's political empowerment (improvement in the capacity or ability of women to demand or raise their voice regarding entitlements and rights in various public forums,as well as their participation a members, president in panchayat raj institutions (ZP/MPP/VP/Gramama Sabha) and other local organisations like village forest, educational and health committees.)'

In Kalyanadurga mandal out of the total, the highest numberr 141 respondents have expressed that they discuss politics and administration during the group meetings. Among these 61.7 per cent respondents are illiterate and 37.3 per cent respondents belong to literate. Only Nine respondents expressed that they don't discuss politics and administration during the group meeting.

In Gorantala mandal, 93 respondents have expressed that they discuss politics during the group meetings. Among these 86.0 per cent respondents are illiterate and 14.0 per cent respondents are literate. On the other hand 57 respondents expressed that they don't discuss politics and administration during the group meetings. Among these 76.2 per cent respondents are literate, 16.5 per cent respondents are illiterate and 5.3 per cent respondents belong to graduate.

In Anantapur rural mandal out of the total, the highest number 146 respondents have express ed that they discuss politics and administration during the group meeting. Among these, 67.5 per cent respondents are illiterate, 27.8 per cent respondents are literate and 2.7 per cent respondents are graduate. Moreover, on the other hand, four respondents have expressed that they don't discuss politics and administration during the group meeting.

The overall observation of the table is that in all the three mandals respondents belonging to illiterate groups have been discussing politics and administration during the group meetings. Further moderate size of percentage respondents belong to literate and graduates are also discussing politics and administration during the group meeting. It is felt that education as a variable has no significance to identify the level of interest toward politics and administration of respondents.

References

1. See Methodology part in Chapter III.
2. Swaran Jayanti Swarojgar Yojna, *op. cit.*
3. Ashok Sorksh,Development through NGOs in Bank Valley, *op. cit.*
4. *Ibid.*
5. T.R. Guerumurthy, New Life to Rural Credit Agencies An Urgent Nedd, Kurukshtra, July, 1995, p. 32.
6. T.R Guerumurthy, *op. cit.* p. 33.

Bibliography

Abbas Bhuiya Micro-Credit and Emotional Well-Being: Experience of Poor Rural Women from Matlab, Bangladesh, World Development Vol. 29, No. 11, 2001.

Acharya, K.C.S., Food Security System of India-Evaluation of the Buffer Action Plan for the year DRDA Anantapur, 1990-200.

Action Plan for Women-2000 A.D., Government of Andhra Pradesh, Hyderabad.

Activities for Women and Children in the State of Andhra Pradesh, Dept. of Women Development and Child Welfare, Hyderabad, 1997.

American Sociological Association (ASA) Sage Publications, 1990.

Andhra Pradesh State Action Plan for Women 1994-2000, Dept. of Women Development and Child Welfare, Govt. of Andhra Pradesh, Hyderabad, 1995.

Andhra Pradesh Women's Co-operative Finance Corporation, A Note on the activities of A.P. Women's co-operative Finance Corporation Ltd., Hyderabad, 1997.

Andhra Pradesh Year Book, Data News Features, Hyderabad, 1994.

Andhra Pradesh Year Book, Data News Features, Hyderabad, 1990.

Andhra Pradesh Year Book, Hyderabad, Data News Features Publication, Hyderabad 2000.

Anitha Anand, "Engendering The Plan," in the Hindu, April 6, 1997.

Annual Action Plan DRDA, Anantapur, 1999-2000.

Apppleby, P.H. 'Policy and Administration' Albana: Albana University Press, 1949.

—Public Administration in India, Report of a Survey, Delhi Government of India, 1953.

Archana Sood "Success Story of Matsyafed Cooperative" Kurukshetra, August, 2000.

Bailey S.K. and Mosher, E.K. ESCA: The Office of the Education Administrators Law, Syracuse University, Syracuse, 1968.

Balaramula, C.H., Administration of Anti-Poverty Programmes: A Study of SFDA, Warangal, Kakatiya School of Public Administration, Ashok Printers, 1984.

Balaramula, C.H. Public Policies: An Evaluation of Integrated Rural Development Programme, Ajanta Publications, Delhi, 1991.

Barbara J. Isely, Women's Roles: Perceptions and Practice in a South Indian Village, Journal of Rural Development Vol. (5), NIRD, Hyderabad, 1992.

Barbara J. Nelson, Public Policy and Administration: An Overview : A Hand book of Political science (ed.,) by Robert E. Goodin and Hans-Dieter Klingemnn, Oxford University Press, 2000.

Bhakshi, P.M. Constitution of India, Indian Law Institute, 1995.

Bhagavan, B.S., Need for Effective Evaluation in Rural Development, Kurukshetra, Vol. XXXII. No. 16 July 1984.

Bhasker Rao (ed.), Development Strategies in India, New Delhi: Khanna Publishers, 1993.

Bhatt, G.D., An Evaluation of IRDP, Rural Development Programmes in India, New Delhi, Shanthi Publishers, 1990.

—From Community Development to Integrated Rural Development, Kurukshetra Vol. XXXII, No. 16, July 1984.

Budget Management 1997-98 (Telgu). Women Development and Child Welfare Government of Andhra Pradesh Press, Hyderabad, 1997.

Buta Singh, Policy Options for Poverty Alleviation, Kurukshetra, Vol. XXXIV No. 2, November, 1985.

C.S.W.I.-The Report of the Committee on the Status of Women, 1974, Central Institute of Research and training in Public Co-operation, The Plan for People's Participation: A Research Study, New Delhi 1997.

Centre for Women's Development Studies, Women's Work and Employment Struggle for a Policy, Selections from Indian Documents, New Delhi, 1990.

Chandrakal, A. Hote, Changing Status of Women in Post-Independent India, Allied Publications, Bombay, 1969.

Charles O. Jones and Robert and D. Thomas. "Public policy-Making In a Federal System", Sage Publications, London, 1976.

Charyulu, U.V.N. and M. Setharam, Role of Rural Workers' of Organisations in Population Family welfare Activities-

Case Study of a Non-Organisation Journal of Rural Development, Vol. (3) NIRD, Hyderabad, 1988.

Chauhan, Indira, Purdha to Profession: A Case Study of Working Women in M.P., Delhi B.R. Publishing Corporation, 1986.

Chawdhry Paul D., Hand book of Social Welfare (Fields of Social Work), Atma Ram and Sons, New Delhi: 1993.

—Women Welfare and Development: A Source Book, Inter India Publications, New Delhi, 1992.

CSD, A Case Study of the Functional Literacy Programme of ICDS, Council for Social Development, New Delhi, 1979.

Dissertation Abstract of India A 61/03, p. 1143, Sep. 2000.

Dissertation Abstract of India A 61/03, p. 1157, Sep. 2000.

Dissertation Abstract of India A 61/03, p. 1181, Sep. 2000.

Dissertation Abstract of India A 61/07, p. 2908, Jan. 2001.

Dissertation Abstract of India A 61/10, p. 4150, Apr. 2001.

Dissertation Abstract of India A 61/10, p. 4158, Apr. 2001.

Dissertation Abstract of India A 61/12, p. 4915, Jun. 2001.

Dissertation Abstract of India A 61/10, p. 4142, Apr. 2001.

Dissertation Abstract of India A 60/08, p. 3123, Feb. 2000.

Dissertation Abstract of India A 60/09, p. 3517, Mar. 2000.

Demko George J & Jackson Michael C (Eds.): "Populations At Risk In America : Vulnerable Groups At the End of the Twentieth Century" : Westview Press, Inc., 1995, pp. 66-76.

Department of Women and Child Development, National Perspective Plan for Women 1988-2000. A.D. (MPPA).

Ministry of Human Resource Development, Government of India, 1988.

Department of Women Development and Child Welfare, Administrative Report, Government of A.P. Hyderabad, 1978.

Department of Women Development and Child Welfare, Status Report 1996, Hyderabad, 1996.

Department of Women's Development and Child Welfare, State Action Plan for Women 1994-2000, Government of A.P., 1985.

Dimensions in Rural Non-Farm Employment of Women: A Case In Andhra Pradesh Journal of Rural Development, Vol. 4(1), NIRD, Hyderabad. 1995.

District Collectorate, Rural Works Programmes, Anantapur District, Anantapur, 1974.

District Rural Development Agency: The Annual Plans of DRDA, IRDP, Anantapur, 1980-81, 1990-94.

District Rural Development Agency: The Report of DRDA, DWCRA, Anantapur, 1989-94.

District Rural Development Agency: The Report of DRDA, NREP, Anantapur, 1980-81, 1985-94.

District Rural Development Agency: The Report of DRDA, PASMA, Anantapur, 1983-84, 1989-94.

District Rural Development Agency: The Report of DRDA, TRYSEM, Anantapur, 1980-81, 191-94.

Dubashi, P.R., Policy and Performance: Agricultural and Rural Development in Post-Independent India, Sage Publishers, New Delhi, 1986.

Dubey, S.N. and Patna Mudra, Administration of Policy and Programmes for Backward Classes in India. Somya Publications Pvt. Ltd., Bombay, 1976.

Dye Thomas R. "Policy Analysis", Alabama: University of Alabama Press, 1976.

—"Understanding Public Policy", New Jersey, Prentice Hall Inc., Englewood Cliff JN: 1971.

Easton David, The Political System, New York, Knopf, 1953.

Economic Empowerment of Women through' Rashtriya Mahila Kosh Scheme Kurukshetra, May-June, 1995.

Everstone Robert, The Thread of Public Policy: A Study in Policy Leadership, Indian Polis: Bobbs Merril, 1971.

Financing A Self Help Groups, A Reference, NABARD, Bangalore, 1999.

Friedrich Carl J. Gangadhra Rao, G. "Man and his Government", New York: Mc Graw Hill, 1963.

Gadgil, D.R., District Development Planning, Asian Publishing House, Bombay, 1967.

Ganapathy, R.S., Ganesh S.R. and others (ed.), Public Policy and Policy Analysis in India, Sage Publications, New Delhi, 1985.

Ganguli, B.N., Social Development Essays in Honour of Smt. Durga Bai Deshmukh, Sterling Publishers Pvt. Ltd., New Delhi, 1977.

Giriappa, S., Role of Women in Rural Development, Sage Publication New Delhi, 1989.

Government of Andhra Pradesh and Department of Women development and Child Welfare, Women Sub-Plan 1997-98 Hyderabad, 1997.

Government of Andhra Pradesh, A.P. State Administrative Report 1986-87, Government Central Press, Hyderabad, 1991.

Government of Andhra Pradesh, Action Plan for Women 2000, Department of Women's Development and Child Welfare, Hyderabad, 1966.

Government of Andhra Pradesh, Andhra Pradesh Administrative Report 1983-84, Director of Printing, Hyderabad, 1987.

Government of Andhra Pradesh, Department of Women Development and Child Welfare, State Empowerment Policy, Hyderabad 1997.

Government of Andhra Pradesh, Fifth Five Year Plan, Andhra Pradesh, Hyderabad, 1975.

Government of Andhra Pradesh, Planning Development of Backward Region (Vol. I), Government Central Press, Hyderabad, 1987.

Government of Andhra Pradesh, Seventh Five Year Plan 1985-90, Hyderabad, A.P. Vol. II, Finance and Planning Department (PLG Wing), 1985.

Government of Andhra Pradesh, Vision-2020 Document, Hyderabad, 2000.

Government of India—"Government of India", a Report of the Committee on the Status of Women in India Towards Equality—Department of Social welfare, Ministry of Education, 1975.

Government of India, Census of India, 1991, New Delhi.

Government of India, Five Year Plan - 1974-79, New Delhi.

Government of India, National Perspective Plan for Women, 1988-2000 AD. Report of the Core Group set up by Department of Women Development and Child Welfare, Ministry of HRD, 1986.

Government of India, Second Five Year Plan-1956-61, New Delhi, 1961.

Government of Andhra Pradesh, District Gazetteers, Anantapur, 1970.

Gulab Singh, From Calories To Capacity Building The Grameen Bank Approach to Poverty Alleviation in Bangladesh, Journal of Rural Development, Vol. 4(4), NIRD, Hyderabad, 1995.

Handbook of Policy and Related Documents on Women in India, National Institute of Public Co-operation and Child Development, New Delhi, 1988.

Hender Mahajan, "Status of Women and Socio Economic Programmes Under India's Seventh Five Year Plan" in R.K. Saptu (ed.) Women and Development, Ashish Publishing House, New Delhi, 1989.

ICSSR, United Nations Plan of Action for Women 1975-85, Programme of Women's Studies, New Delhi, 1977.

Indira Misra, "Self-Employment through IMY", in Yojna, Vol. 41, No. 4, April 1997.

Indira Misra, "Reaching Out to Poor Women: RMK's Mission", Kurukshetra, August, 1995.

International Encyclopaedia of Social Sciences-The Mac Millan Company and the Free Press, 1968.

Jain C.K. (ed.), Women Parliamentarians in India, Lok Sabha Secretariat, : Surjeet Publications, New Delhi 1993.

James E., Public Policy Marketing, Praegar publications, New York, Anderon, 1975.

Jayawera, Programme of Non-Formal Education for Women, Indian Journal of Adult Education, Vol. 40, 1979.

Joshi, S.C. "Indira Mahila Yojna: Empowerment of Women", Kurukshetra, March 1996.

Joyee M. Mitechell, William C. Mitchel R and M.C. Nully and "Political Analysis and Public Policy: An Introduction to Political Science", Chicago, 1969.

Kalbagh, C. (ed.), Policies and Programmes for Women's Development, Discovery Publishing House, New Delhi: 1992.

Kar, G.D. Poverty: Some Conceptual Consideration, Journal of Rural Development, Vol. 8(3), NIRD, Hyderabad, 1989.

Key V.O. Jr. "Public Opinion and American Democracy", New York, Kaopf, 1967.

Kistaiah (ed.), Public Policy and Administration, Sterling Publications New Delhi, Pvt. Ltd., 1986.

Kitchlu T.N. "Women's Rights, Legislative Measures", In Yojana, Nov. 15, 1991, Vol. 35, No. 20, New Delhi, 1991.

Krishna Haldipur, Women's Literacy and Empowerment Some Suggestion, IASSI Quarterly Vol. 17, No. 2, 1997.

Krishna Raj Maithreyi, Women and Development: The Indian Experience Pune: Shubhadra Swaraswat Mumbabee, 1988.

—Women Development. Indian Context, Monograms on Sociology, SNDT Women's University, 1990.

Krishna Rao. V., Communism in Andhra Pradesh: Rise and Decline, Kaveri Publishers, Hyderabad, 1989.

Kusum Lata Tiwari, "Women and Development", Kurukshetra, August, 1995.

Laswell Harold D. "The Policy Orientation of Political Science", Laxmi Narayan Agarwal, Agra, 1971.

Laswel, Harold D. and Abraham Kaplan, Power and Society, New Heaven: Yale University Press, 1970.

Madhubal Nath, Women's Issues: From the Periphery to the Centre, Journal of Rural Development, Vol. 11(5), NIRD, Hyderabad, 1992.

Mahanth. K, Rural Industrialization in India-Policy, Programmes and Prospects, Journal of Rural Development, Vol. 7, No. 2 March 1988.

Meenakshi, Apte, 'Rural Women and Development in India', Indian Journal of Social Work, Vol. 39, 1979.

Meenaxi Anand Chaudhry, "Empowerment Strategies for Rural Women in India" Kurukshetra, March, 1996.

—All About Mahila Samriddhi Yojana, Kurukshetra Sept. 1994.

Ministry of Rural Development, Government of India and UNICEF June 1992-Marketing of Products of Rural Women's Group. New Delhi.

Murali Manohar K., Socio-economic Status of Indian Women, Seema Publications, Delhi, 1983.

Nandan, S.C., 'Role of Women in Rural Development', Kurushetra, Vol. 30., July 16th, 1982.

Narayan Reddy, Reddy G., Women and Child Development Contemporary Issues, Chugh Publishers, Allahabad, 1987.

National Bank, NABARD, Annual Report, Mangalore, 1990-1991.

Neera Desai and Maithreyi Krishna Raj, Women and Society in India, Ajanta Publications, Delhi, 1987.

Neera Desai, Amit Kumar Gupta (ed.), "Changing Status of Women, Policies and Programmes in Women and Society, Developmental Perspective", New Delhi, 1986.

Nehru and Rural Development, Nehru 135th Century, Kurukshetra, October 1989.

O.P. Srivastava, Public Administration and Management Vol. 1, Himalaya Publishing House, Bombay, 1991.

Paul D. Chowdhery, Women Welfare and Development: A Source Book, Inter India Publications, New Delhi: 1992.

Planning Commission, Draft Five Year Plan: Community Programmes - A Draft Outline, Report of the Royal Commission of Agriculture, 1928.

Prakash, B., And Raju, M., Rural Development; Issues to Ponder, Kurushetra, Vol. 32, No. 4, January 1984.

Provisional Population, Paper 2 AP, Census of India, 2002.

Ram Reddy, G. Hara Gopal, G. Public Policy and the Rural Poor in India, Concept Publishing Co., New Delhi, 1985.

Rama Kishore. K, Caste Class and Rural Political Leadership: A Case Study of Khammam District, Unpublished Ph.D Thesis, Kakathya University, 1994.

Rama Kumari, K., Women Welfare Programmes in Andhra Pradesh (1970-96)-A Policy Analysis, Unpublished Ph.D Thesis, Osmania University, 1998.

Rama Majumdar, Poverty Alleviation Programme and Rural Women, Kurukshetra, April, 1988.

Ramaiah, P., Veera Venkataiah and Mohan Reddy, Impact of IRDP on Rural poor—A Micro Study, Kurukshetra, Vol. XXXVI, No. 12, September 1988.

Ramesh Sachithananda P. Women's Rights, Myth and Reality, Printwell, Jaipur, 1984.

Rastramlo Mandala Vyavasta ; Eenadu, Telugu Daily, Tirupathi, 13th January, 1987.

Rath N. Womens Specific Legislations in India and Germany: A Comparative Study, nabak Usha Chaudhary Centre for Krishnadevaraya Developmental Studies, Occasional paper No. 10, Bhubaneshwar, Orissa, 1994, p. 97.

Ravinder, D. Politics of Rural Development in Andhra Pradesh, A Case Study of IRDP in Mahabubnagar District, Unpublished Ph.D Thesis Osmania University, 1996.

Report of Andhra Mahila Sabha Silver Jubilee Celebration (1958-1983), Hyderabad.

Report of the National Committee on the Status of Women, Status of Women in India, The Indian Council of Social Sciences Research, New Delhi, 1971.

Report on India's Administrative System: Comments and Reactions, Delhi, 1956.

Report on Study Team on District Administration (Chairman: T. Jain) Administrative Reforms Commission, Government of India, Ministry of Planning, New Delhi, 1967.

Ripley Randall, Policy Analysis in Political Science, Nelson Hall Publishers, Chicago, 1987.

Robert, E. Goodin and Hans Dicter "A New Handbook of Political Science", Oxford Klingemann (Ed.) University Press, 2000.

Rose Richard (ed.), Policy-Making In Great Britain, London: Mc Millan Co., 1969.

Samarendra K. Singh and S.N. Ambedkar, National Rural Employment Programme: Performance And Prospects, Journal of Rural Development, Vol. 8(1), NIRD Hyderabad, 1989.

Santha, S.K. and Mandal, S., Integrated Rural Development Programme, Problems and Prospects, Kurukshetra, Vol. XXXVI, No. 12. September, 1988.

Scheme for the Protection of Girl Children : Deccan Chronicle, Sept. 13, 1997.

Sha, S.M., Where we have failed in Rural Development, Kurukshetra, Vol. XL, No. 1, October 1991.

Status of Women and Children in Andhra Pradesh, Centre for Economic and Social Studies, Begumpet, Hyderabad, 1990.

Stri Sisuvula Rashana Pathakam : Eenadu, Oct. 4, 1997.

Stuart S. Nagel, "Policy Analysis", in G. Ronald Gilbert (ed.), "Making and Managing Policy", Marcel Dekkar, New York, 1984.

Suresh Bhargava, Empowering Women At the Village Level, UNICEF Representative Andhra Pradesh., Karnataka,

Suvarna Rani, G. "Development and Rural Woman of India", Kurukshetra, Aug. 1995.

Swaranjayanti Gram Swarojgar Yojna, Guidelines Government of India, Ministry of Rural Development, New Delhi, 1999.

Syed Masud Ahmed, Mushtaque Chowdhury, Micro-Credit and Emotional Well Being: Experience of Poor Rural Women from Matlan, Bangladesh, World Development Vol. 29, No. 11. 2001.

Syndicate Report: Development Administration: Concepts, Principles and Approaches, 78th Orientation Course, National Institute of Community Development, Hyderabad 1972.

The Myrada Experience: Self Help Groups Reading Materials and Related Literature, Gulbarga, 2001.

The Report of the National Committee on the Status of Women. "Status of Women in India", The Indian Council of Social Science Research, New Delhi, 1971-74.

Thomas, R. Dye, Understanding Public Policy, Englewood Cliffs, N.J. Prentice-Hall, 1972.

Umesh Samuel, A., and Paul Ray, S., 'Role of Official and Participation in Rural Development Schemes', Kurukshetra, Vol. XXXIX, No. 8, May 1991.

Verma, B.M. Decentralisation in Administration, Public Policy for Eradication of Poverty, Uppal Publishing House, New Delhi, 1990.

Verma Sudhir, Women's Development: Policy and Administration, Aalekh Publishers, Jaipur, 1992.

Verma, S.L, Research Methodology in Political Science, Rawat Publishers, Jaipur, 1989.

Vina Mazembdar (ed.), Symbols of Women's Power, Study on the Political Status of Women in India, Allied Publishers Pvt. Limited, Bombay, 1979.

Wilkinson, T.S. and P.L. Bhandarkar, and P.L. Bhandarkar, Methodology and Techniques of Social Research, Himalaya Publishing House, Bombay, 1984.

Index

Nanhi Shop
Online Shopping..
Www.nanhishop.com